IMAGES
of Rail

Sioux City Railroads

On the cover: This scene is the Chicago, Milwaukee, St. Paul and Pacific Railway roundhouse and shop complex north of the Riverside section of Sioux City. The photograph dates from the 1920s. The Big Sioux River and the state of South Dakota are the background to the complex and freight yard. The roundhouse, property, and other buildings are now the museum of the Siouxland Historical Railroad Association. One can visit the Great Northern steam locomotive *Chief Iron Horse*, listen to programs on railroad history, and take train rides around the property. (Courtesy of the Jack P. Fleckenstein Collection.)

IMAGES
of Rail

SIOUX CITY RAILROADS

Rudolph Daniels

ARCADIA
PUBLISHING

ISBN 978-0-7385-5222-4

Published by Arcadia Publishing
Charleston, South Carolina

Printed in the United States of America

Library of Congress Catalog Card Number: 2007943011

For all general information contact Arcadia Publishing at:
Telephone 843-853-2070
Fax 843-853-0044
E-mail sales@arcadiapublishing.com
For customer service and orders:
Toll-Free 1-888-313-2665

Visit us on the Internet at www.arcadiapublishing.com

Sioux City Railroads *is dedicated to the citizens of Sioux City, Iowa.*

Contents

ACKNOWLEDGMENTS

There are so many people to acknowledge in preparing *Sioux City Railroads*. First of all George and LouAnn Lindblade of G. R. Lindblade and Company Productions contributed many photographs and did the preparations of others. They have also shared railroad artifacts that they have collected. The Lindblades have preserved many subjects and objects of Sioux City history over the years.

Bill Metz permitted me to read and to copy the trackage agreement between the Illinois Central and the Sioux City and St. Paul Railroad companies. George Berkstresser actually sent his medium format negatives of his many fine railroad photographs he took in the 1940s and 1950s.

Matt Andersen processed and prepared all the photographs from the Sioux City Public Museum. John Schultz searched through the Siouxland Historical Railroad Association archives. He also processed and copied many needed photographs. I am honored to have Paul H. Reistrup's willingness to help with the project and contribute photographs. Mr. Reistrup is a Sioux City native and was the second president of Amtrak.

Richard Donaway contributed the 1950-era maps and other paper artifacts, and Jim Adamson of Depot Renovation, Inc., Cherokee, Iowa, permitted use of the 1911–1917 maps and a copy of the 1888 State of Iowa Board Report. Paul Fleckenstein furnished photographs from his father's company of Woodworth Commercial Photography as the Jack P. Fleckenstein Collection.

Larry Obermeyer of the Siouxland Historical Railroad Association served as a reader and assisted with acquiring of the association's photographs. Mr. Obermeyer contributed his time and talent as a reader of the proof draft. Rick Alleley of the City of Sioux City Economic Development Department also served as a reader. Bill Sibley made suggestions on the first draft. Kim Walsh of the Sioux City Public Library recommended archival material.

Arcadia editor Ted Gerstle was most patient in answering my many questions and providing (much needed at times) encouragement during the project.

I am greatly indebted to Steve Paulson of Steve's Studio. Steve prepared all of the photographs digitally for publication. I would not have been able to do so with my limited experience and equipment. He also made text suggestions from his knowledge of Sioux City. He was most patient as I was seeking sources and making changes. I owe him a lot for the preparation of the photographs for the book.

I wish to thank the officials of the *Sioux City Journal* for granting me permission to use photographs which may have appeared in the newspaper. They may also have the copyright on photographs which may have been taken by such photographers as George Newman.

INTRODUCTION

During the 19th century, Sioux City was vital to the settlement of the interior of the United States and for the country's economic development. At first, Sioux City was in an ideal location for exploration of the northern Great Plains. Later settlers came to the city to work in its commercial enterprises while others established farms in its hinterland. By the end of the century, Sioux City could claim to be one of the fastest growing municipalities in the world, and its products crossed the seven seas. These accomplishments were made possible by the railroads.

Sioux City history can be roughly grouped into three periods that reflect its population growth and economic well-being. The first stage was from its establishment until the arrival of the railroads. The second followed basically the passenger era of the great railroad companies. The third, or last, is from the 1970s to the present.

Before Sioux City was founded, the famous Lewis and Clark Expedition camped in the area in 1804. In fact, one of its members, Sgt. Charles Floyd, was buried within the city's future boundaries. When Theophile Bruguier built a trading post in the location in 1849, its only source of transportation and contact with the rest of the country was the Missouri River. There was a growing population in eastern Iowa, but Sioux City was cut off from it by several hundred miles of wilderness. Soon others settled around Brugier's trading post, and a town was established prior to the Civil War. It became a supply center for explorers, hunters, and miners of the northern Great Plains.

The arrival of the railroads in the 1870s ushered in a new era. Sioux City now had an all-season mode of transportation. The railroads permitted people to settle in the area and to be able to export agricultural products to the nation and to the world. During the 1880s, a stockyard and meatpacking industry developed. These industries encouraged more railroad growth, which permitted competition and a greater opportunity for business ventures to thrive.

Railroads had been planned to go through Sioux City even before the Civil War. It is an irony that the city had three chances to be on the first transcontinental line. During the 1830s, shortly after the demonstration of the practicality of a steam railroad was developed, there was the idea of laying tracks to California. One of the early studies ran the line through Iowa territory. In the 1840s, J. H. Plombe separately planned a transcontinental line running through Dubuque, Iowa, and then straight across the state. The tracks, therefore, would run through the present site of Sioux City.

The United States government began a study for the construction of a transcontinental railroad in the 1850s. The project was headed by Jefferson Davis, the future president of the Confederacy. A U.S. Army lieutenant was sent to the new town of Sioux City to look over the topography as to the possibility of running the transcontinental main line through it. He reported back, however, that construction was not possible due to the mountain ranges to the immediate west of the town. One must wonder what the lieutenant had in mind: the nearest mountains are over 600 miles away from Sioux City.

In spite of the lieutenant's report, Sioux City was still considered for a major role in the future transcontinental railroad. According to the original Pacific Railroad Act of 1861, there were three rail lines to merge into a single one near the future North Platte, Nebraska. One of these lines verged southwest out of Sioux City. Pres. Abraham Lincoln later revised the plan and eliminated the Sioux City trackage. He directed all the railroads from the east to converge on Council Bluffs, Iowa, rather than in central Nebraska.

When the citizens of Sioux City learned that the transcontinental route would pass them to the south and the anticipated arrival of the Illinois Central Railroad was delayed, business people invested capital to build their own line to connect with it near Missouri Valley, Iowa. This Sioux City and Pacific Railroad began operation in 1868, almost a year before the completion of the transcontinental. The Illinois Central arrived in the city a bit later. The Illinois line was a more direct link with Chicago and eastern carriers. Another railroad to the north, the Sioux City and St. Paul Railroad came shortly thereafter. It made an agreement to use the Illinois Central tracks for over 20 miles from Le Mars to Sioux City. The Sioux City and St. Paul joined with and built other lines in Nebraska and in the 1880s became the Chicago, St. Paul, Minneapolis, and Omaha Railway. It was commonly called the Omaha Road in its territory.

Sioux City was originally to be the western terminus of the Chicago, Milwaukee, and St. Paul Railway. It turned, however, to cross the Big Sioux River at Canton, South Dakota. It wanted to position itself to build in Dakota Territory. The Milwaukee Road, as it became known, came to Sioux City through the purchase of the Sioux City and Dakota Railroad. It built another entrance during the 1880s from its main line in central Iowa. Those tracks from out of Manilla completed the circuit. The Milwaukee Road used this southern track as its main line from Sioux City to Chicago.

Railroad traffic to the stockyards and other growing industries encouraged Sioux Citians to build their own railroad to points north. Toward the end of the 19th century, Sioux Citians built their own interstate railroad to connect with Duluth, Minnesota. This Sioux City and Northern Railroad was constructed to Garretson, Minnesota, before it went bankrupt during the panic of 1893. It was taken over by the Great Northern Railway shortly thereafter. The last major company to build to Sioux City was the Chicago, Burlington and Quincy. The Burlington Route, as it was called, entered by the Omaha Road bridge in 1916.

These railroads built branch lines during the years prior to World War I. These tracks radiated outward as spokes in a wheel to connect the numerous small towns with the growing agricultural center of Sioux City. The main attractions were the stockyards and meatpacking companies. Farmers rode with their cattle and hogs in the caboose—which was also known as the drover's car. They sold their animals at the stockyards auction, enjoyed an overnight stay in the big city, and then picked up supplies and took the train home.

The railroads and the meatpacking industry caused Sioux City to grow by leaps and bounds. Prior to the arrival of the railroads, Sioux City's population was approaching about 4,000. By the middle of the 1880s, it reached almost 20,000. By 1890, the population grew to 50,000, and the city had 60 passenger trains a day running in every direction. Another economic barometer was the price of land. Before the arrival of the railroad, land in and around Sioux City was worth about $2 an acre. Shortly after the first rail companies built to Sioux City, an acre was valued at $7. With most trackage constructed by the 1890s, and the huge population growth, the price of an acre rose to $300!

With its phenomenally rapid growth, some citizens believed that Sioux City would quickly eclipse Chicago as the Midwest's most prominent city. The city fathers expanded the borders in the belief that the population growth of the 1880s would continue into the foreseeable future. Some historians consider Sioux City to have been the 10th largest rail center in the United

States at that time. That estimate is believable as Sioux City was the home to the sixth largest meat processing complex in the entire world.

Because of the many rail companies and tracks in the city, investors constructed their own local railroad company to move cars from one railroad to another within the city limits. The Sioux City Terminal Railway was every bit as important as its counterparts in Kansas City, St. Louis and Chicago. To avoid the numerous rail crossings in the approach to the downtown and to the stockyards, Sioux City constructed the nation's third elevated steam railway. The Sioux City El was a model for the famous tourist landmark in present-day Chicago.

Huge changes in transportation came during the mid-years of the 20th century. The Sioux City Terminal Railway ceased operation in 1970. Cattle and hogs arrived at the stockyards and the finished products now moved by truck. The stockyards soon declined as farmers sold their animals directly to the packing companies. The whole meatpacking scene changed in the city. Iowa Beef Processors opened a plant in Dakota City, Nebraska, while in Sioux City one packinghouse after another closed. By the beginning of the 21st century, Home Depot built a store on the grounds formerly occupied by the once largest roofed stockyards in the world. In 1971, Amtrak was formed, and Sioux City was not on any of its routes. The last passenger train left Sioux City on the Illinois Central just before the National Rail Passenger Corporation was created.

Sioux City is still a very important rail center. With the mega mergers through the 1990s, BNSF (the official name of the former Burlington Northern Santa Fe), Union Pacific, and Canadian National rail companies have tracks to Sioux City. Even without the stockyards and large meatpacking industry, these three Class I railroads still operate in the municipality. Canadian National has taken over the Illinois Central, the Burlington Route's and Great Northern's successor BNSF has a major north-south line through Sioux City as an important western connection. With its takeover of the former Chicago and Northwestern, the Union Pacific has a primary shortcut from the Pacific coast to Minneapolis through Sioux City.

With the decline of private railroad company passenger trains, Sioux City's growth also slowed down. Its industry changed during the second half of the 20th century. Through trains still stop in the city to change crews. Others actually are made up in Sioux City. There is plenty of rail activity, but it is freight only. Freight builds commerce, and Sioux City's current great rail system holds the promise for a growing economy and a bright future.

One

The Early Railroads

As the first transcontinental line was being constructed out of Omaha and out of Sacramento simultaneously, Sioux Citians waited for the rails of the Illinois Central Railroad to arrive from the east. It was hoped that the Illinois Central would turn south out of Sioux City to connect with the Union Pacific. If not, Sioux City would lose connections with the Pacific coast. There were numerous delays, however, in the westward progression of the Illinois Central. Seeing the necessity of rail connections, the citizens of Sioux City took matters into their own hands.

Several Sioux City businessmen invested their money and built their own Sioux City and Pacific Railroad. Even though the *Pacific* portion was part of its name, this railroad was not planned to build to the West Coast. The second part of the name was more of a symbolic gesture. The line went south and connected with the then Chicago and Northwestern Railway's Iowa district near Missouri Valley. This connection permitted the linking with trains that went both east to Chicago and west to California.

The Sioux City and Pacific Railroad opened up Sioux City to the nation. The town was no longer cut off from the rest of Iowa and the country as a whole. There would be a steady and permanent arrival and departure of people, supplies, and goods to and from northwest Iowa's largest city. Sioux Citians could now read in their newspapers what happened only hours before anywhere in the United States due to the telegraph connections that accompanied railroad growth.

The railroads brought Sioux City another great advantage. By the 1880s, there was significant development in the design of stock cars and ice-cooled cars. Humane livestock cars were being built with established rules on taking care of animals in transit to slaughterhouses. At the same time a network of icing stations emerged throughout the nation to keep these cars cooled to ship carcasses to markets without fear of their spoilage en route. In fact, there developed an industry to safeguard the transporting of meat products. The railroad connections, along with new technologies of meat products transport, placed Sioux City in an ideal position for economic development in the meat-processing industry. And Sioux City took complete advantage of these new opportunities.

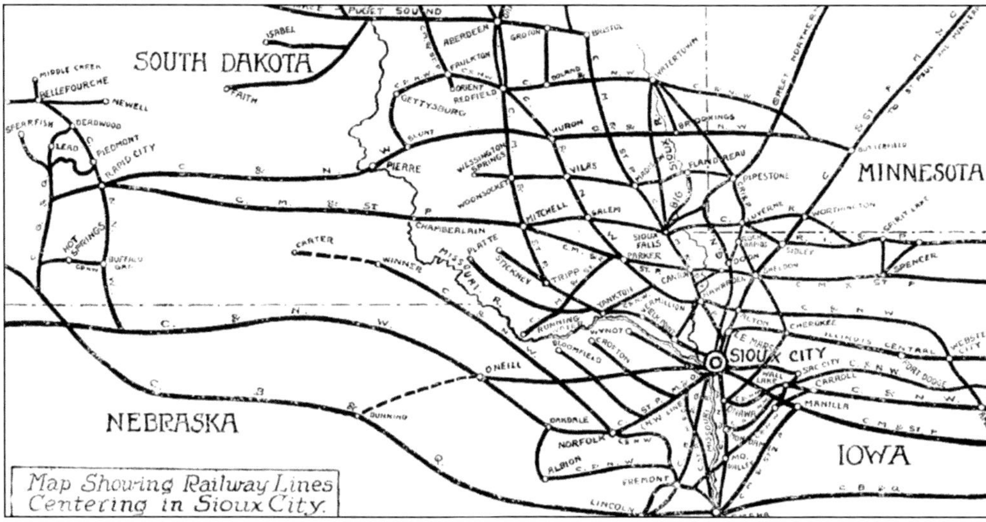

This map was created for a Sioux City promotional page sometime around 1920. As shown here, the Chicago, Burlington and Quincy Railroad completed its line from Lincoln through Fremont, Nebraska, to Sioux City in 1916. The Illinois Central has tracks completed to Sioux Falls, South Dakota. They were mistakenly left out on this map. (Courtesy of George R. Lindblade.)

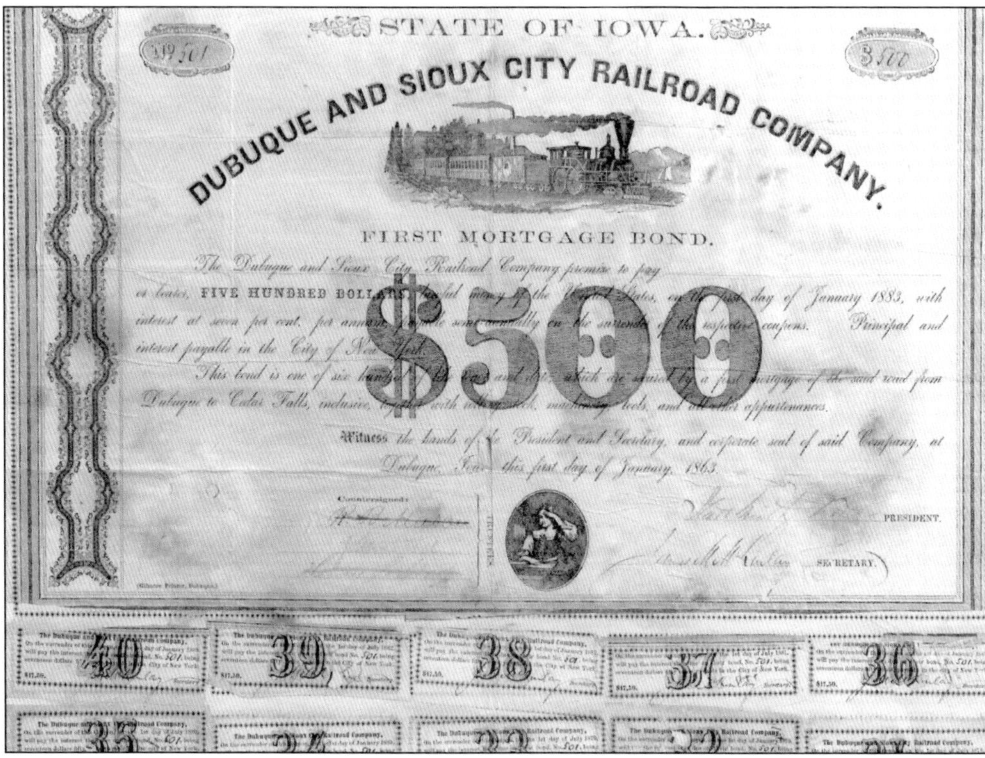

The Dubuque and Sioux City Railroad was the first district company of the Illinois Central in Iowa. The railroad, however, went bankrupt and construction was halted. The railroad magnate John Blair later took over and reorganized the company and completed construction to Sioux City. Blair was truly a railroad creator. He had been president of the huge Pennsylvania Railroad Company. (Author's collection.)

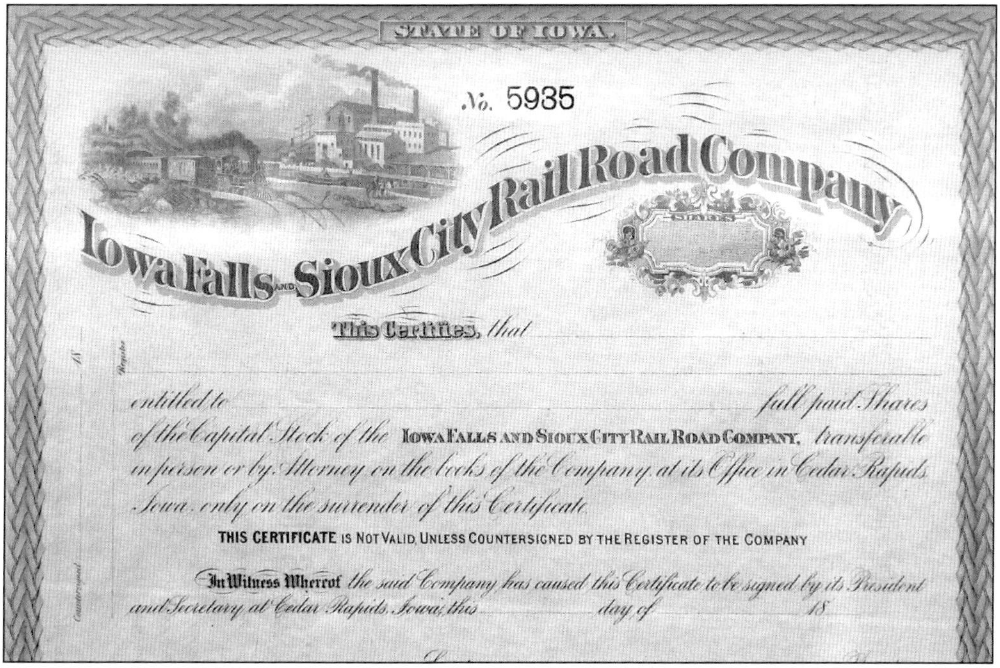

STATE OF IOWA.

No. 5935

Iowa Falls and Sioux City Rail Road Company

Shares

This Certifies, that

entitled to full paid Shares of the Capital Stock of the IOWA FALLS AND SIOUX CITY RAIL ROAD COMPANY, transferable in person or by Attorney on the books of the Company, at its Office in Cedar Rapids Iowa, only on the surrender of this Certificate.

THIS CERTIFICATE IS NOT VALID, UNLESS COUNTERSIGNED BY THE REGISTER OF THE COMPANY

In Witness Whereof the said Company has caused this Certificate to be signed by its President and Secretary at Cedar Rapids, Iowa, this day of 18

The Iowa Falls and Sioux City Rail Road Company was a continuation of the Illinois Central's trek across Iowa. The Iowa Falls and Sioux City existed as a legal entity after the construction to Sioux City was completed. Such regional or district parts of a larger railroad company were common in the 19th century. (Courtesy of Richard Donaway.)

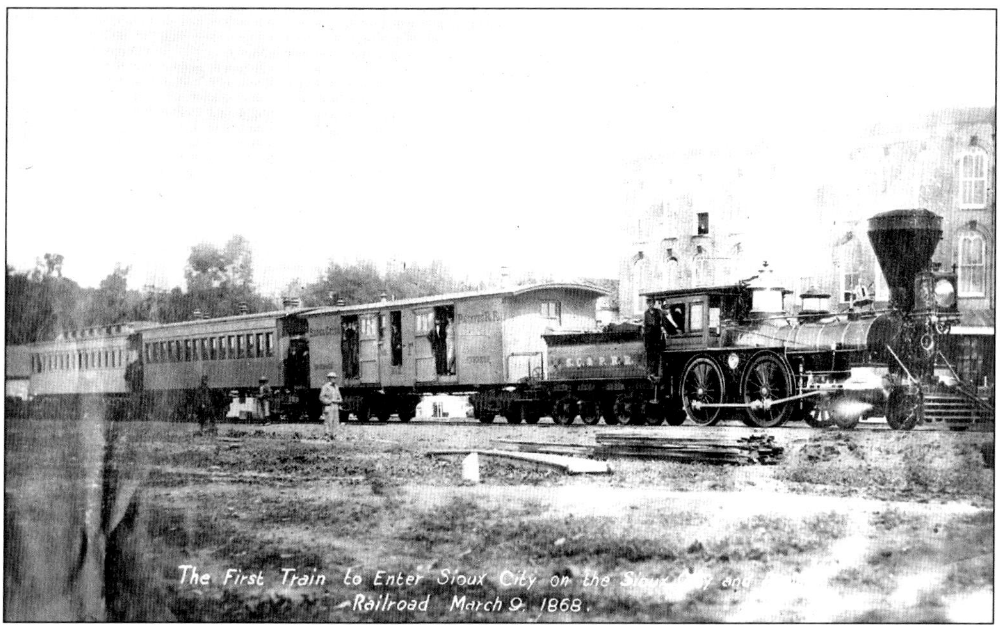

The arrival of the first train in any community was a great occasion. In March 1868, Sioux City had a transportation and communication link with the rest of the country. The Sioux City and Pacific Railroad ran between Sioux City and near Missouri Valley, Iowa. It was constructed with investments from Sioux City businessmen. (Courtesy of the Sioux City Public Museum.)

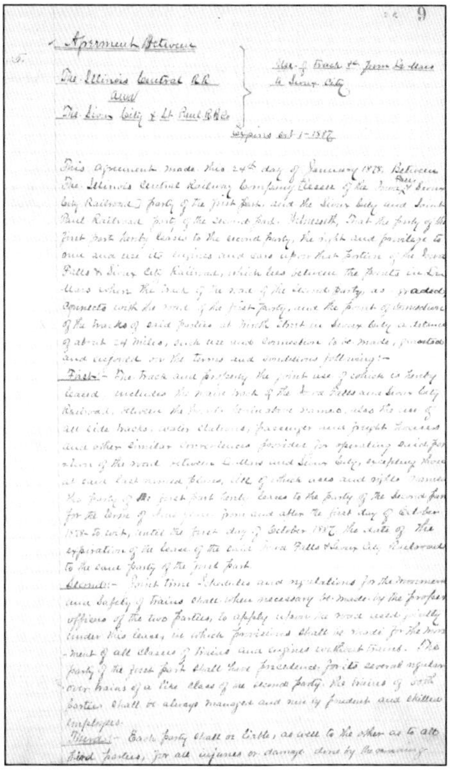

Before typewriters (not to mention computers) everything not printed by press was handwritten. This page opened the agreement for the Sioux City and St. Paul Railroad to use the Illinois Central tracks from Le Mars to Sioux City for a distance of 25 miles. The agreement has been renewed to this day. It is now between the Canadian National Railway and the Union Pacific. (Courtesy of Bill Metz.)

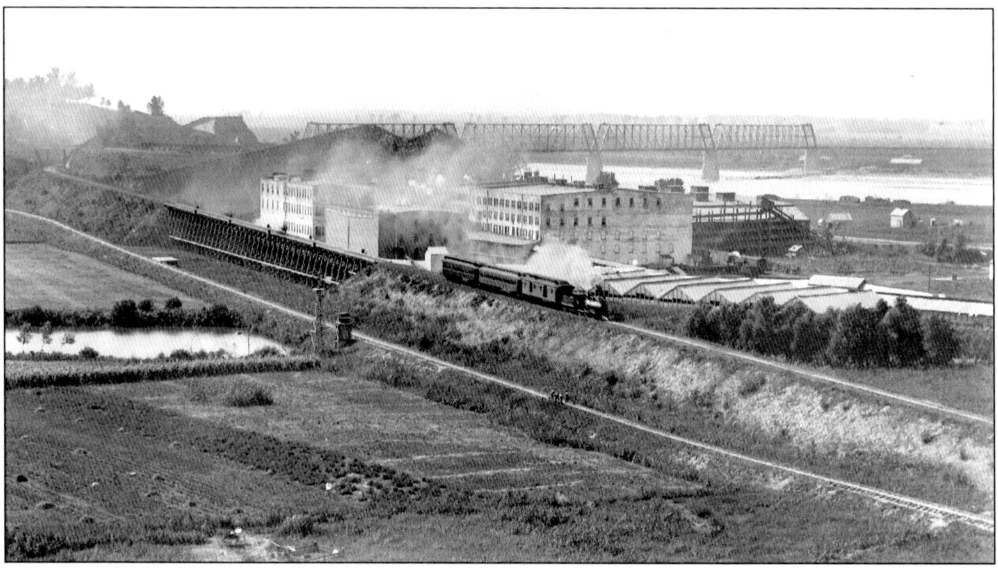

The scene is probably from the early 1890s. In all likelihood, a Chicago, St. Paul, Minneapolis and Omaha Railway train is entering Sioux City from the south. There is also a crew of the Sioux City El working on its ground-level tracks leading to the Morningside suburb. The large building behind the train is the Silberhorn Meat Packing Company. (Courtesy of the Sioux City Public Museum.)

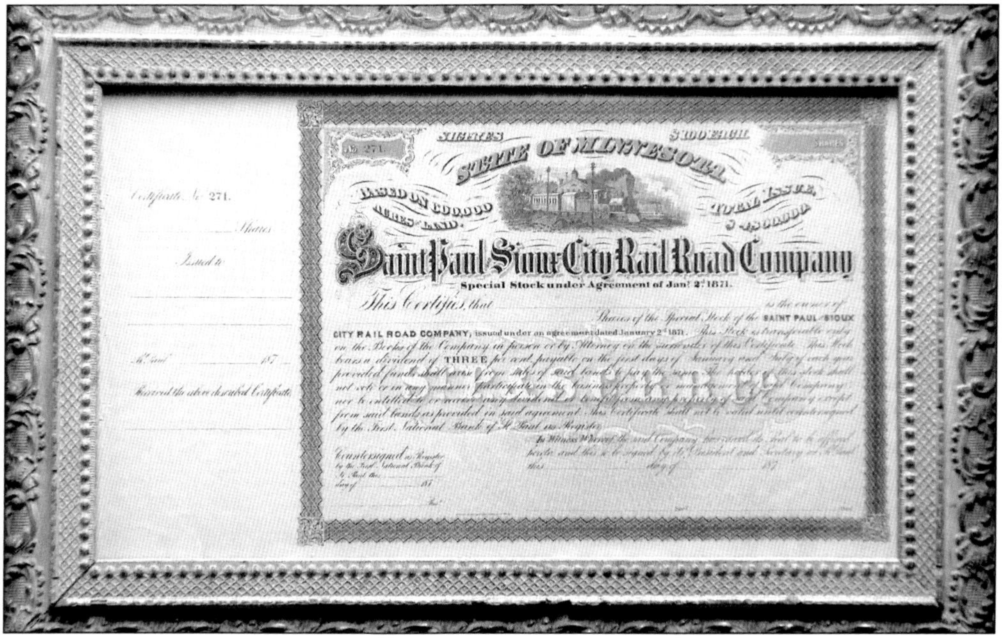

The St. Paul and Sioux City Rail Road Company was the Minnesota predecessor of the Chicago, St. Paul, Minneapolis and Omaha Railway. Railroads in the 19th century issued volumes of stock particularly during their first or start-up years. It met the Sioux City and St. Paul Railroad at the Iowa and Minnesota border. (Courtesy of Richard Donaway.)

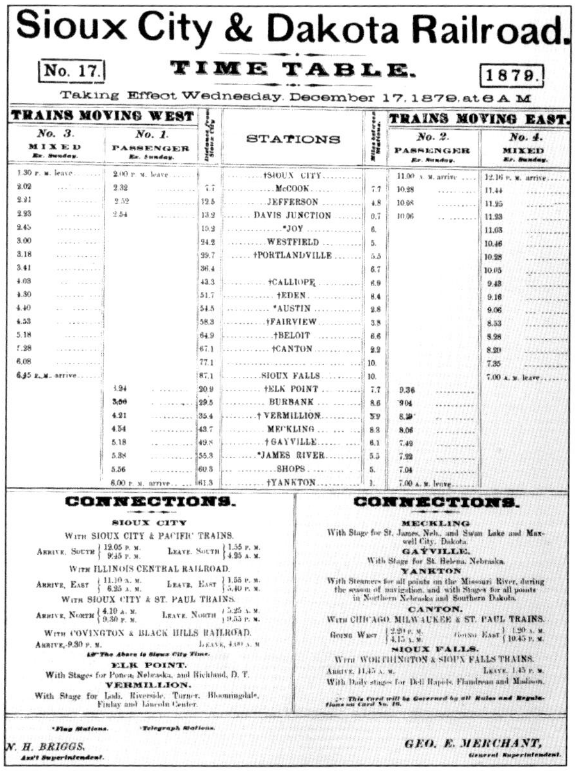

Sioux City & Dakota Railroad.

No. 17. **TIME TABLE.** 1879.

Taking Effect Wednesday, December 17, 1879, at 6 A M

TRAINS MOVING WEST No. 3. MIXED Ex. Sunday.	No. 1. PASSENGER Ex. Sunday.	Distance from Sioux City	STATIONS	Miles between Stations	TRAINS MOVING EAST. No. 2. PASSENGER Ex. Sunday.	No. 4. MIXED Ex. Sunday.
1.30 P. M. leave	2.00 P. M. leave		†SIOUX CITY		11.00 A. M. arrive	12.16 P. M. arrive
2.02	2.32	7.7	McCOOK	7.7	10.28	11.44
2.21	2.52	12.5	JEFFERSON	4.8	10.08	11.25
2.23	2.54	13.2	DAVIS JUNCTION	0.7	10.06	11.23
2.45		19.2	*JOY	6.		11.03
3.00		24.2	WESTFIELD	5.		10.46
3.18		29.7	†PORTLANDVILLE	5.5		10.28
3.41		36.4		6.7		10.05
4.03		43.3	†CALLIOPE	6.9		9.48
4.30		51.7	†EDEN	8.4		9.16
4.40		54.5	*AUSTIN	2.8		9.06
4.53		58.3	†FAIRVIEW	3.8		8.53
5.18		64.9	†BELOIT	6.6		8.28
5.28		67.1	†CANTON	2.2		8.20
6.08		77.1		10.		7.35
6.45 P. M. arrive		87.1	SIOUX FALLS	10.		7.00 A. M. leave
	3.24	20.9	†ELK POINT	7.7	9.36	
	3.56	29.5	BURBANK	8.6	9.04	
	4.21	35.4	† VERMILLION	5.9	8.39	
	4.54	43.7	MECKLING	8.3	8.06	
	5.18	49.8	† GAYVILLE	6.1	7.49	
	5.38	55.3	*JAMES RIVER	5.5	7.22	
	5.56	60.3	SHOPS	5.	7.04	
	6.00 P. M. arrive	61.3	†YANKTON	1.	7.00 A. M. leave	

CONNECTIONS.

SIOUX CITY

WITH SIOUX CITY & PACIFIC TRAINS.

ARRIVE, SOUTH { 12.05 P. M. 9.45 P. M. LEAVE, SOUTH { 1.55 P. M. 4.25 A. M.

WITH ILLINOIS CENTRAL RAILROAD.

ARRIVE, EAST { 11.10 A. M. 6.25 A. M. LEAVE, EAST { 1.55 P. M. 5.40 P. M.

WITH SIOUX CITY & ST. PAUL TRAINS.

ARRIVE, NORTH { 4.10 A. M. 9.30 P. M. LEAVE, NORTH { 5.25 A. M. 9.55 P. M.

WITH COVINGTON & BLACK HILLS RAILROAD.

ARRIVE, 9.30 P. M. LEAVE, 4.40 A. M.

The Above is Sioux City Time.

ELK POINT.

With Stages for Ponca, Nebraska, and Richland, D. T.

VERMILLION.

With Stage for Lodi, Riverside, Turner, Bloomingdale, Finlay and Lincoln Center.

CONNECTIONS.

MECKLING

With Stage for St. James, Neb., and Swan Lake and Maxwell City, Dakota.

GAYVILLE.

With Stage for St. Helena, Nebraska.

YANKTON

With Steamers for all points on the Missouri River, during the season of navigation, and with Stages for all points in Northern Nebraska and Southern Dakota.

CANTON.

WITH CHICAGO, MILWAUKEE & ST. PAUL TRAINS.

GOING WEST { 2.20 P. M. 4.15 A. M. GOING EAST { 1.20 A. M. 10.45 P. M.

SIOUX FALLS.

WITH WORTHINGTON & SIOUX FALLS TRAINS.

ARRIVE, 11.45 A. M. LEAVE, 1.45 P. M.

With Daily stages for Dell Rapids, Flandreau and Madison.

This Card will be Governed by all Rules and Regulations on Card No. 16.

*Flag Stations. †Telegraph Stations.

N. H. BRIGGS, Ass't Superintendent.

GEO. E. MERCHANT, General Superintendent.

The Sioux City and Dakota Railroad opened up the Dakota Territory to Sioux City markets by the end of the 1870s. At first, train schedules were placed on placards in various places before the printing and distribution of timetables. Shortly after its formation, the Sioux City and Dakota was taken over by the Chicago, Milwaukee and St. Paul Railway. (Author's collection.)

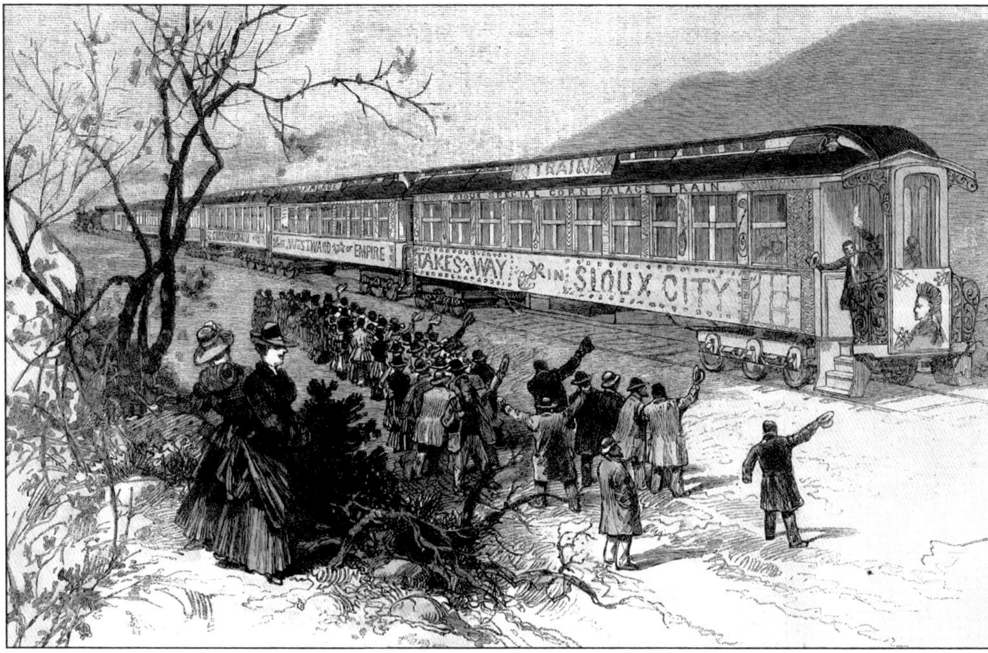

This postcard sketch illustrates the "Sioux City Corn Train." Citizens of Sioux City chartered a train to ride to the inauguration of Pres. Benjamin Harrison in 1889. The cars had drawings of Sioux City agricultural products along the coach sides. It was a unique marketing tool for Sioux City—all the way to Washington, D.C. (Courtesy of George R. Lindblade.)

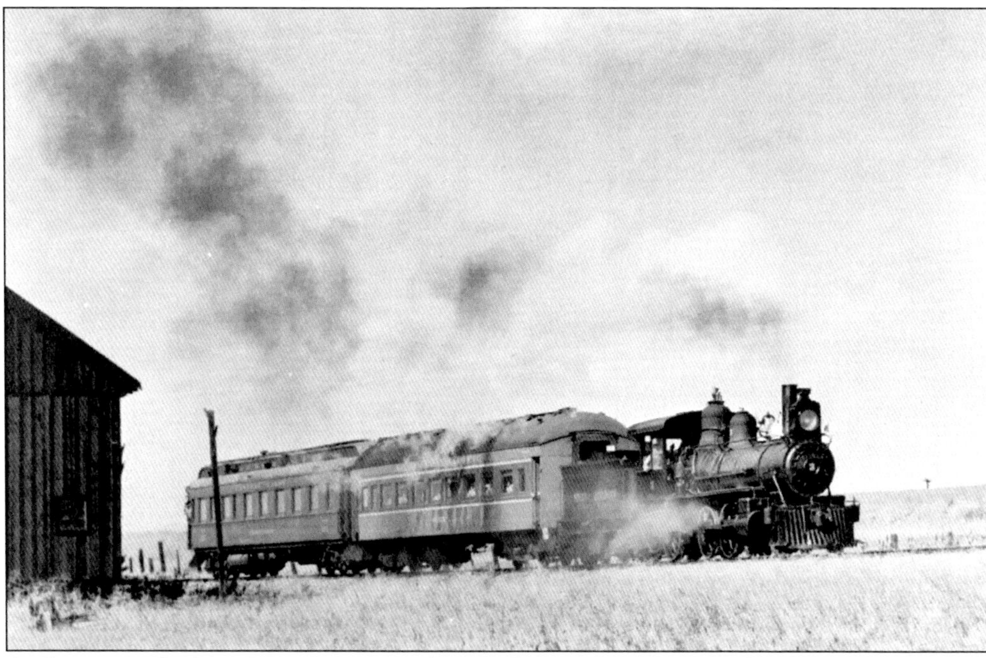

A classic standard or American type of steam locomotive enters or leaves Sioux City. This photograph was taken before 1890, as the headlight oil lamp on the locomotive was electrified at the end of the 19th century. Coaches converted to electric lights by the 1920s. (Courtesy of George R. Lindblade.)

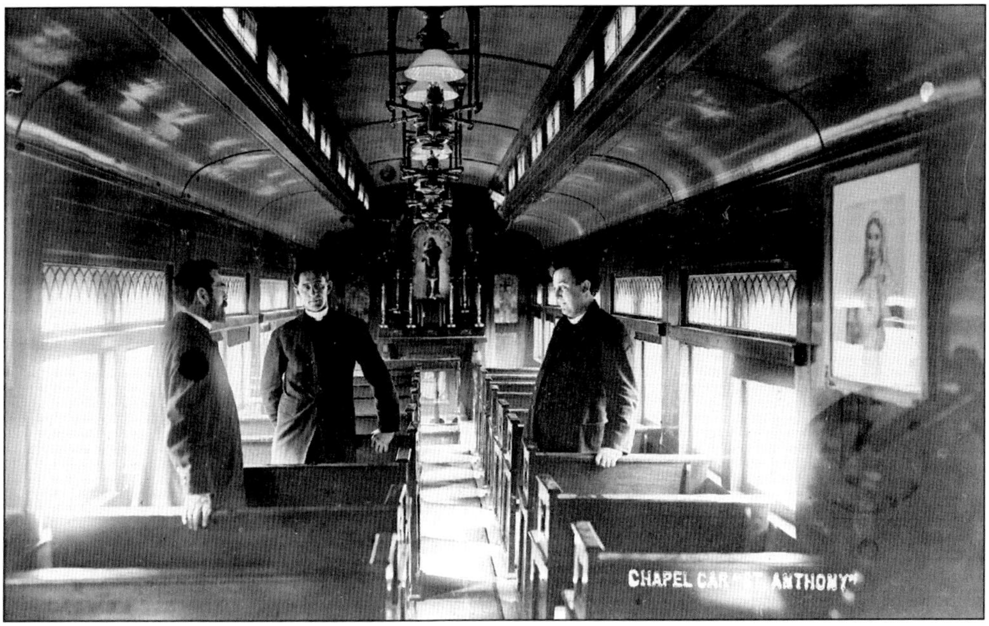

Several religious denominations had chapel cars to bring ministers and priests to hold services in remotely located towns. The Catholic chapel car *St. Anthony* was stationed in Sioux City for a period of time—possibly for repairs. The altar is clearly visible in this photograph. The car had a small living quarters for the priest and a confessional. (Courtesy of the Sioux City Public Museum.)

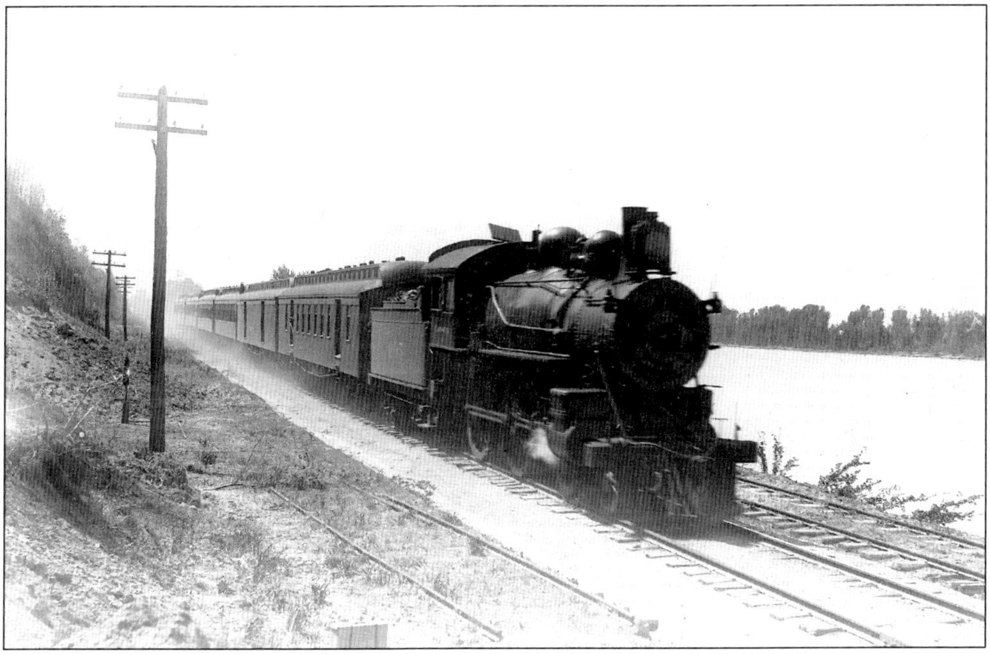

This image is an archetypical photograph of a Sioux City and Pacific Railroad passenger train approaching downtown Sioux City from the south. The Missouri River is in the background. The line was double tracked at the end of the 19th century when this photograph was taken. (Courtesy of the Sioux City Public Museum.)

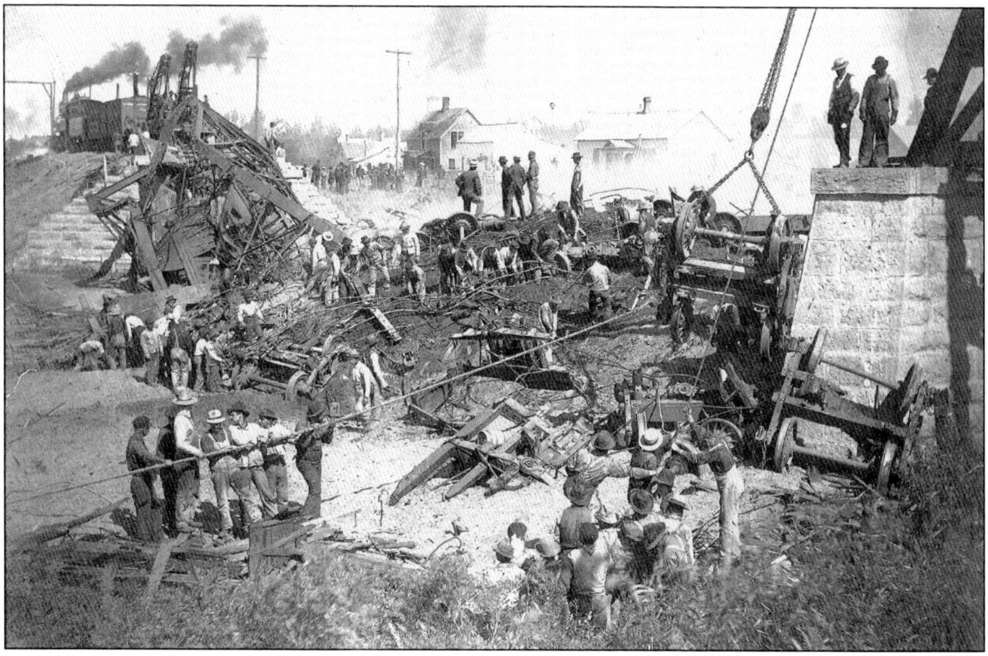

Bridge collapses in the 19th century were not uncommon. Many were hastily constructed and with flawed materials. Locomotives and passenger cars became heavier, and the old structures were not able to accommodate them. The exact site is unidentified. (Courtesy of the Sioux City Public Museum.)

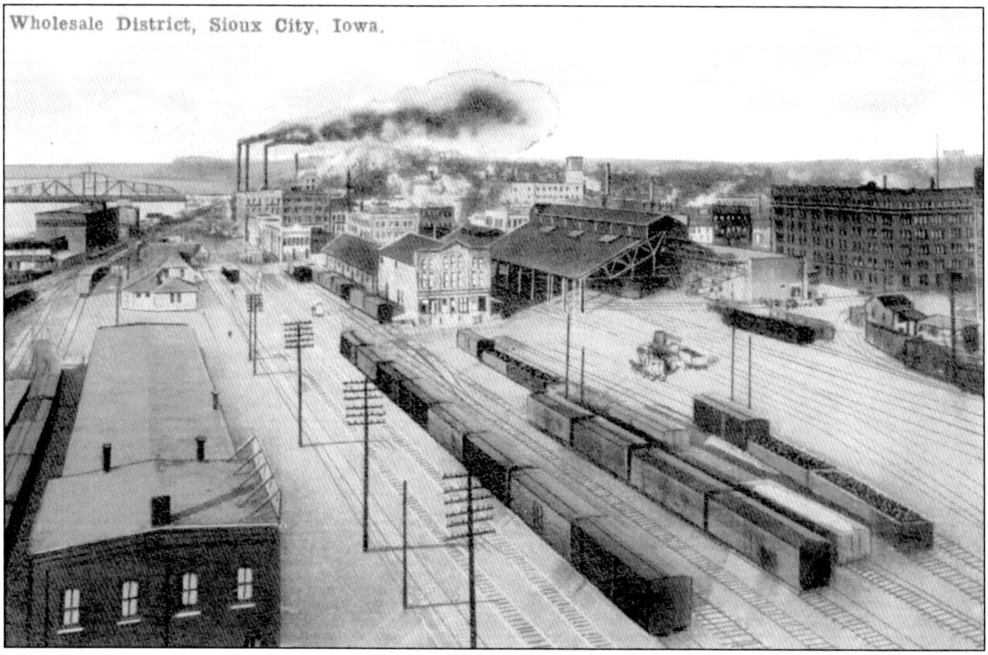

This postcard shows the downtown area and the large number of tracks that led to local businesses. The Combination Bridge can be seen at the upper-left corner. The sketch is probably just prior to World War I. It is clear that the railroad dominated the downtown scene. (Courtesy of George R. Lindblade.)

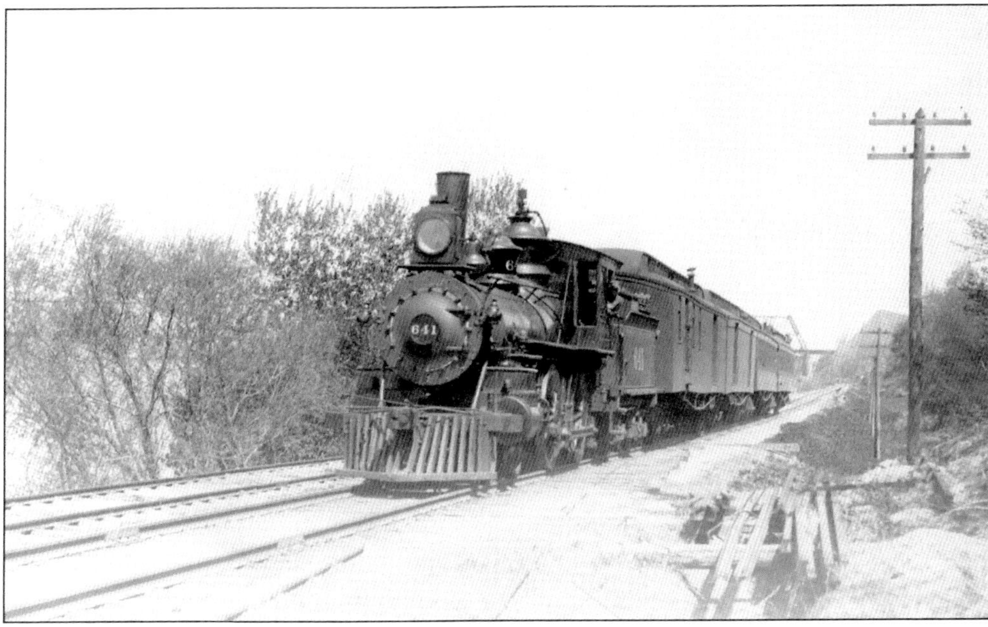

This classic early-20th-century 4-4-0 American-type steam locomotive is leaving Sioux City on its way to Missouri Valley. (The numbers 4-4-0 is a classification that means four wheel swivel front truck, four larger drive wheels, and no wheels under the steam locomotive cab.) The Missouri River is on the left of the locomotive. At Missouri Valley, Sioux Citians could take trains to Chicago or to San Francisco. (Courtesy of George R. Lindblade.)

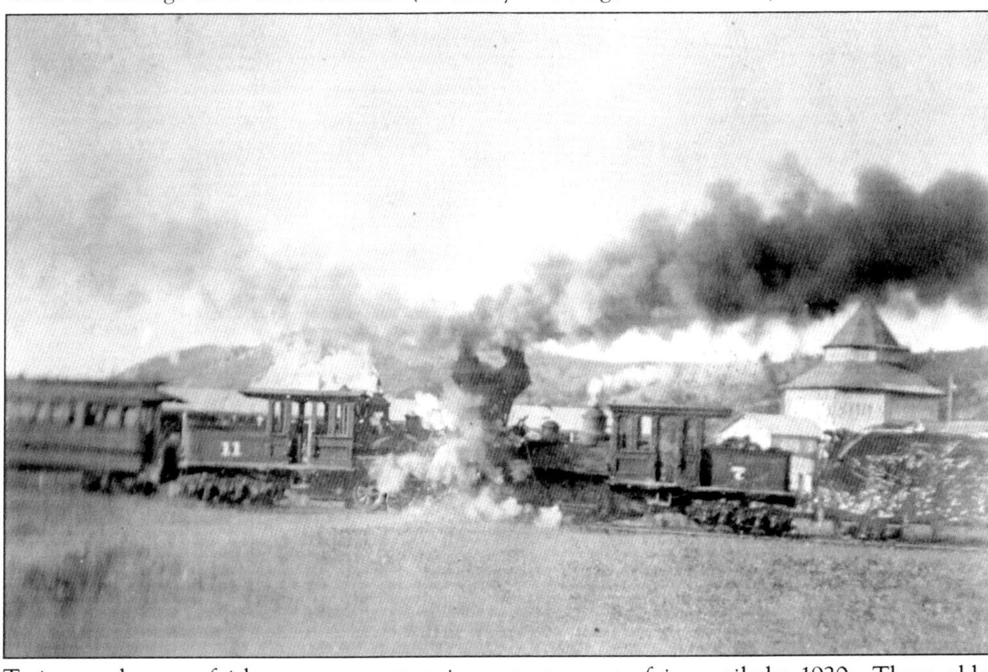

Train wrecks were fairly common entertainment at county fairs until the 1920s. These older locomotives ran into each other at full throttle on a mile long track in Sioux City in 1896. These events were dangerous. Bystanders could be killed by exploding boilers and flying parts. (Courtesy of the Sioux City Public Museum.)

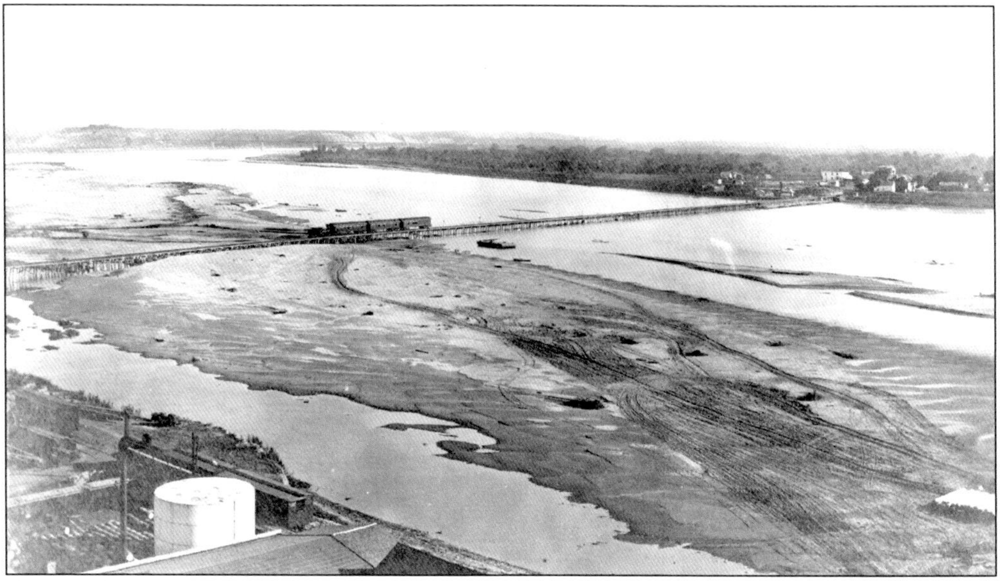

The Combination Bridge Company built a railroad trestle across the Missouri River to transport construction materials to both banks. South Sioux City at that time was known as Covington. The tracks on the trestle were the only rails built by the Pacific Short Line Railroad. (Courtesy of the Sioux City Public Museum.)

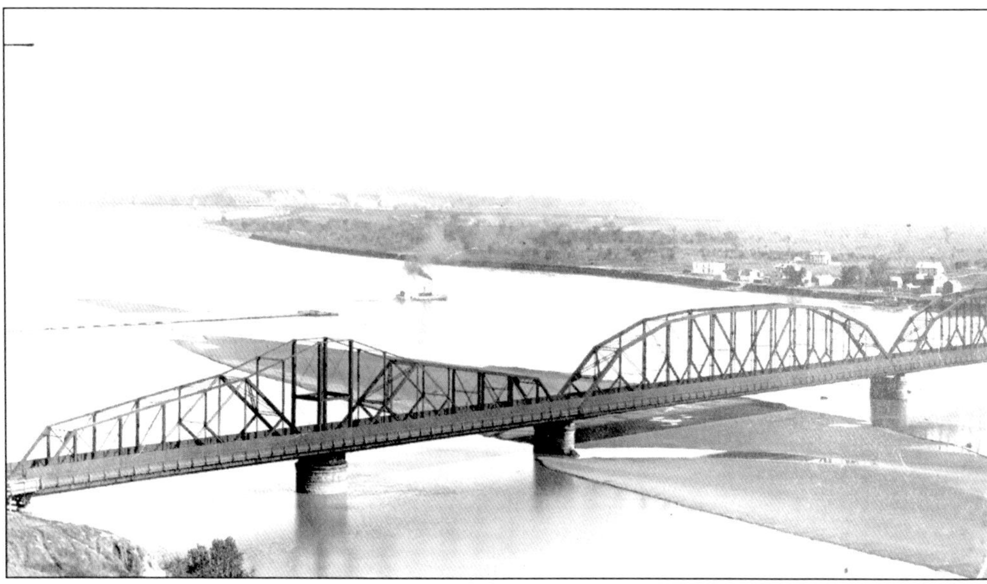

The Combination Bridge was originally built for the Pacific Short Line Railroad. It stood for over 70 years and was used mostly for automobile traffic. Trains never crossed on it. It was replaced by the Siouxland Veterans Bridge for automobiles and pedestrians in 1981. (Courtesy of the Sioux City Public Museum.)

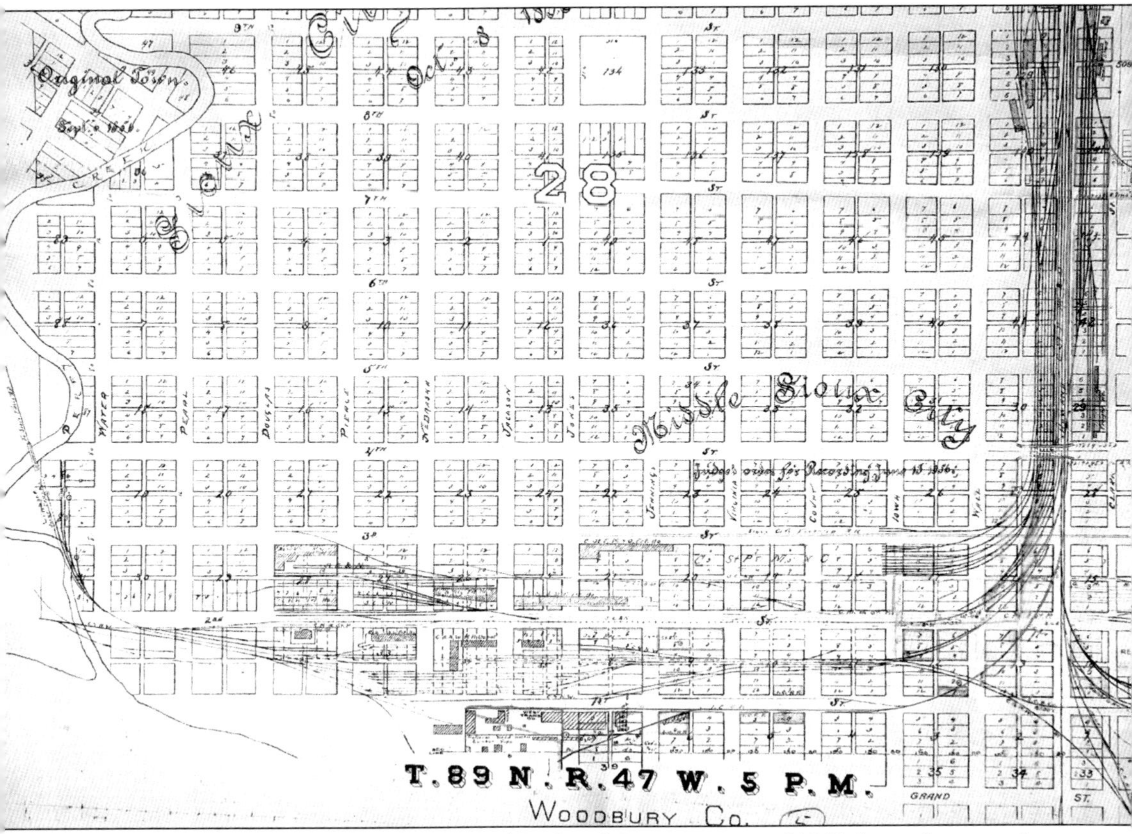

This track map printed for the Illinois Central Railroad Company around 1917, shows the myriad of tracks in the immediate downtown of Sioux City. It covered an area from a block east of Wall Street to just west of Water Street. (Courtesy of Jim Adamson and the Depot Renovation, Inc., Cherokee, Iowa.)

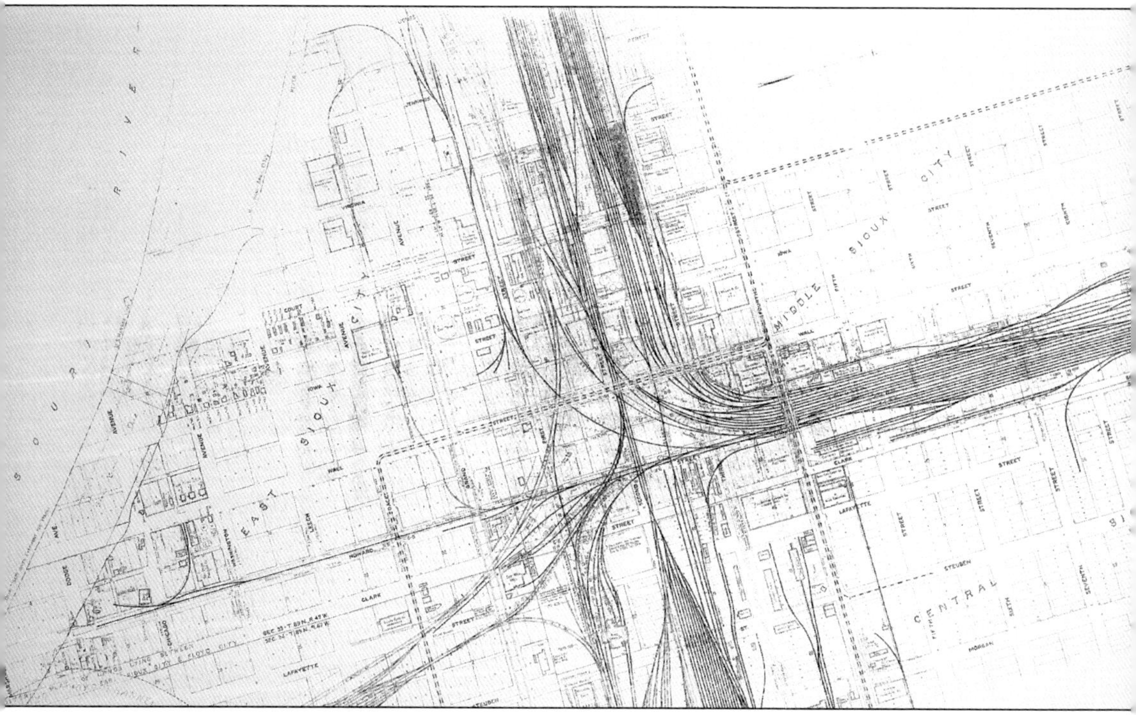

Sioux City still had a large number of tracks in the downtown area in 1950. The entrance to the meatpacking complex rail yard is to the lower left on this map. By the year 2000, there was only one track through downtown Sioux City. (Courtesy of Richard Donaway.)

Two

The Chicago and Northwestern Railway

The Chicago and Northwestern Railway had the most extensive system of branch lines around Sioux City. The railway also owned controlling stock shares of the Chicago, St. Paul, Minneapolis, and Omaha Railway. Sioux City's first railroad, the Sioux City and Pacific Railroad, joined with the Chicago and Northwestern on its main east–west line northeast of Omaha. The Sioux City and Pacific eventually merged into the larger system in 1903, during a flurry of such purchases. The Chicago and Northwestern also purchased, built, and extended other branch lines to Sioux City by the early 20th century.

The Chicago, St. Paul, Minneapolis, and Omaha Railway came to Sioux City by the tracks of two interconnecting companies. In Minnesota, it was originally the St. Paul and Sioux City Railroad, and in Iowa, it was known as the reverse, the Sioux City and St. Paul Railroad. Its growth to Omaha was made possible by purchases and mergers with companies in eastern Nebraska. Known in the area affectionately as the Omaha Road, its first link in Nebraska was on the roadbed of the former Covington, Columbus and Black Hills Railroad. The Omaha Road connected the agriculturally rich eastern Nebraska with Sioux City. It constructed a bridge across the Missouri River at Sioux City in 1886. At the same time, it eventually charged high toll fees to other railroads that wanted to use the bridge. Both the Union Pacific and the Fremont, Missouri, and Elkhorn Valley Railroads shared these tracks to bring passenger trains to Sioux City in the 1890s. The Chicago, Burlington and Quincy Railroad needed the Omaha Road's bridge when it constructed to Sioux City just before America's entry into World War I.

The Chicago and Northwestern gained controlling ownership in the Omaha Road as early as 1882. The Omaha had the status of "leased carrier" with its parent until 1952. The Chicago and Northwestern made complete acquisition in 1972. Until that time, the Omaha Road kept its own identity, although it did use the outline of the Chicago and Northwestern as its herald. Why the Chicago and Northwestern did not merge the Omaha into its parent company in the early 1900s has been a mystery to railroad historians.

The Chicago and Northwestern Railway system provided a vital service with its eastern and western links, and it prided itself on its slightly over 10 hour passenger schedule to Chicago on its appropriately named train, the *Corn King*.

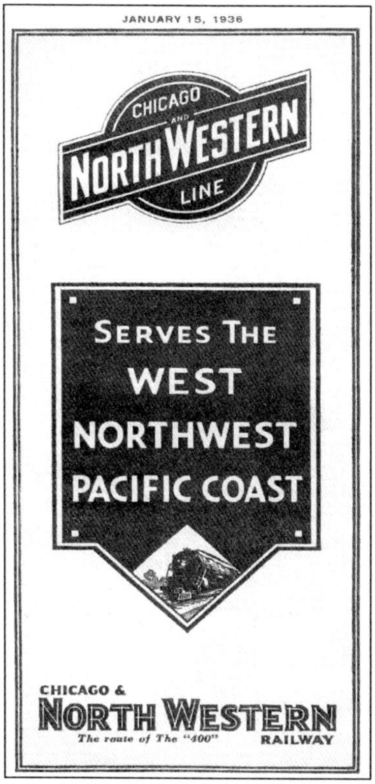

The Chicago and Northwestern Railway used a slanted cigar band–type herald. It is similar in style to the New York Central Railroad system's level, horizontal design. The Chicago and Northwestern timetable is the thickest of the companies that served Sioux City. It had the most branch lines around the city. It included the trains of the Chicago, St. Paul, Minneapolis, and Omaha Railway. This edition is from 1936. (Author's collection.)

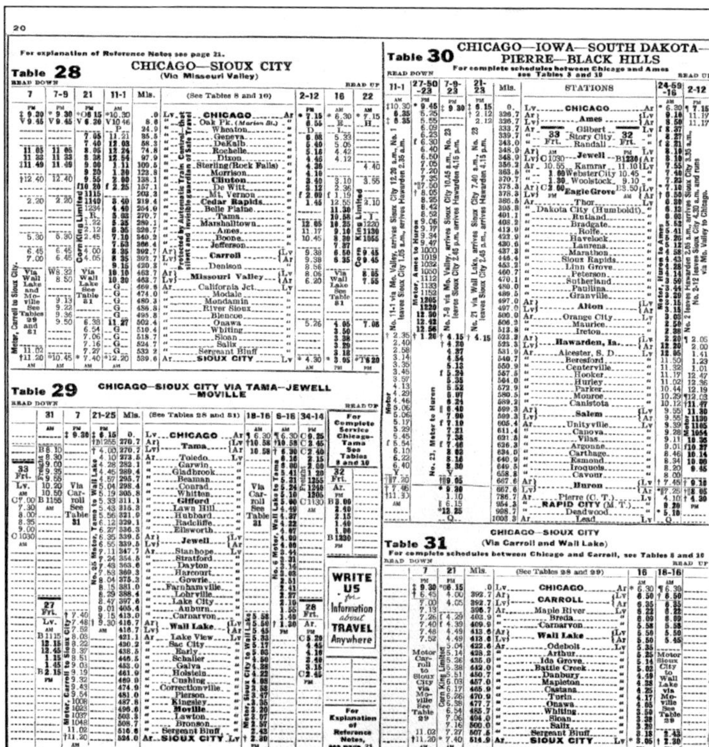

The Chicago and Northwestern offered two train schedules to Chicago that featured different routes. During World War II the Sioux City to Missouri Valley route had a faster-than-10.5-hour train to Chicago. The Wall Lake, Jewell and Tama route took significantly longer. (Author's collection.)

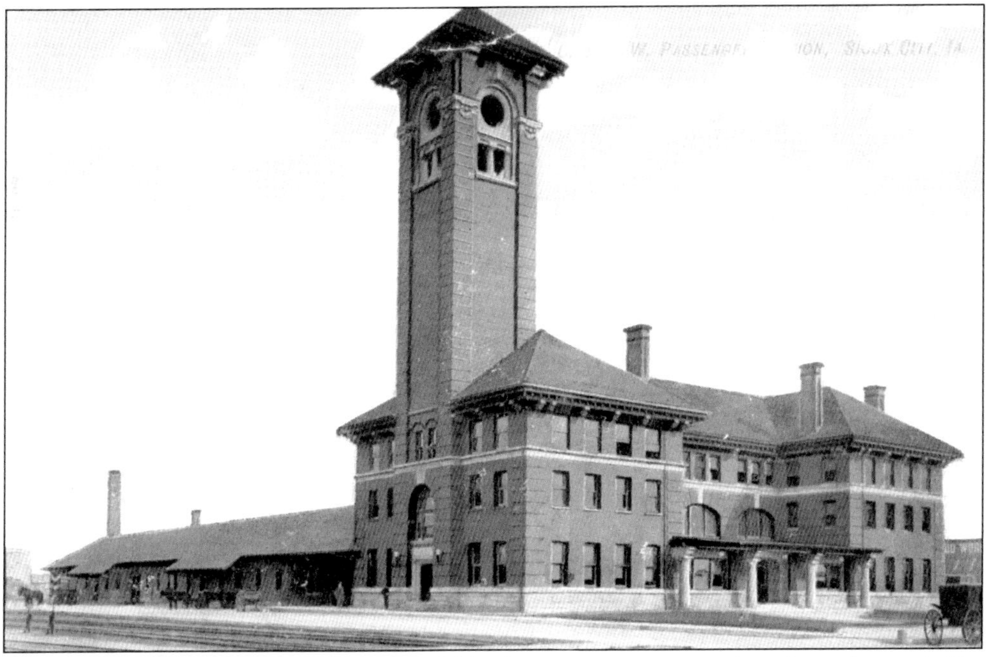

This first photograph of the Chicago and Northwestern station is taken from the trackside. With the horses and carriage in the picture, it was probably taken at the beginning of the 20th century. (Courtesy of the Jack P. Fleckenstein Collection.)

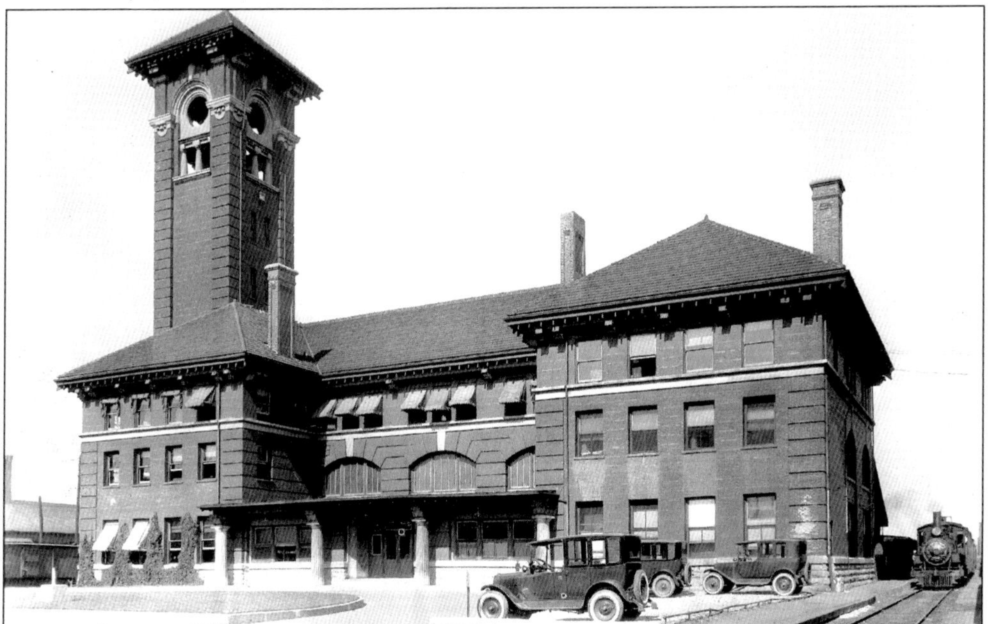

A train is approaching the Chicago and Northwestern passenger station. The scene is from the 1920s. As part of the Northwestern system, the Chicago, St. Paul, Minneapolis, and Omaha Railway used the facility. Until the last years of passenger service in Sioux City, the Illinois Central also picked up and discharged passengers at this station. (Courtesy of the Jack P. Fleckenstein Collection.)

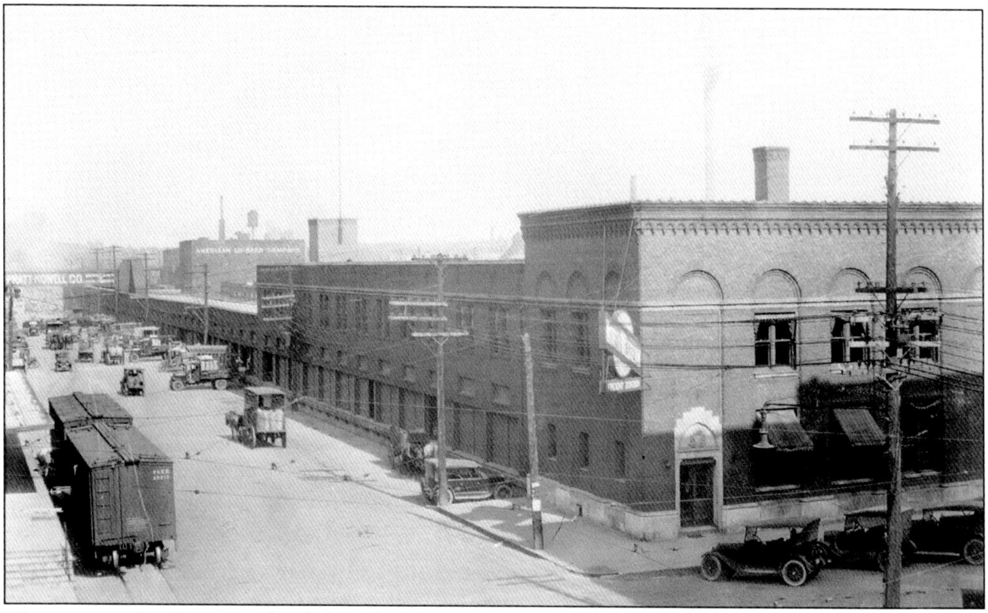

The street-side photograph of the Chicago and Northwestern depot was taken probably around the beginning of the 20th century. The boxcars in the street testify to the many rail spurs to warehouses and other places of deposit and pick up in downtown Sioux City. (Courtesy of George R. Lindblade.)

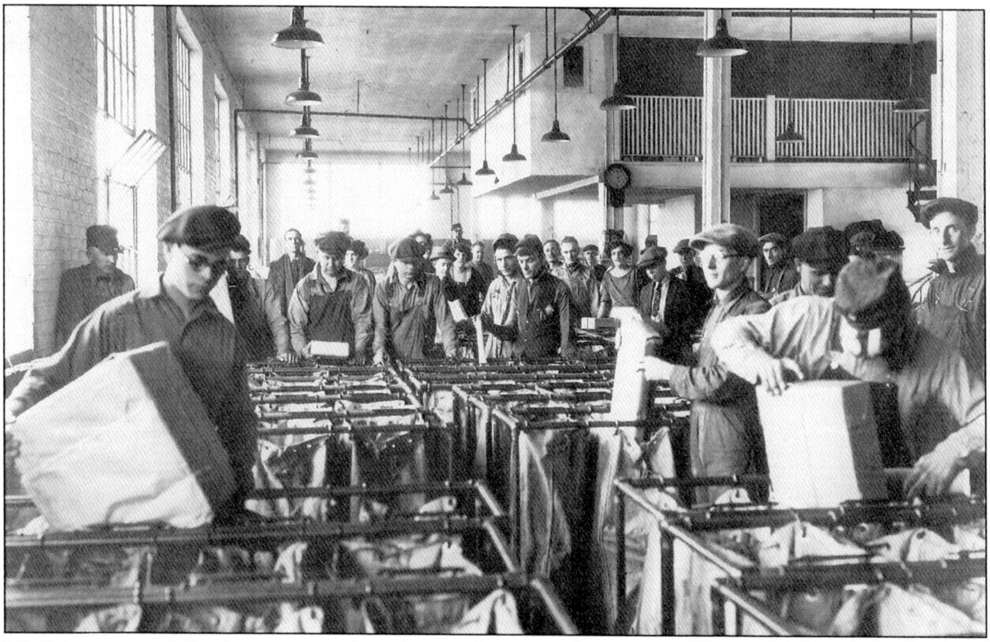

Mail is prepared for being carried and sorted on a railway post office car. The photograph is from the 1920s. The three women are Clara Schmidt Hilton, Henrietta Schmidt Berg (who were sisters), and Hazel McGrath. The federal government insisted on the employment of women. The four men in the foreground are, from left to right, George DeWit, Henry Michaelson, James Humphreys, and Burleigh Fordyce. (Courtesy of the Siouxland Historical Railroad Association.)

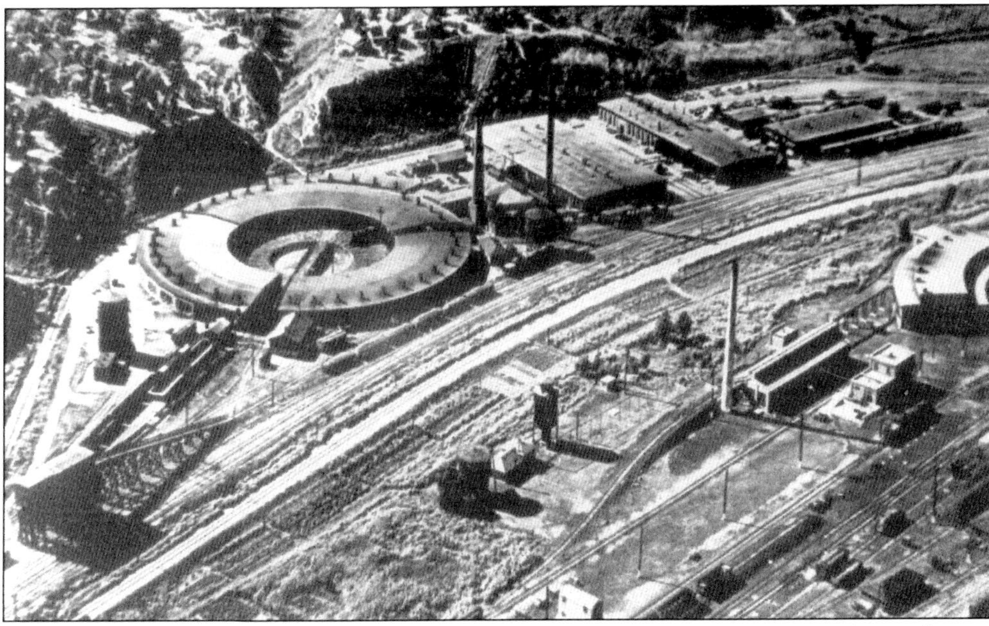

This excellent aerial view of the Chicago and Northwestern and Illinois Central roundhouses shows the railroad complex to the northeast of the downtown. The larger roundhouse on the left belonged to the Chicago and Northwestern and the Chicago, St. Paul, Minneapolis, and Omaha Railway. The smaller one, which is partially cut off, was for the Illinois Central. (Courtesy of the Siouxland Historical Railroad Association.)

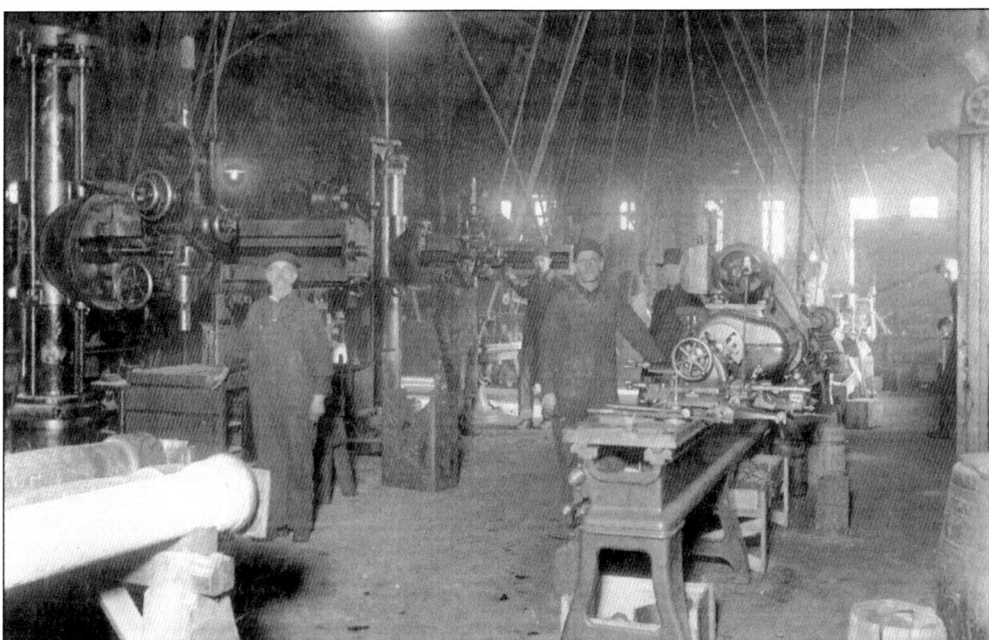

The Chicago, St. Paul, Minneapolis, and Omaha had its carpenter shops at Eighteenth and Howard Streets. The man at the lathe is identified as machinist Jensen. The other workers are unidentified. The photograph is dated January 1917. (Courtesy of the Siouxland Historical Railroad Association.)

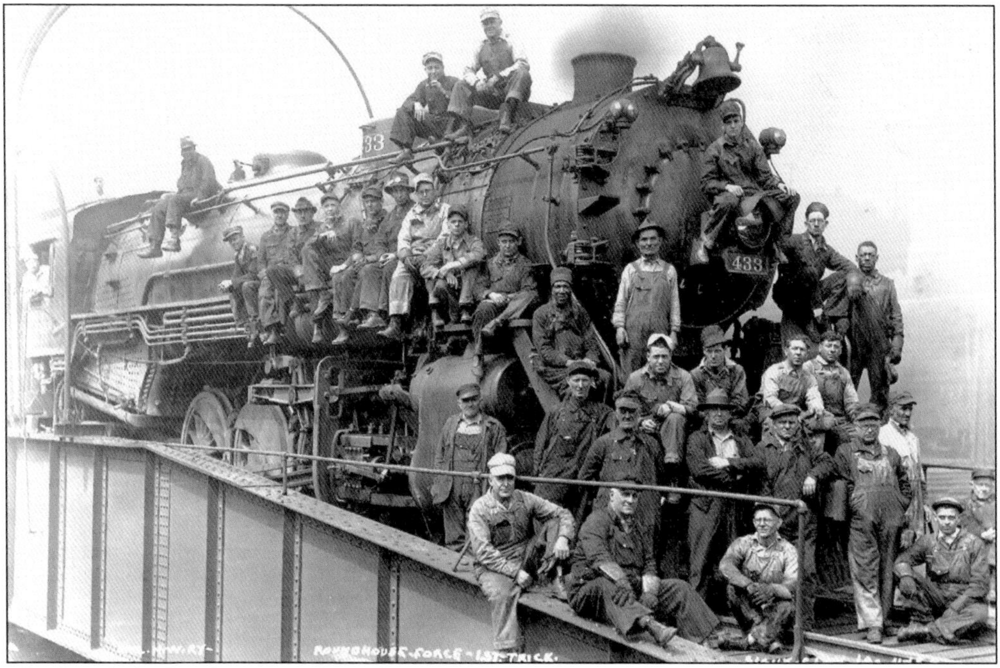

The first shift of a Chicago and Northwestern roundhouse crew paused for a photograph in 1916. They are seated around and perched on a freight locomotive placed on the turntable. At the time of this photograph, railroads accounted for 20 percent of the nonagricultural workforce in the United States. They employed a large population of any town at that time. (Courtesy of the Sioux City Public Museum.)

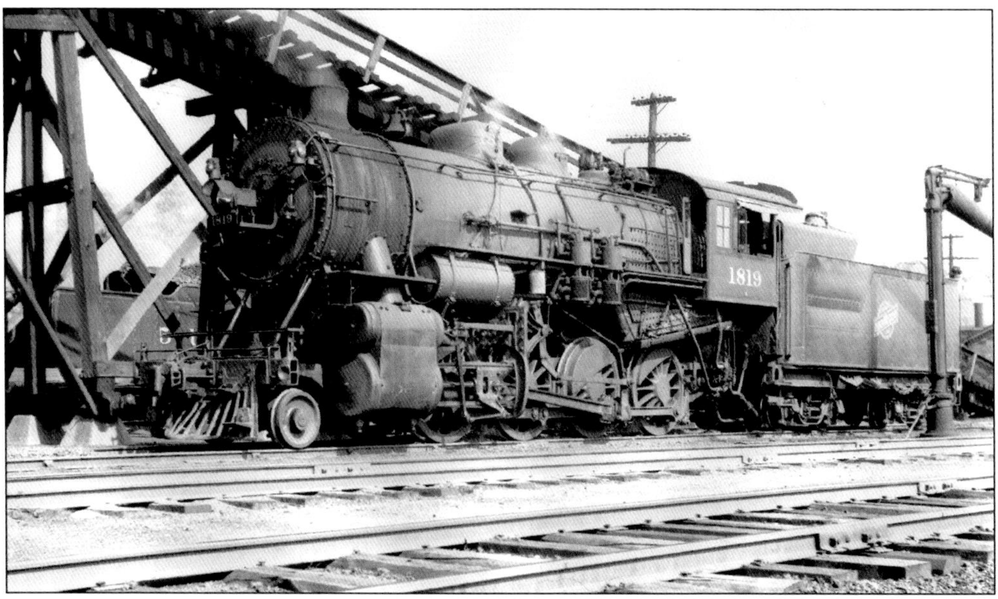

The Chicago and Northwestern Railway No. 1819 freight locomotive is approaching a coal-loading dock. Notice that no coal is visible at the top of the tender. The tender of a second locomotive is visible on the other side of the coaling facility. The photograph dates from June 1949. (Courtesy of the Siouxland Historical Railway Association.)

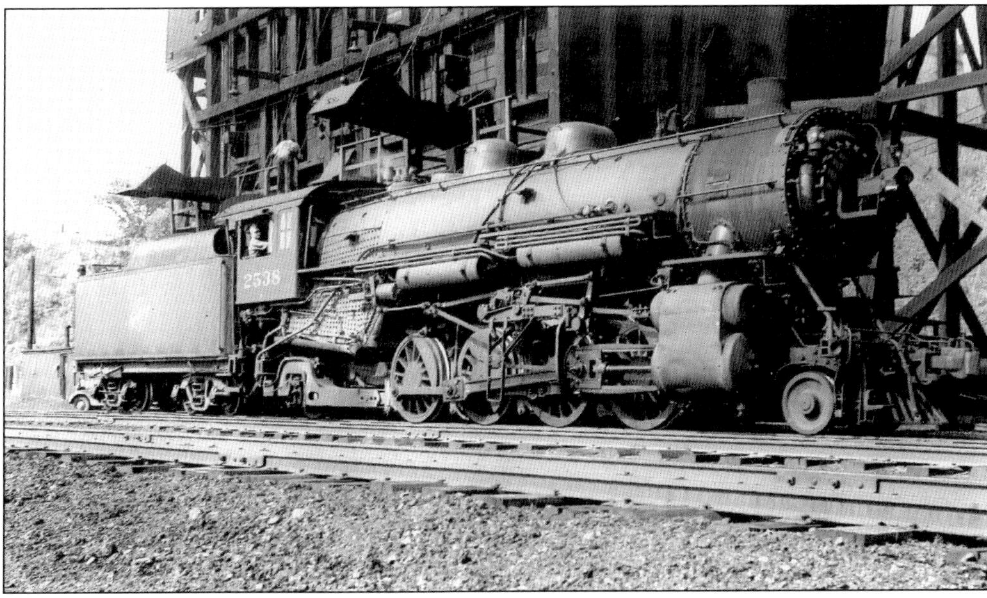

The Chicago and Northwestern 2-8-2 freight locomotive No. 2538 stands in front of the coaling chute in 1940. The locomotive is preparing probably to run south to Missouri Valley and then east or west. (Courtesy of the Siouxland Historical Railroad Association.)

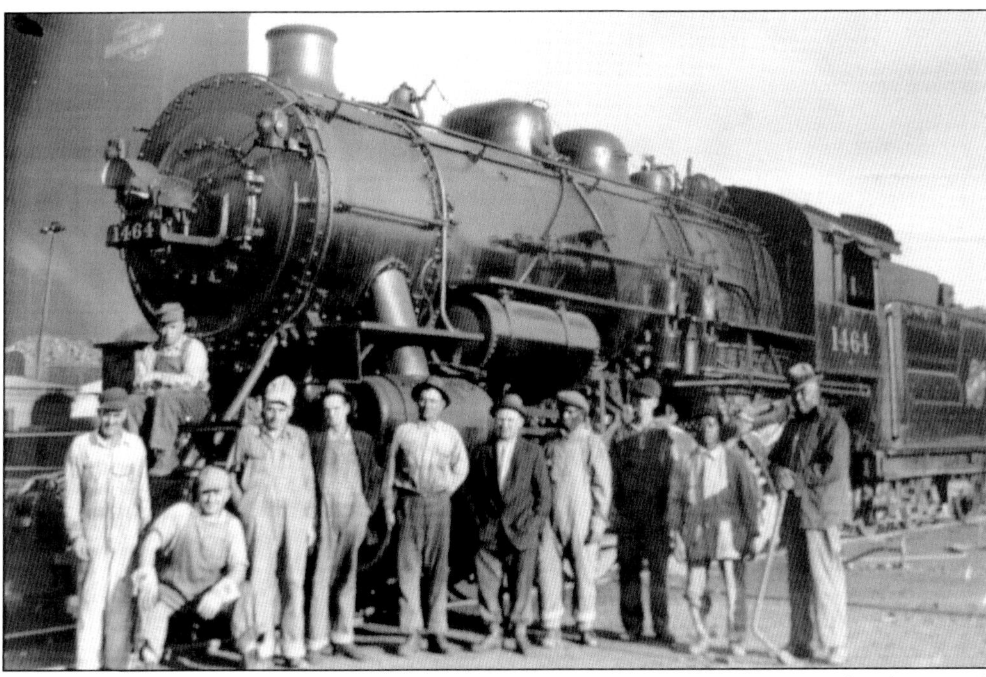

A group of railroaders stand in front of a Chicago and Northwestern locomotive. The photograph appears to be from the 1920s. It took eight workers to keep a steam locomotive running. Each was a skilled craftsman. (Courtesy of the Siouxland Historical Railroad Association.)

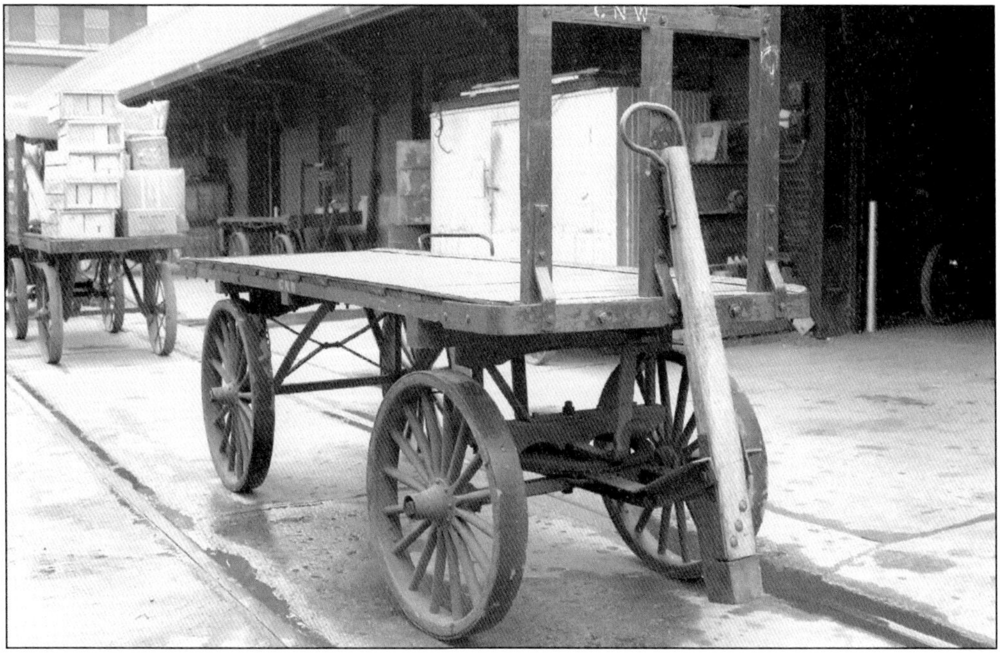

These hand-pulled baggage carts were a common sight all over the United States in the passenger railroad era. These stand at the Chicago and Northwestern depot in downtown Sioux City. Even though they look cumbersome, they were easy to maneuver. The handle was weighted to swing upwards when released. (Courtesy of George R. Lindblade.)

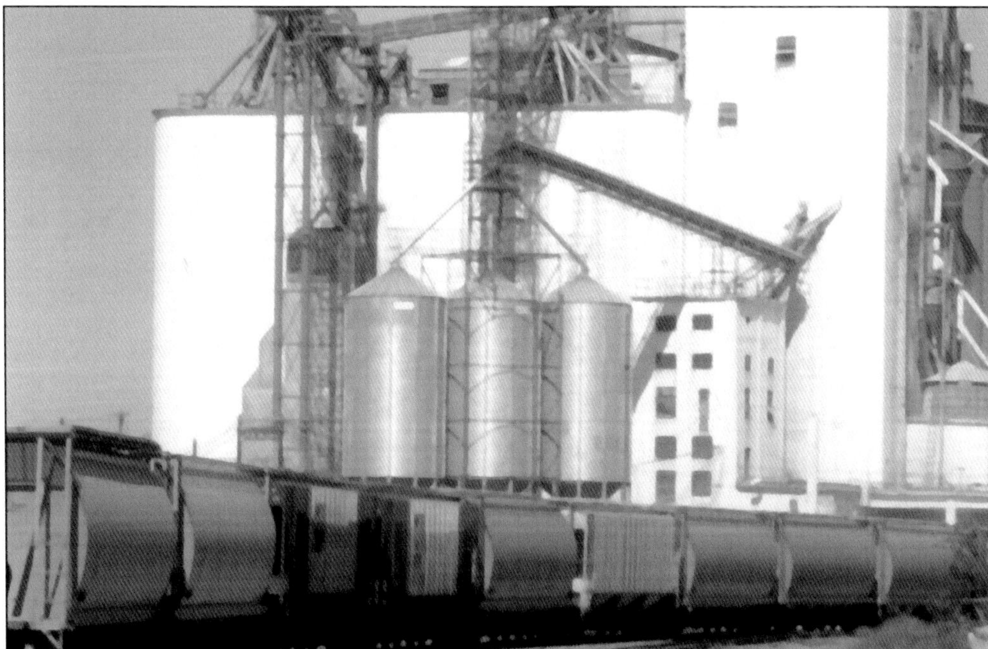

These closed-hopper cars are lined up at a local plant to take on grain or some other commodity. The Chicago and Northwestern was known as a granger railroad due to its service to farmers and the agriculture industry. (Courtesy of George R. Lindblade.)

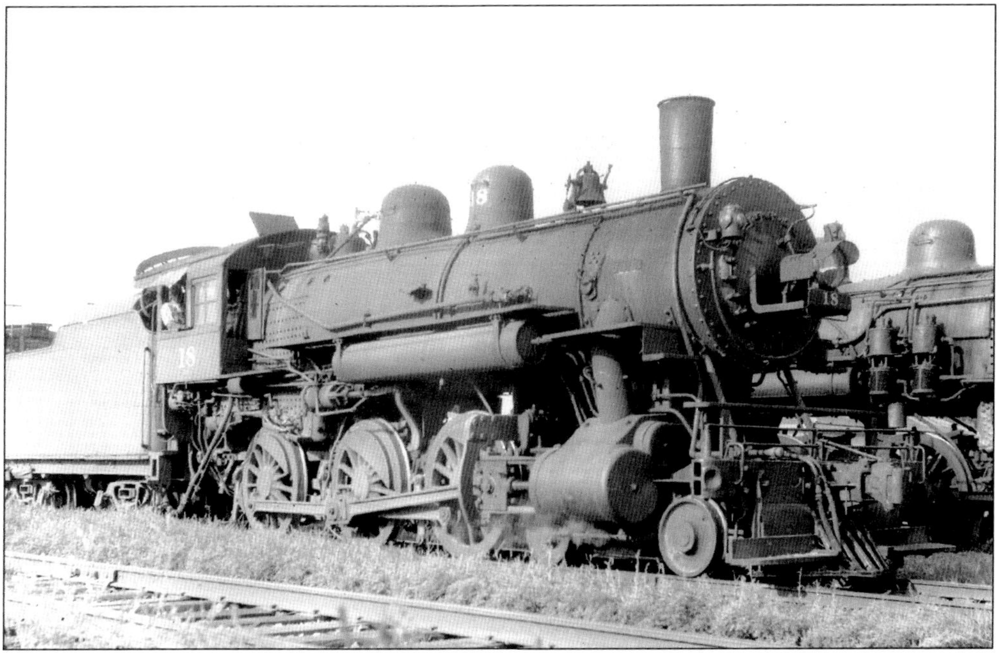

The Chicago and Northwestern No. 18 could be used in branch line passenger service. With the lack of coal at tender height level, it would be arriving in Sioux City after a run. (Courtesy of the Siouxland Historical Railroad Association.)

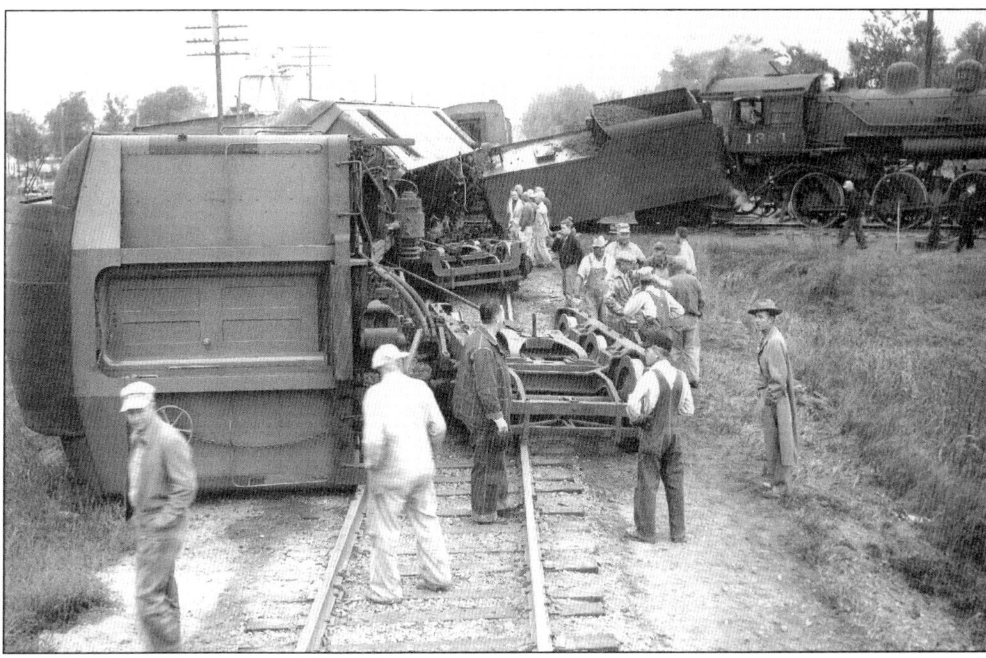

A Chicago and Northwestern locomotive plowed into a Chicago, Milwaukee, St. Paul and Pacific Railway passenger train in Sioux City. No date was listed. It appears that the locomotive backed into the passenger train at a meeting and crossing of two tracks called a diamond. (Courtesy of the Siouxland Historical Railroad Association.)

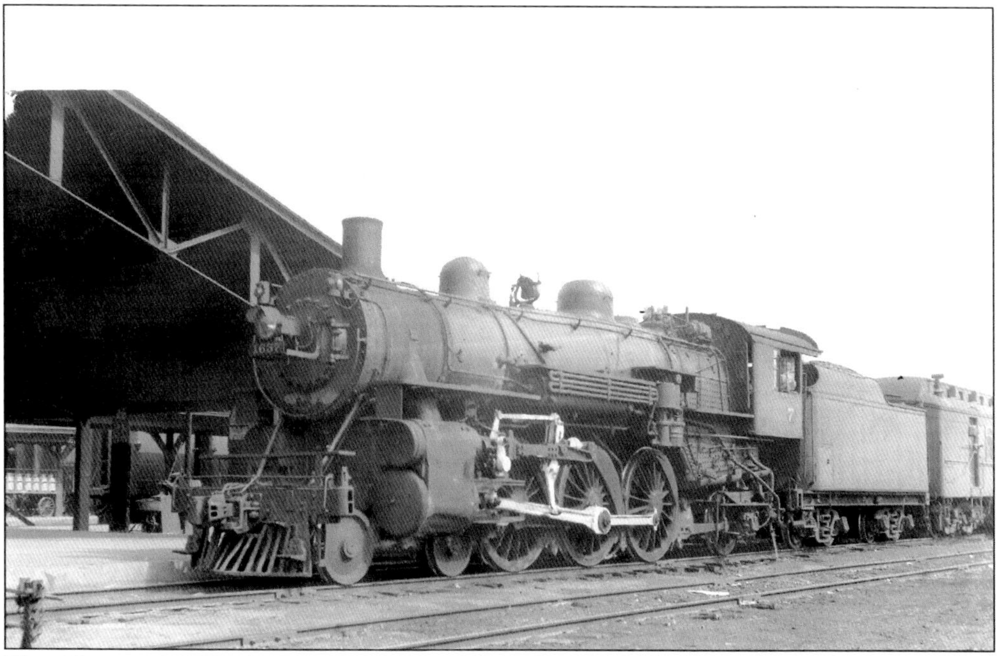

This Chicago and Northwestern Pacific-type locomotive is pulling up to the depot on a March day in 1941. It has stainless steel driving rods. Notice the cart in the background with old-style milk cans. An early-morning train that made frequent stops was often referred to as a milk run. (Courtesy of the Siouxland Historical Railroad Association.)

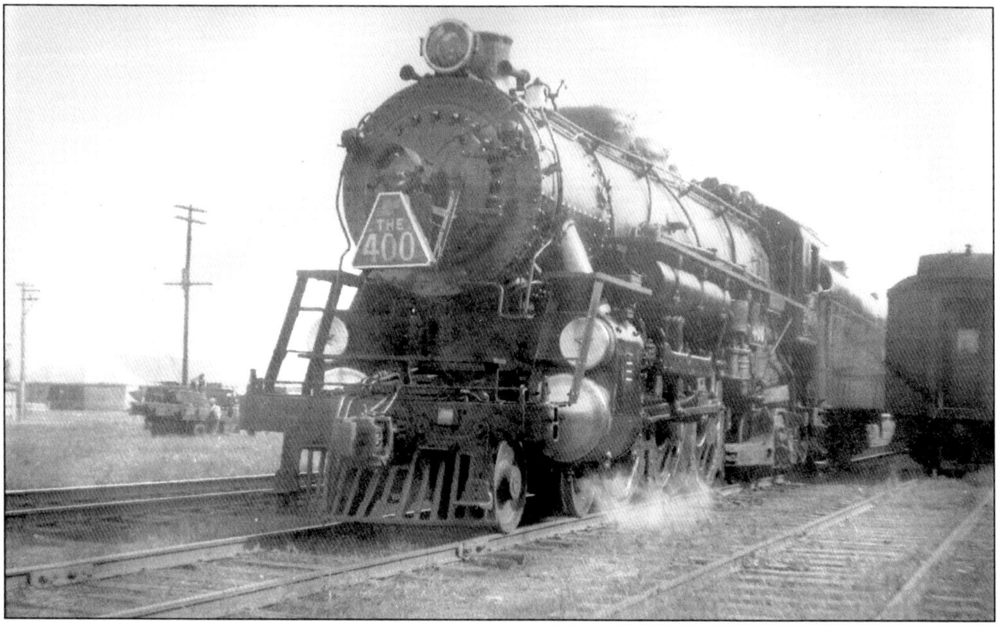

A heavy-duty Chicago and Northwestern Pacific–type locomotive is in motion in the Sioux City yard. The smoke box bears the emblem of "the 400," which was the insignia of the Chicago to Minneapolis streamliners. Any railroad will move motive power where needed, and Minneapolis was a short distance to Sioux City on the Omaha Road. (Courtesy of the Siouxland Historical Railroad Association.)

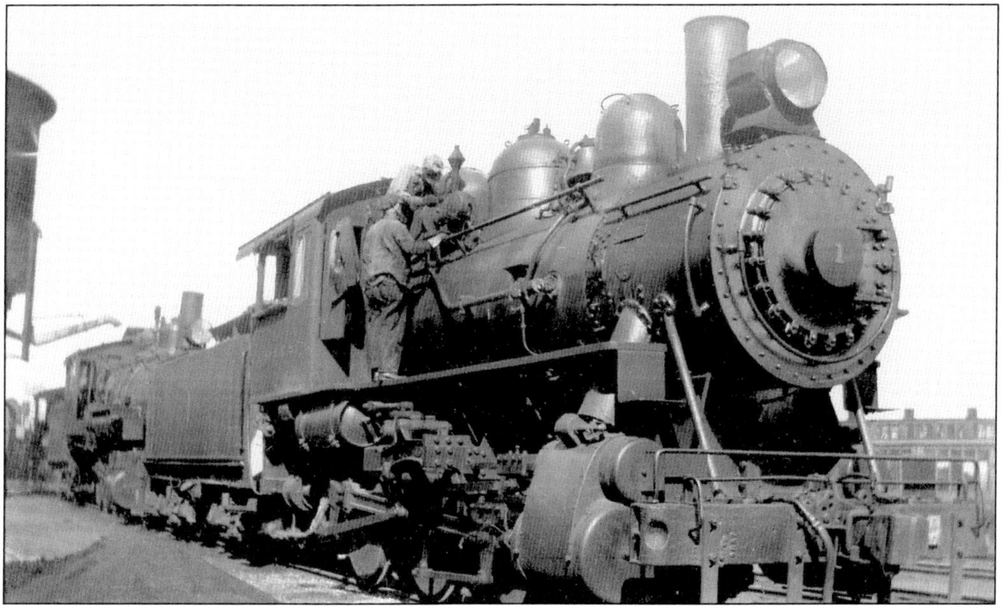

This Chicago, St. Paul, Minneapolis, and Omaha No. 1 switch locomotive is a prime example of a "yard goat," which is railroad slag for a yard-switching locomotive. It appears that the railroad men are working on the steam generator atop the locomotive. It was built by the Baldwin Locomotive Works of Philadelphia, Pennsylvania, in 1913. (Courtesy of the Siouxland Historical Railroad Association.)

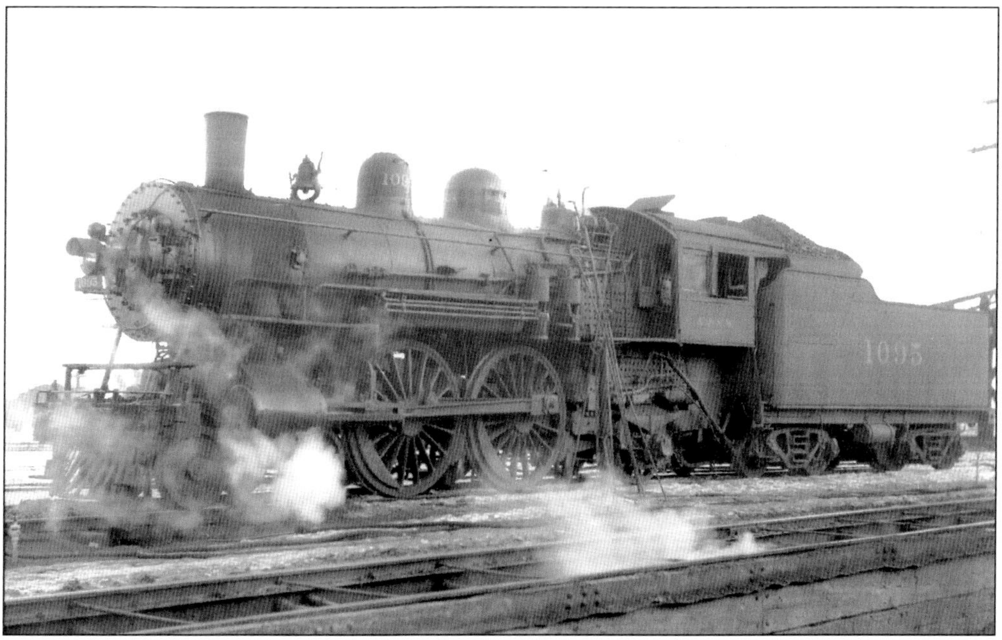

The No. 1095 was a Chicago and Northwestern "high stepping" Atlantic-type locomotive used in fast passenger service. While this type of locomotive was a genuine speedster, it was not capable of pulling the longer, heavier passenger trains that came into fashion during the 1930s. They would then be used on shorter, local passenger schedules. (Courtesy of the Siouxland Historical Railroad Association.)

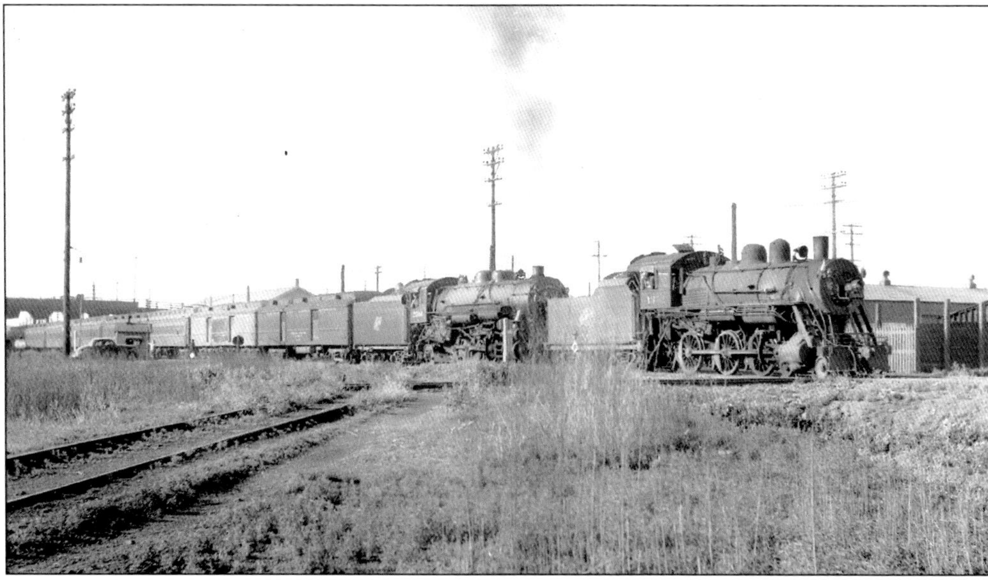

The double-headed passenger train is entering Sioux City probably in the 1940s. The Chicago and Northwestern maintained a fast schedule to Chicago during World War II. A double-headed train could save quite a bit of time by accelerating much more quickly from a stop or slow order. (Courtesy of the Siouxland Historical Railroad Association.)

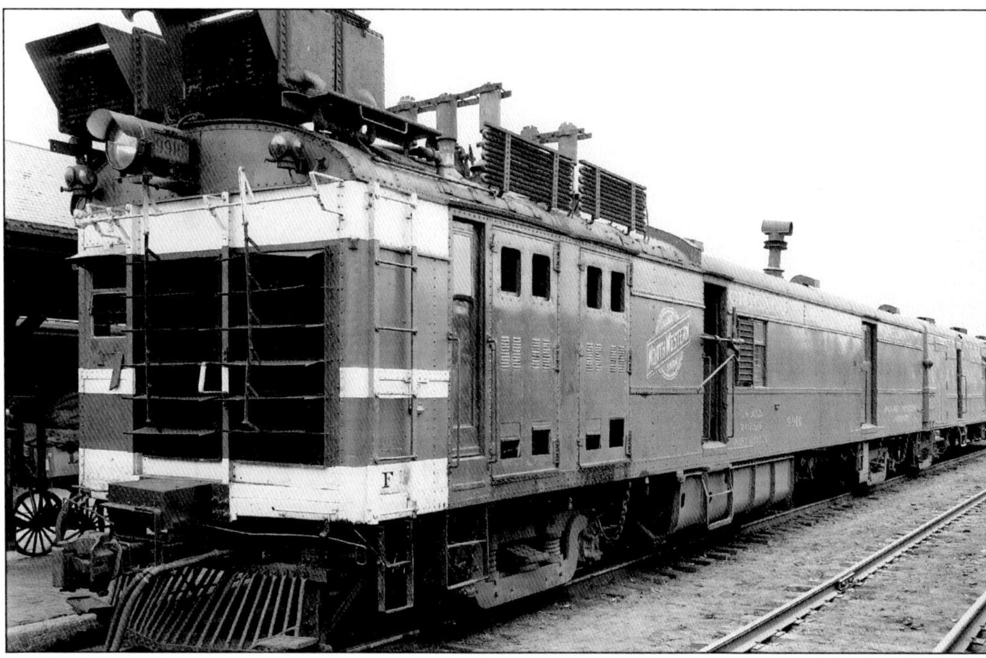

The Chicago and Northwestern also purchased, built, and extended branch lines to Sioux City. Some of these tracks originated or led to Ames and Maple River, Iowa, and Iroquois, South Dakota. The Chicago and Northwestern Railway furnished Sioux City with a "doodlebug" or self-contained locomotive and baggage car unit. It was used primarily in branch line service or on secondary tracks to small towns. Some railroaders called them "galloping geese" or something similar. (Courtesy of the Sioux City Public Museum.)

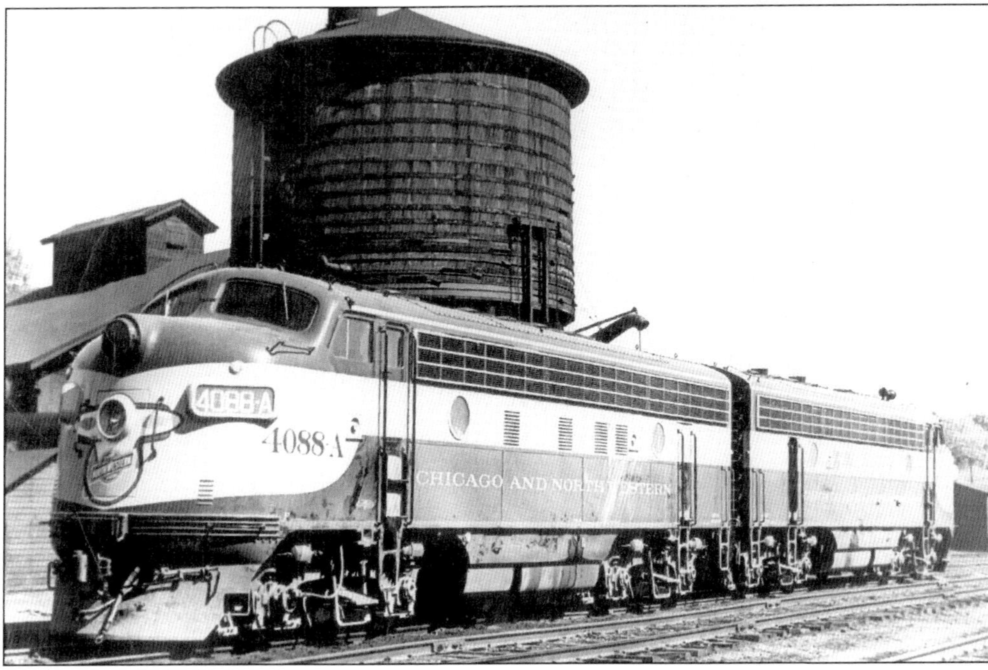

These beautiful F7 A units of the Chicago and Northwestern stand in the yard near the water tower. (An A unit had an engineer's cab, and a B unit was an engine without a cab.) These early diesel electrics were the engines that first replaced steam locomotives on city-to-city runs. They did not need to take on water—except for steam boilers used in passenger service during winter. (Courtesy of the Siouxland Historical Railroad Association.)

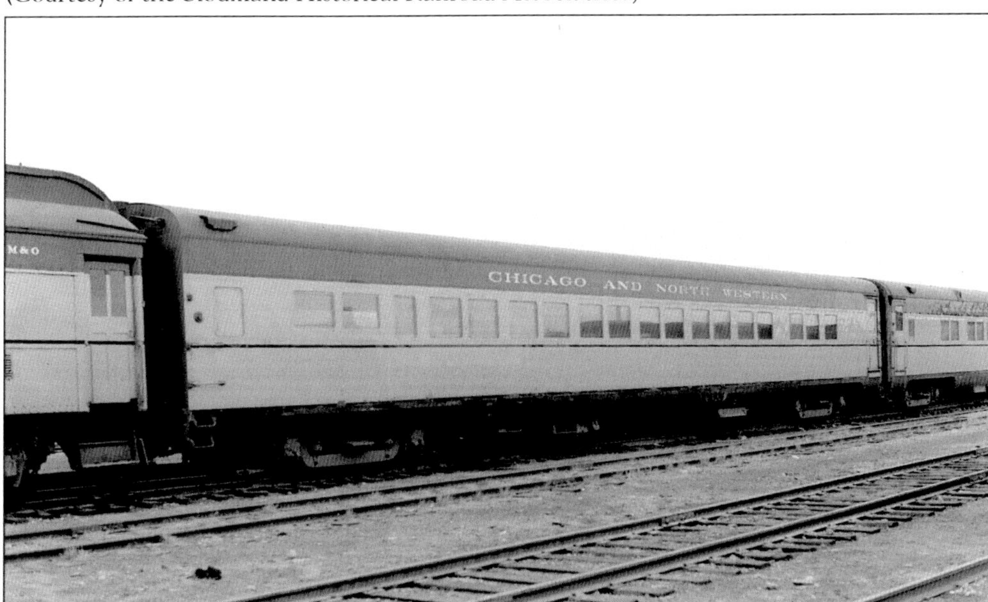

These Chicago and Northwestern passenger cars await their clientele in the yard. The long-distance coaches were smooth riding and very comfortable—all the way to Chicago. Most passenger equipment in the United States was made by the Pullman Company, the Budd Company, or American Car and Foundry. (Courtesy of George R. Lindblade.)

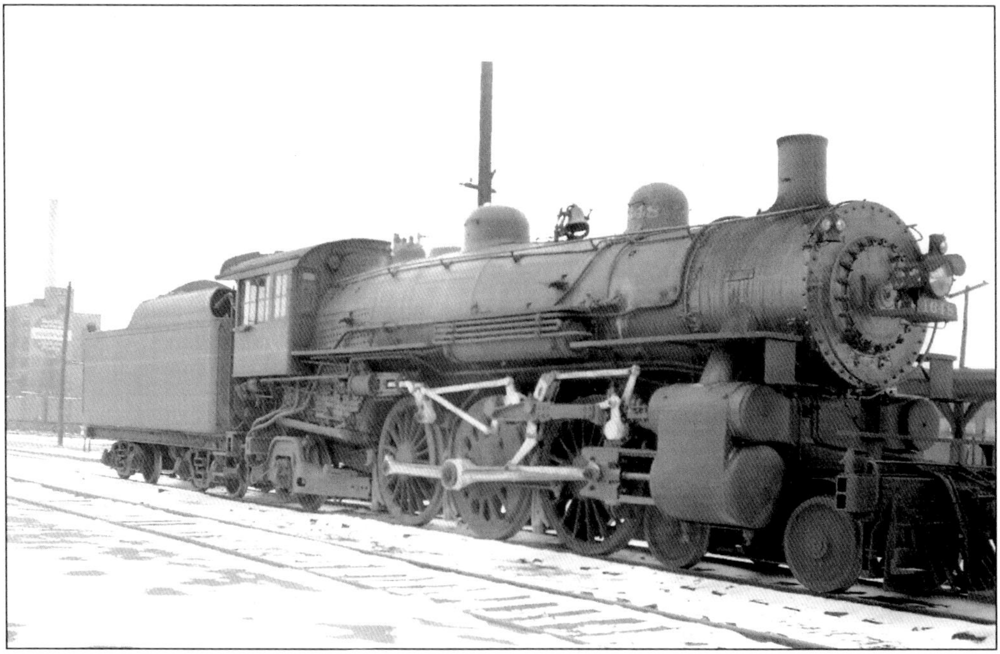

This Chicago and Northwestern Railway 4-6-2 Pacific has stainless steel drive rods and eccentrics. These mechanical devices transfer the power from the steam cylinder to the larger wheels that propel the locomotive. This locomotive is ready for a passenger consist on a cold February day in 1941. (Courtesy of the Siouxland Historical Railroad Association.)

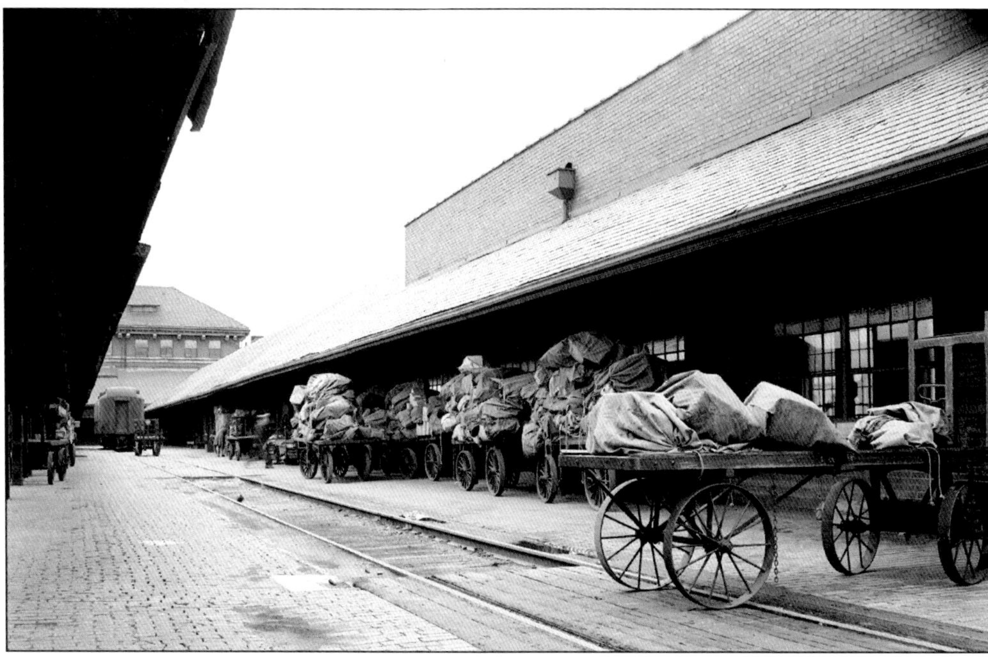

Mail and railroad baggage sit on station carts at the Chicago and Northwestern depot. Railroads carried the mail by act of Congress since 1838. Mail was sorted en route even through street address for some cities. It had its own special car with mail slots for communities along the schedule. (Courtesy of the Sioux City Public Museum, George Newman Collection.)

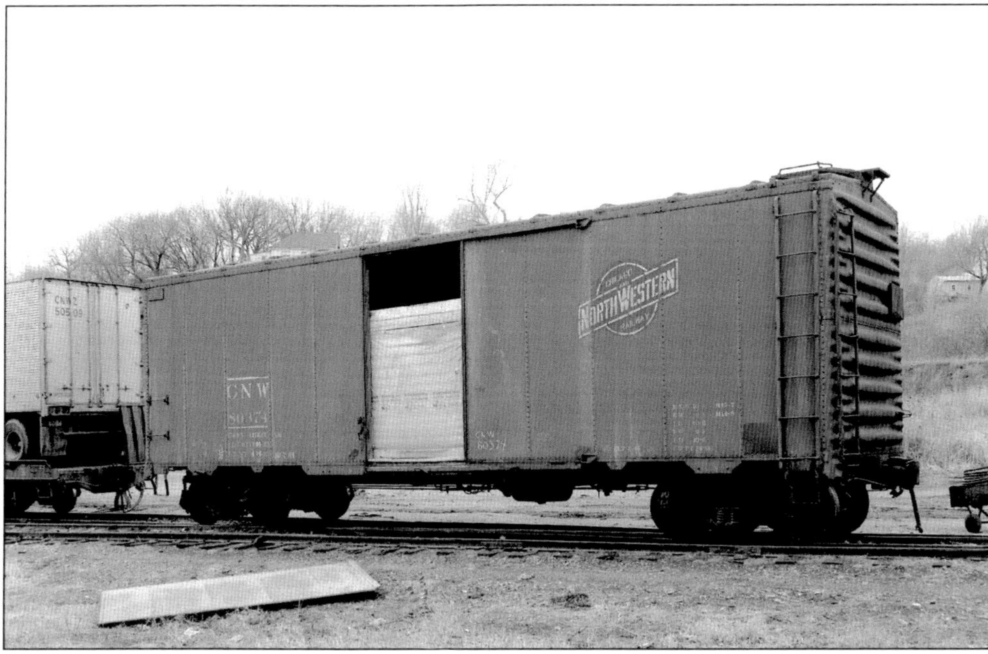

Boxcars carried just about anything! This Chicago and Northwestern car is delivering lumber to a yard in Sioux City. Lumber yards were often located near the tracks. Notice the piggyback flatcar that is attached. It is in the yard waiting to be shunted to the proper lumber business. (Courtesy of George R. Lindblade.)

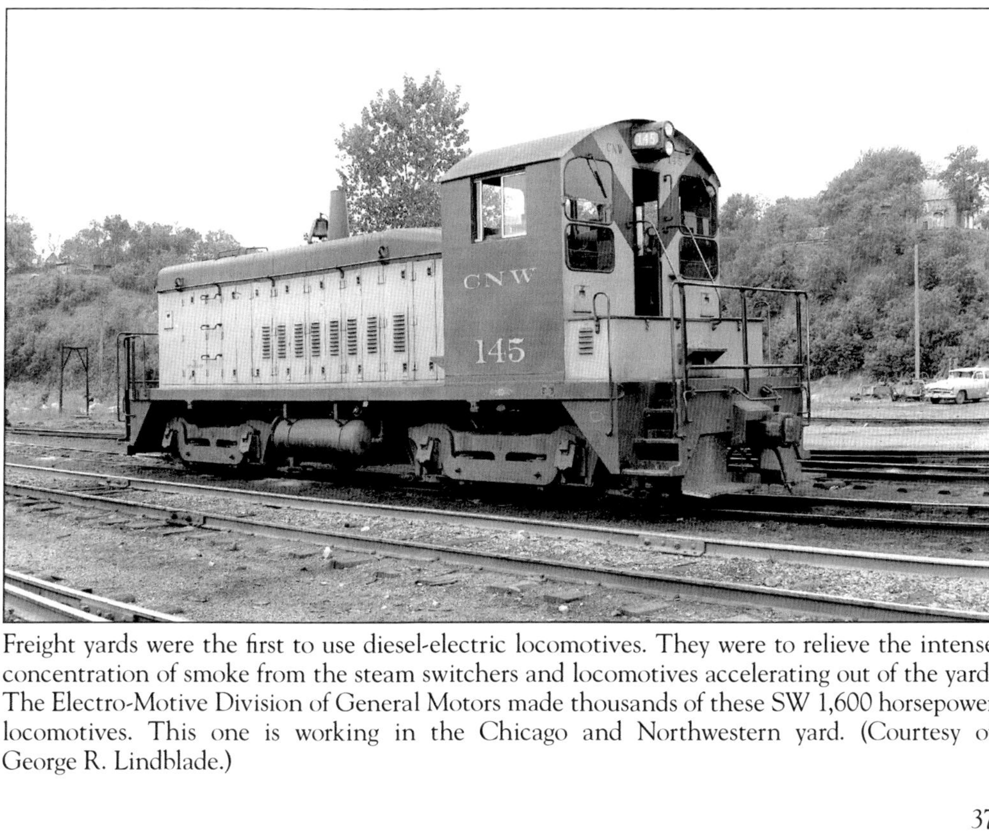

Freight yards were the first to use diesel-electric locomotives. They were to relieve the intense concentration of smoke from the steam switchers and locomotives accelerating out of the yard. The Electro-Motive Division of General Motors made thousands of these SW 1,600 horsepower locomotives. This one is working in the Chicago and Northwestern yard. (Courtesy of George R. Lindblade.)

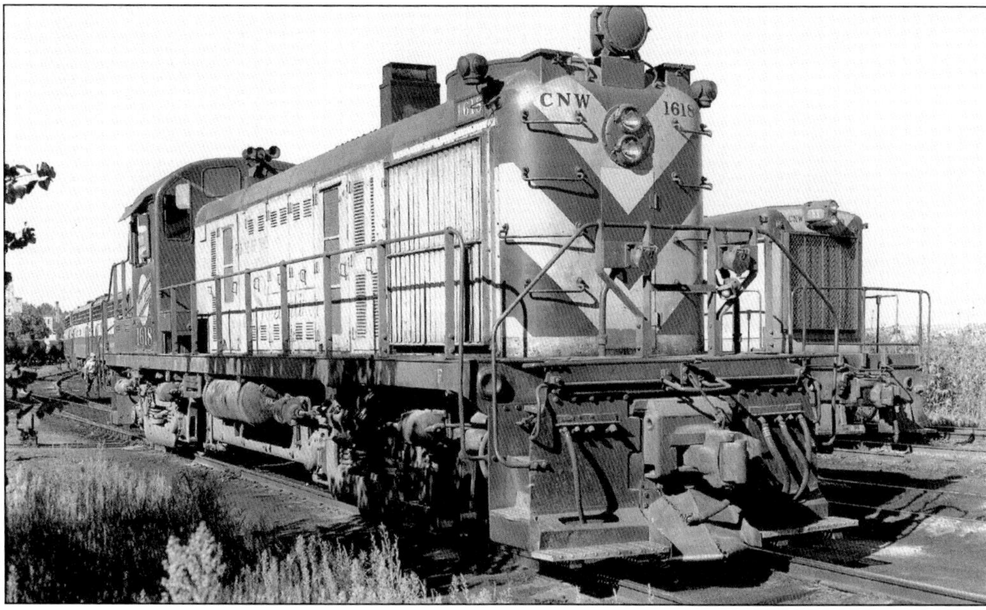

There are three different diesel-electric locomotives in this photograph. One made by the American Locomotive Company (Alco) is in the foreground. At the right is the nose of an Electro-Motive switch engine, and in the left background there is an Electro-Motive E Unit. General Electric Corporation did the motors and electric components for Alco. (Courtesy of George R. Lindblade.)

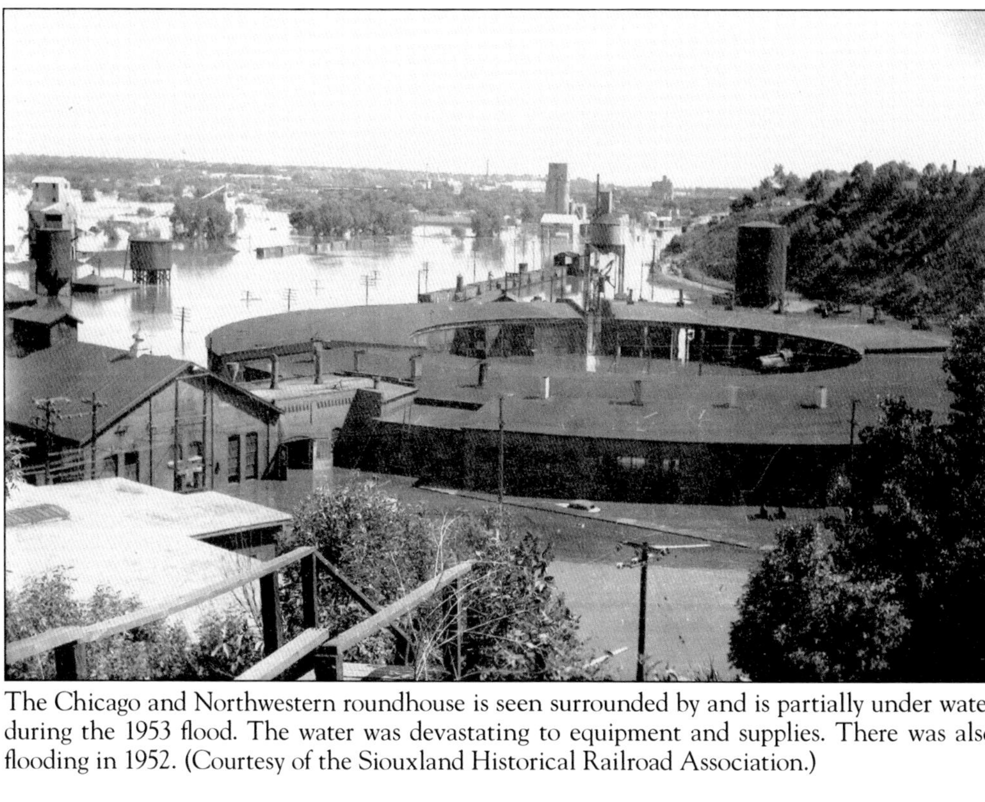

The Chicago and Northwestern roundhouse is seen surrounded by and is partially under water during the 1953 flood. The water was devastating to equipment and supplies. There was also flooding in 1952. (Courtesy of the Siouxland Historical Railroad Association.)

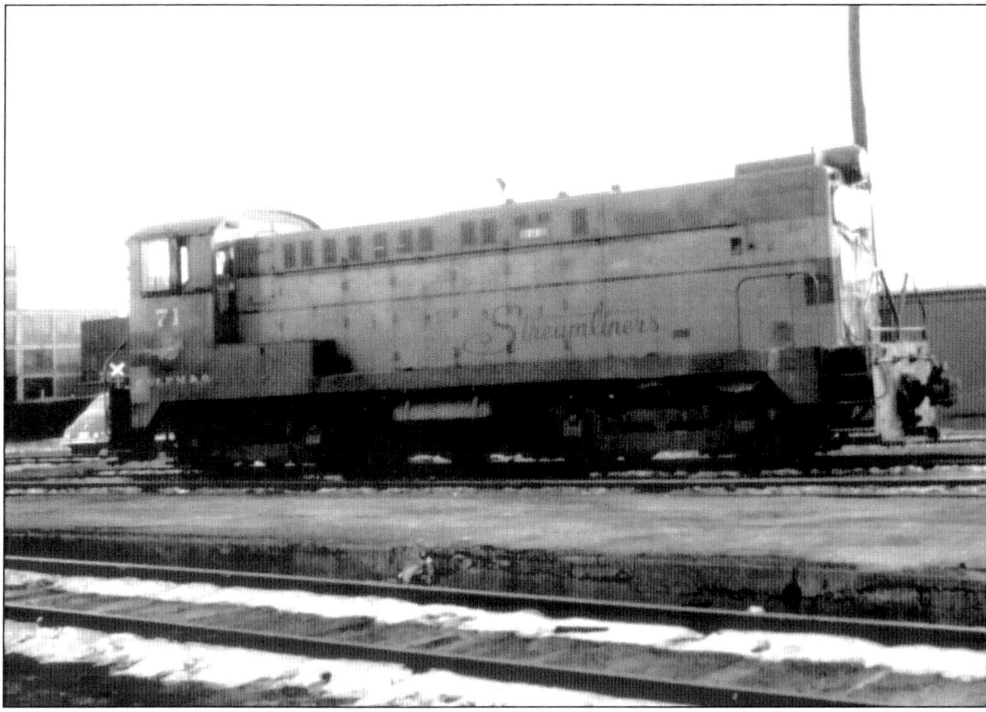

The Chicago, St. Paul, Minneapolis, and Omaha diesel-electric road switcher advertises the Chicago and Northwestern streamliners along its side. The Chicago and Northwestern used the Omaha Road tracks from Chicago to Minneapolis. The switcher appears to be a Baldwin VO 1000. (Courtesy of the Siouxland Historical Railroad Association.)

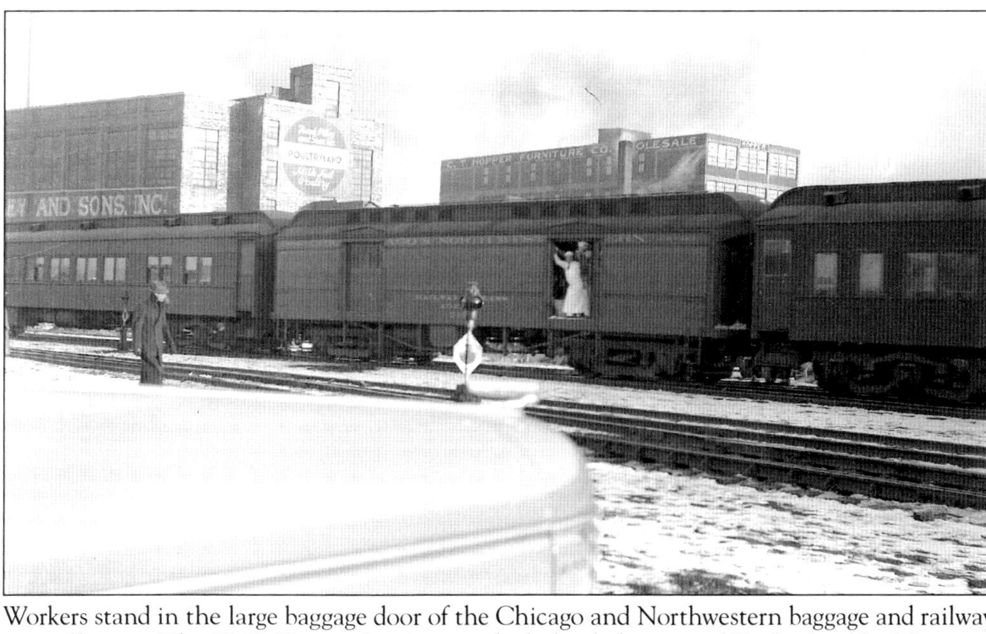

Workers stand in the large baggage door of the Chicago and Northwestern baggage and railway post office car. The C. T. Hopper furniture and wholesale house and Poultryland buildings are in the background. (Courtesy of the Siouxland Historical Railroad Association.)

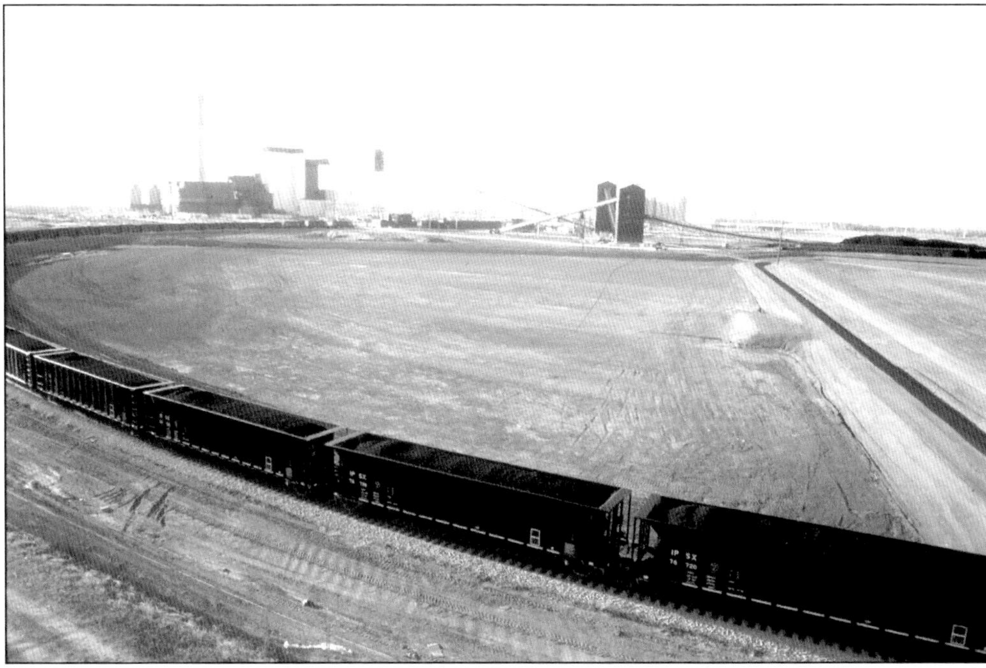

This string of coal cars is being unloaded at the former Iowa Public Service plant just to the south of Sioux City along the Missouri River. When all cars are the same and have the same loading and delivering points, it is called a unit train. (Courtesy of George R. Lindblade.)

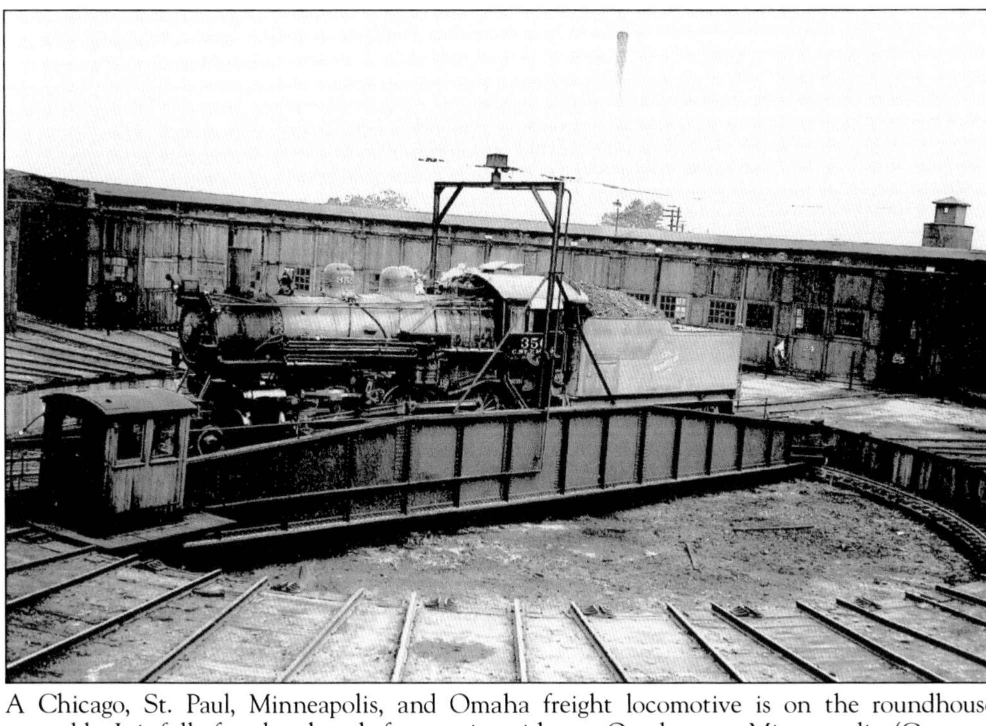

A Chicago, St. Paul, Minneapolis, and Omaha freight locomotive is on the roundhouse turntable. It is full of coal and ready for running either to Omaha or to Minneapolis. (Courtesy of the Sioux City Public Museum, George Newman Collection.)

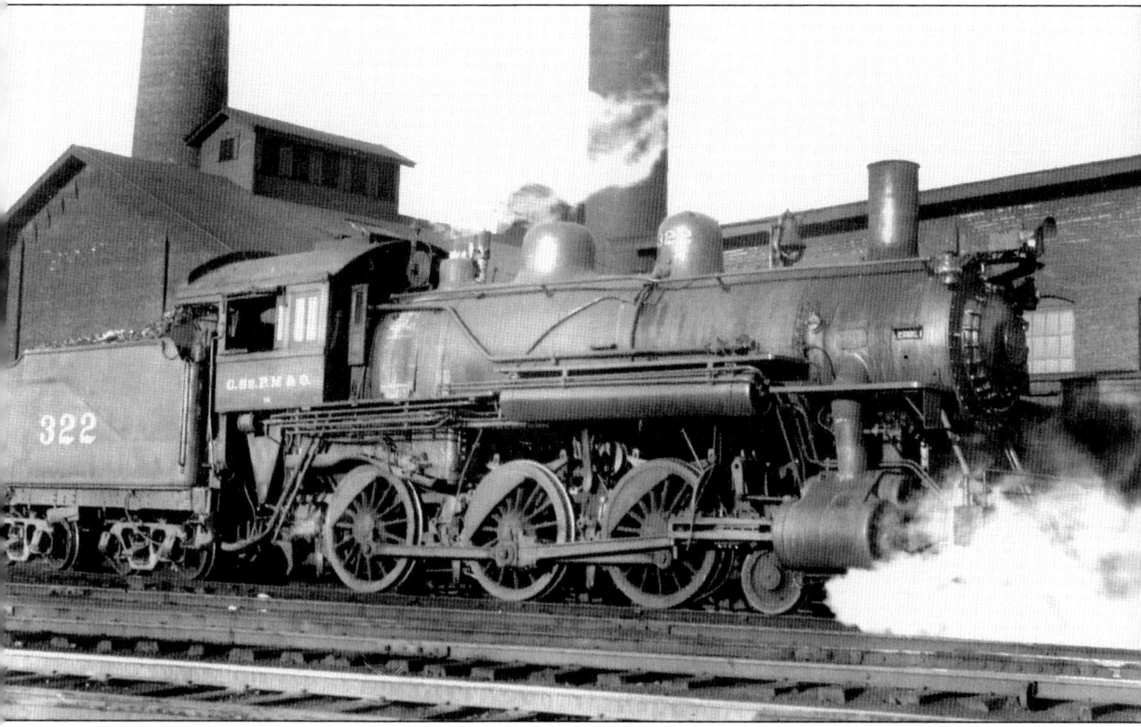

The Chicago, St. Paul, Minneapolis, and Omaha No. 322 has a tender full of coal. All locomotives in the Midwest burned bituminous coal. Anthracite coal–burning locomotives were exclusively in the mid-Atlantic states. It is emitting steam to clean the pipes and valves. It looks like it is ready for a passenger run. (Courtesy of the Siouxland Historical Railroad Association.)

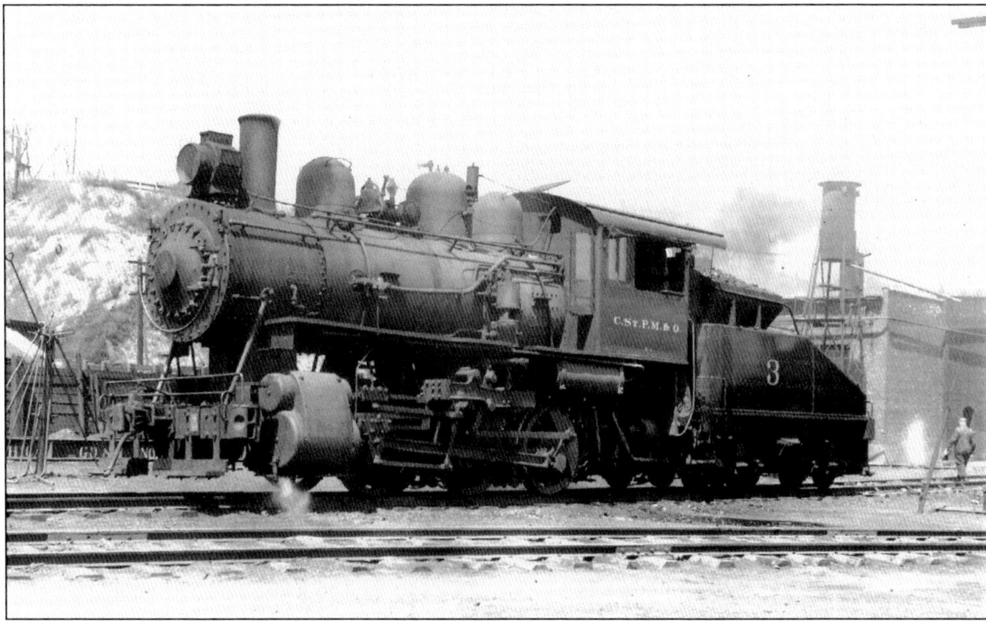

The Chicago, St. Paul, Minneapolis, and Omaha 0-6-0 No. 3 "yard goat" is off to its duties in the Sioux City yard. Yard switchers usually had smaller tenders as they could pause to take on coal and water at almost anytime. The photograph is dated May 1940. (Courtesy of the Siouxland Historical Railroad Association.)

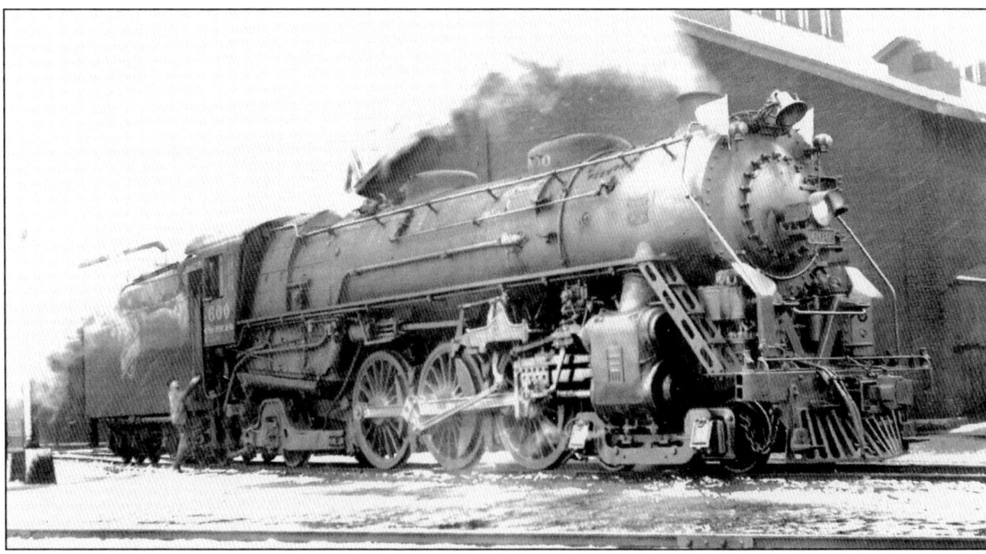

The No. 600 was the Chicago, St. Paul, Minneapolis, and Omaha's largest Pacific type of locomotive. This Alco-built was in fact the largest Pacific type ever constructed. The white flags indicate a special or unscheduled run in April 1940. (Courtesy of the Siouxland Historical Railroad Association.)

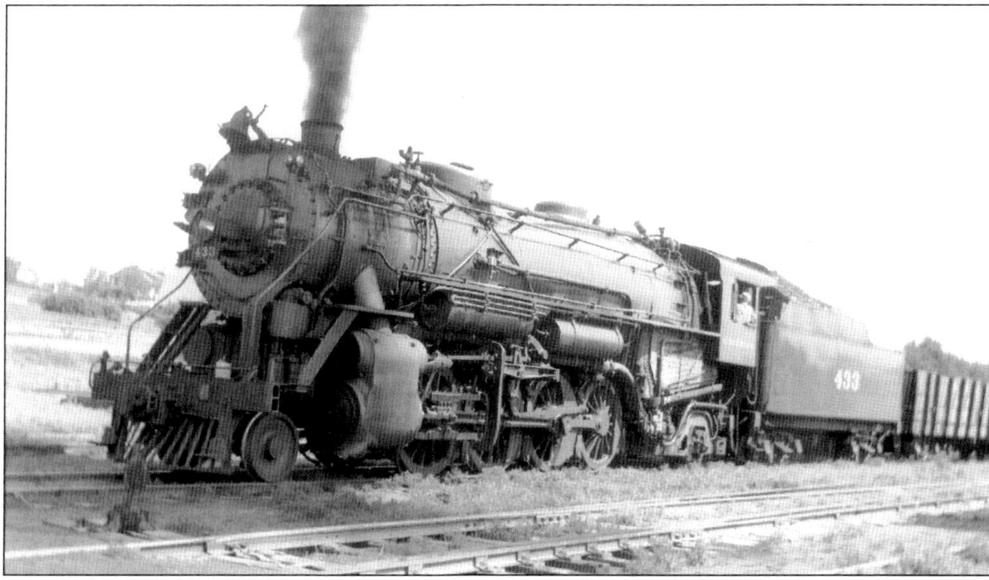

The No. 433 of the Chicago, St. Paul, Minneapolis, and Omaha is spewing a full head of coal smoke in pulling a freight out of Sioux City. The fireman is seen leaning backwards at the window on a June day in 1939. (Courtesy of the Siouxland Historical Railroad Association.)

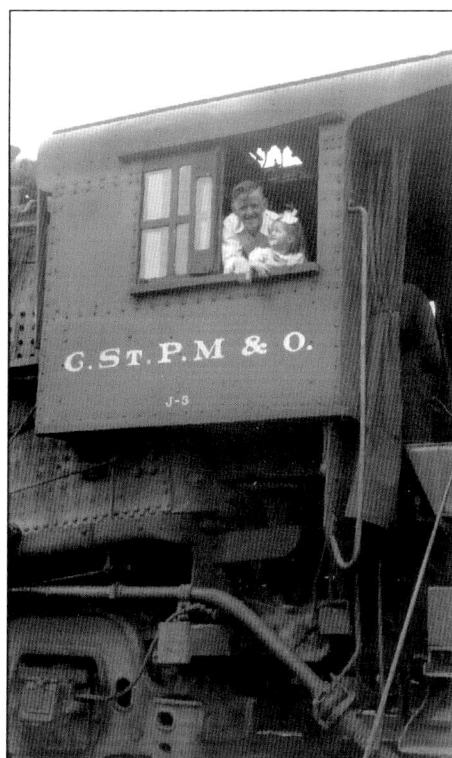

An unidentified man and little girl are looking out the fireman's window of an Omaha Road locomotive. They are probably a father and daughter. The locomotive is noted to be a J-3 class. The young lady will probably remember the event for the rest of her life. (Courtesy of the Siouxland Historical Railroad Association.)

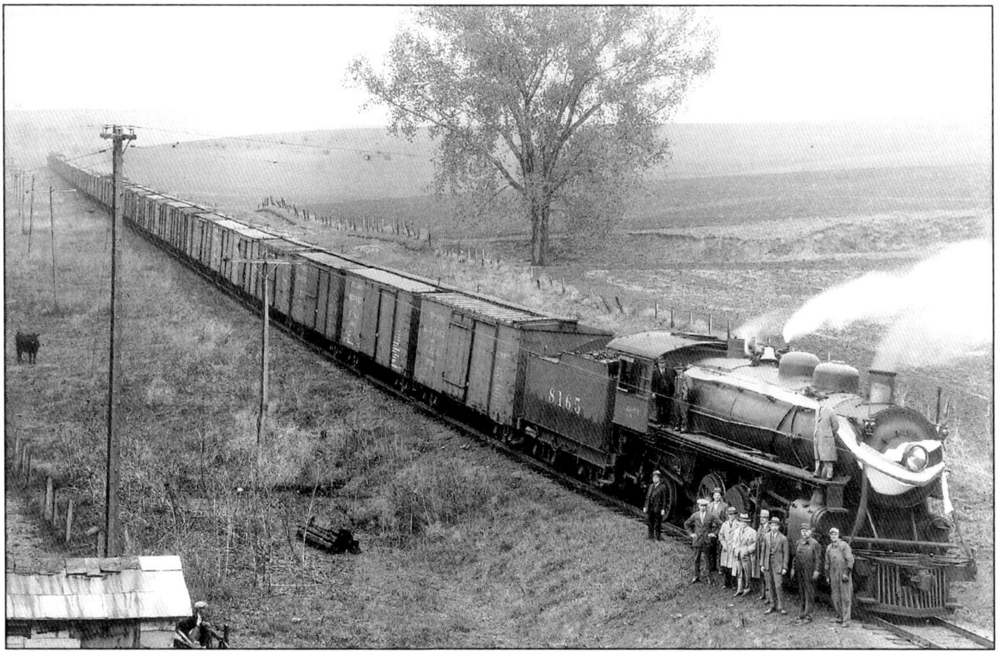

Before modern Thrall cars transport automobiles, they were carried to dealers in standard boxcars. These cars, however, had an elaborate system of pulleys and gears to fit four or more cars. Ryal Chevrolet, at the beginning of the 21st century, remains in the same family that owned it in 1922. The train was on the Omaha Road. (Courtesy of Knoepfler Chevrolet.)

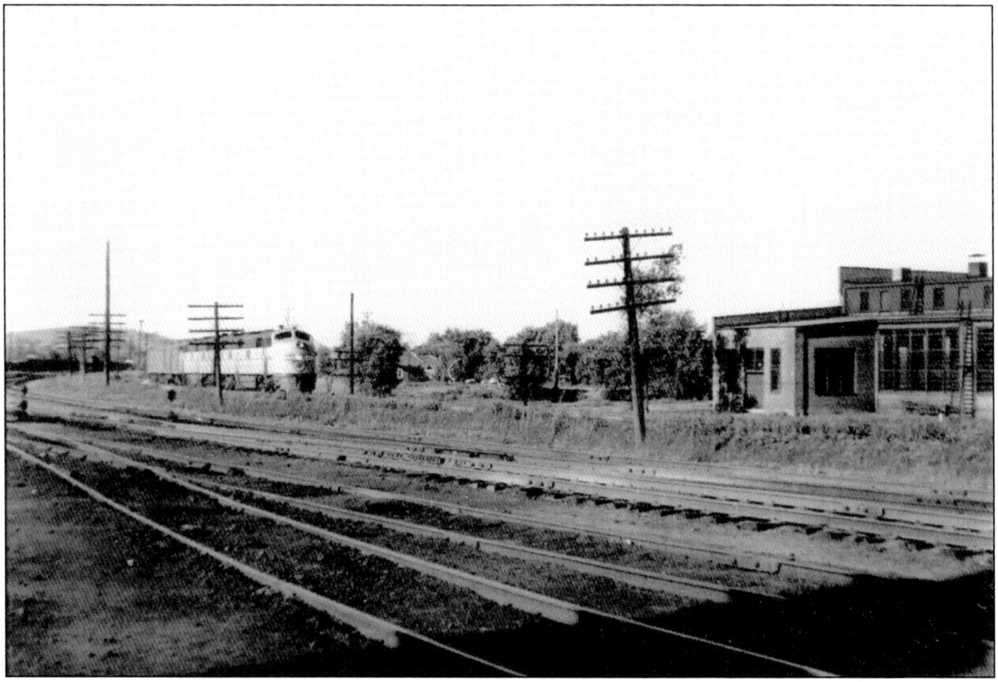

Two Chicago and Northwestern passenger E7 locomotives race to Sioux City from Minneapolis on the Omaha Road track. The Illinois Central roundhouse is on the right. The train will arrive at the Northwestern station in just a few minutes. (Courtesy of Paul H. Reistrup.)

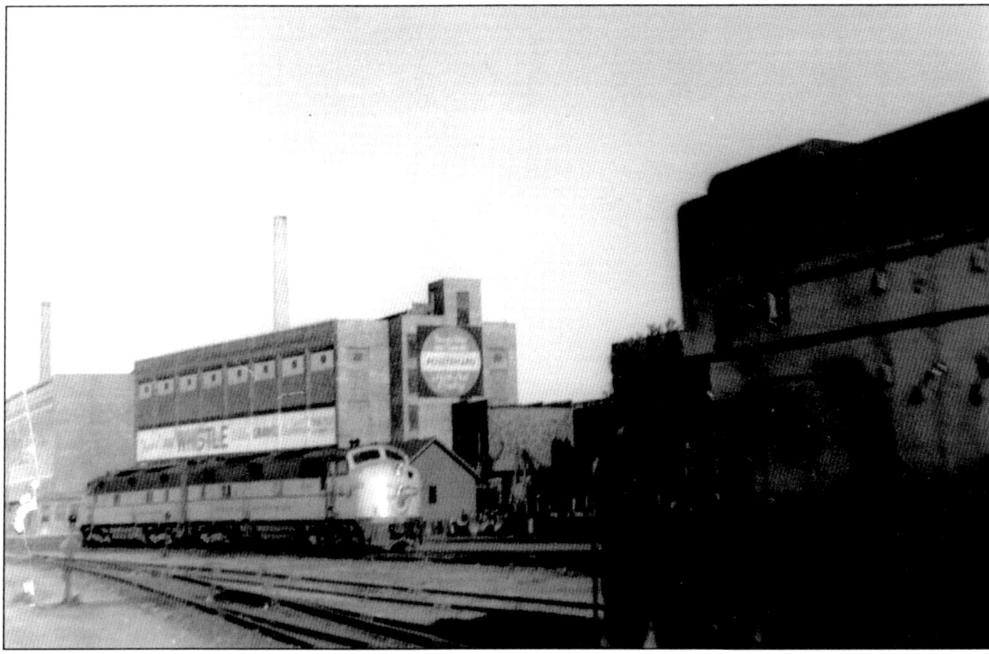

Two Chicago and Northwestern E7 units are parked near the Chicago and Northwestern station waiting for their passenger consist. A switch locomotive is in the foreground. These brightly painted diesel-electric units were hoped to increase railroad passenger riders. (Courtesy of Paul H. Reistrup.)

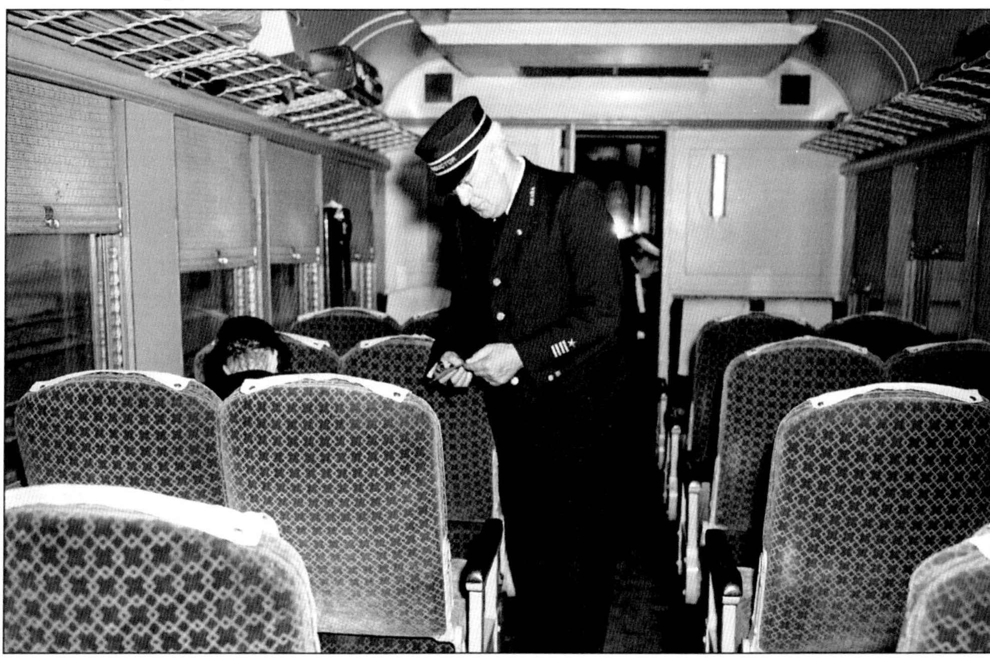

A veteran Chicago, St. Paul, Minneapolis, and Omaha conductor punches a ticket on a train leaving Sioux City. Railroad tickets became a practice in the years just before the Civil War. Each conductor had his own punch symbol on a run or particular railroad. (Courtesy of the Sioux City Public Museum.)

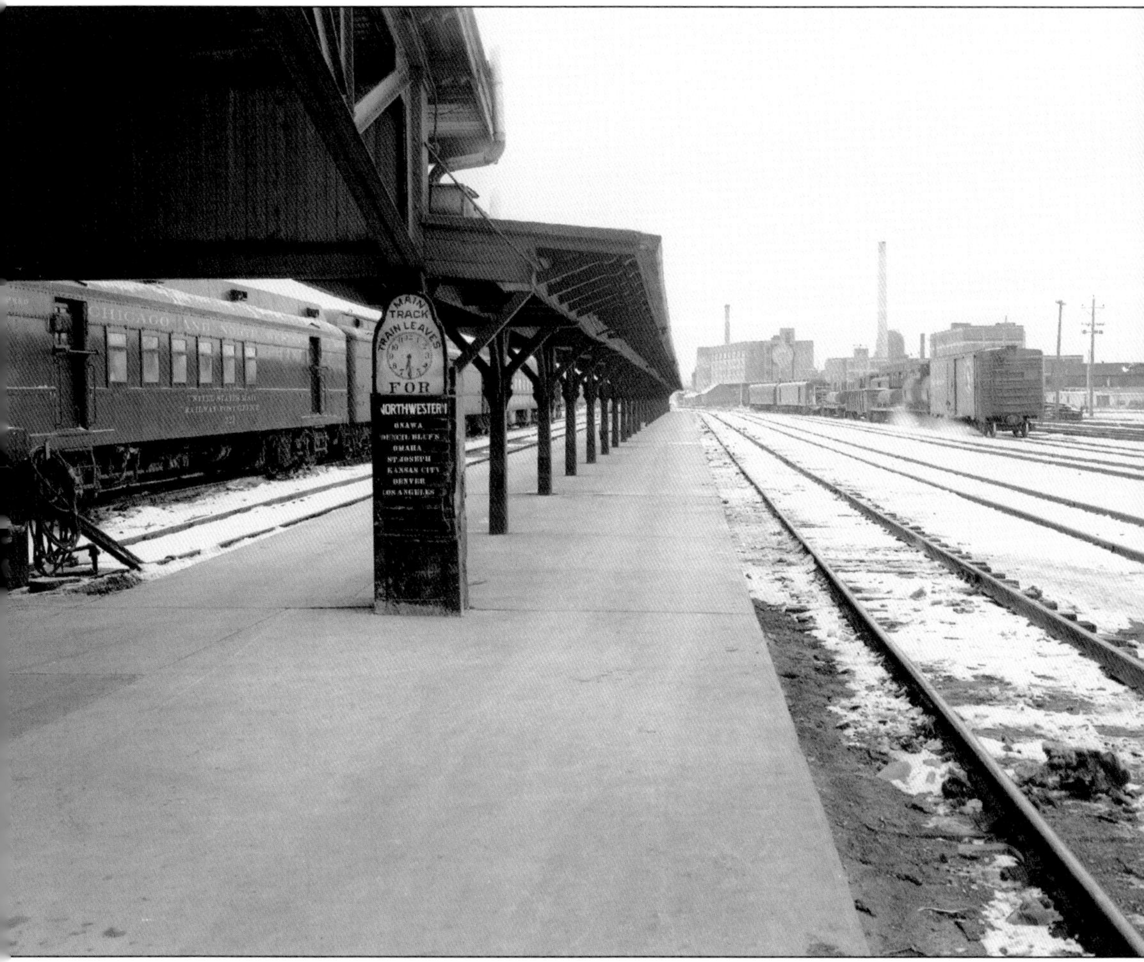

"You can get anywhere from here!" The train announcement at the Chicago and Northwestern Sioux City station indicates a train for Omaha, Kansas City, Denver, and Los Angeles. Of course, one could also travel to Chicago and then anywhere east. The Illinois Central also used the station in its glory days. In some cases, when going westward, one's coach or sleeper would be transferred to another railroad company so that the passenger would not have to change trains. This photograph is from the 1920s. A new railroad station was planned to be built in the early 1930s. It was to be used by all Sioux City railroad companies. It was never built—a victim of the Great Depression. (Courtesy of the Jack P. Fleckenstein Collection.)

Three

The Illinois Central

Considered early on to become a transcontinental railroad, the Illinois Central was Sioux City's direct line to Chicago. The railroad began as the first large-scale direct land grant company in the nation. Its first tracks ran from Galena to Cairo, Illinois, in the 1850s. It later expanded to Chicago and to Dunleith (the early name for East Dubuque), Illinois. By the mid-1850s, the Illinois Central built from Dubuque to Dyersville, Iowa. In 1859, it reached Independence as the Dubuque and Pacific Railroad. One of its major stockholders, Sen. Stephen Douglas of Illinois, had plans to build the railroad all the way to the Pacific coast—right through Sioux City.

Overall, the Illinois Central and its subsidiaries experienced numerous delays and bankruptcies during its construction in Iowa. It re-created itself as the Dubuque and Sioux City Railroad before it stagnated again near the center of the state at Iowa Falls. In 1867, the famous railroad magnate John Blair took over the project. He created the Iowa Falls and Sioux City Railroad to complete the job. Construction now gained pace with the laying of track from both directions of Iowa Falls and of Sioux City. The connection was made near Storm Lake, and the long-anticipated line opened to Sioux City by the end of 1870. From one account, 27,000 people rode the Illinois Central to Sioux City during its first six months of operation.

With its transcontinental hopes dashed, the Illinois Central still had a connection with the Union Pacific through the Sioux City and Pacific Railroad and the Chicago and Northwestern Railway. Sioux City lost some importance in 1886, as the Illinois Central built a line to Onawa to meet the Sioux City and Pacific about 37 miles to the south of western Iowa's largest city. Two years later, the railroad built another line just west of Fort Dodge to Omaha. The Illinois Central had trackage out of Cherokee, Iowa, to Sioux Falls, South Dakota, for a brief period of time. Sioux City, nevertheless, was its chief northwest terminus. Sioux City still had the important connections to the Pacific northwest.

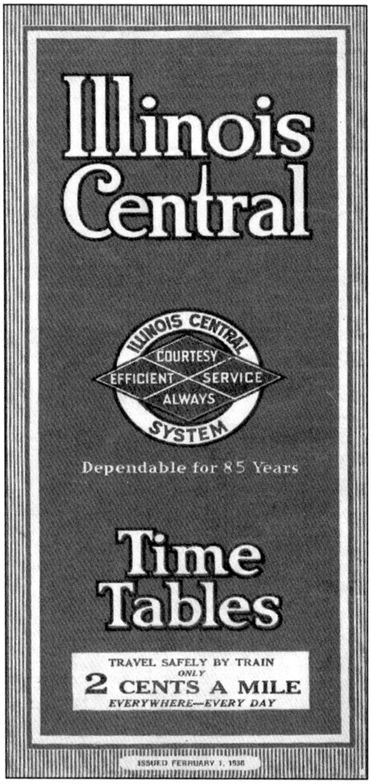

The cover of the Illinois Central time table is colored green. Its symbol was the green diamond. The Illinois Central had a central point at Cherokee where lines branched out to Sioux Falls, South Dakota, and to Onawa, Iowa. The Onawa line was taken up for scrap metal during World War II. The Chicago and Northwestern and the Milwaukee Road had more direct trains from Sioux City to these towns respectively. This edition is from 1936. (Author's collection.)

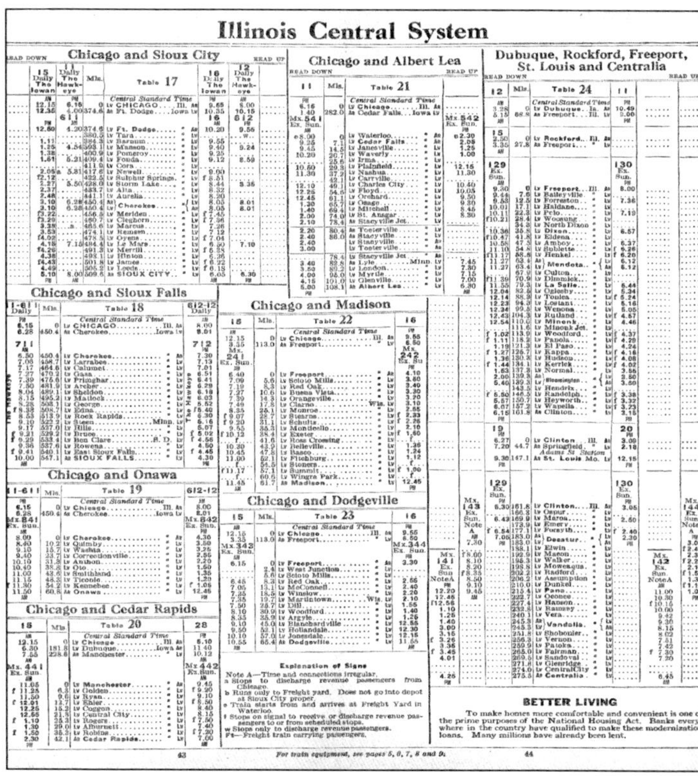

The two important Iowa trains for the Illinois Central were the *Hawkeye* and the *Land of Corn*. The Illinois Central featured New Orleans–style cooking in the dining car. It was the only direct, main-line train schedule to Sioux City's "mirror city" on the Mississippi, Dubuque. (Author's collection.)

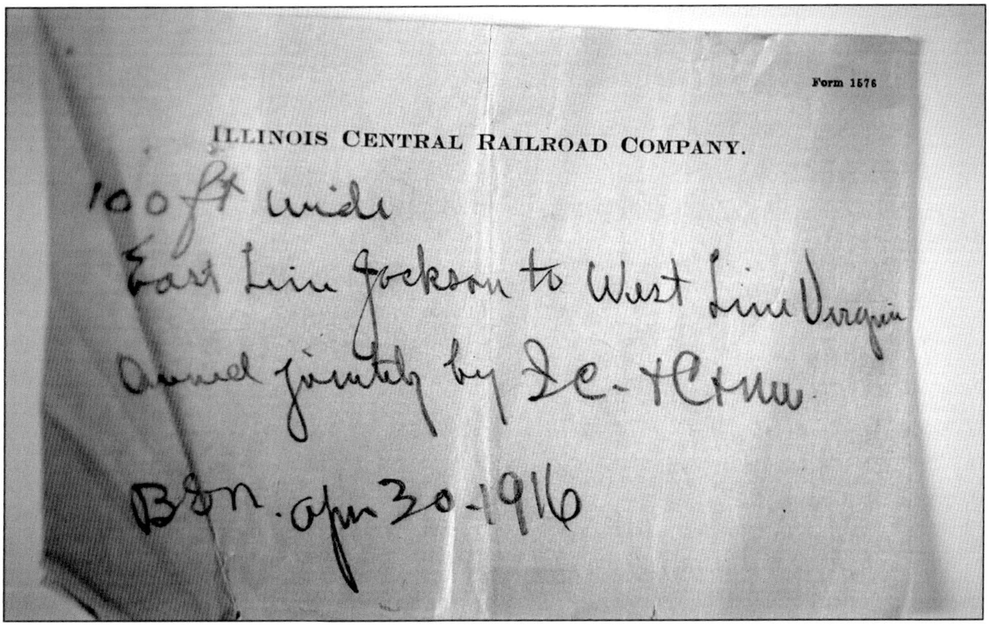

Form 1576

ILLINOIS CENTRAL RAILROAD COMPANY.

100 ft wide
East Line Jackson to West Line Virginia
Owned jointly by I.C. + C&NW.
B&N. Apr 30-1916

The Illinois Central granted trackage rights to the Omaha Road from Le Mars to Sioux City. This notation was to remind Sioux City employees that the Chicago and Northwestern Railway and the Illinois Central had joint ownership of tracks in the downtown. The Illinois Central used the Chicago and Northwestern depot for passenger traffic, mail, and baggage. (Courtesy of George R. Lindblade.)

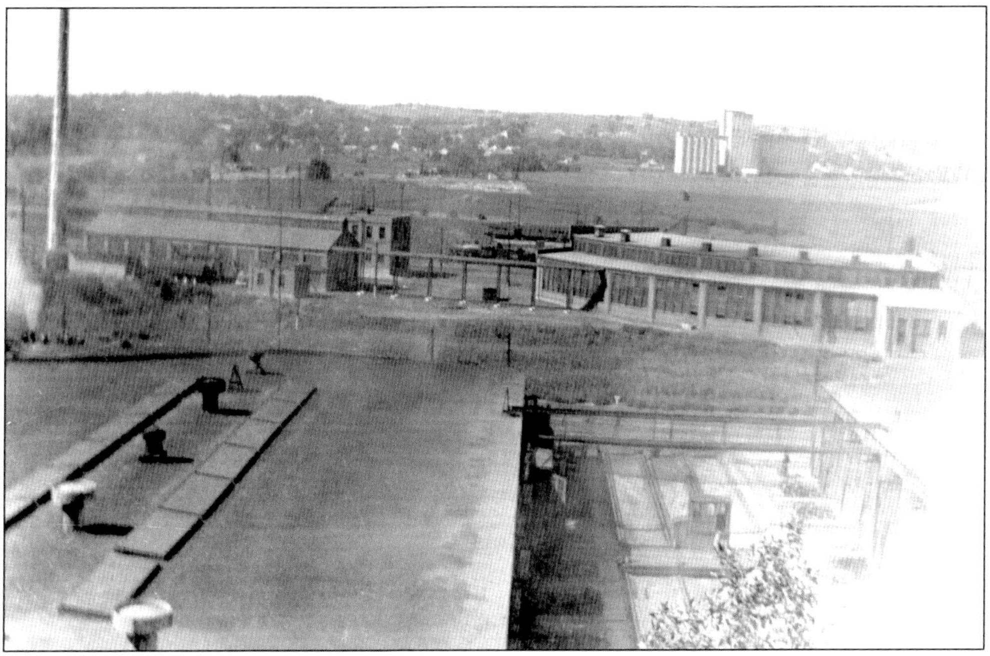

The Illinois Central roundhouse, although smaller than others in Sioux City, was more than adequate for its purposes. Roundhouses were located at strategic industrial towns along trackage. A stockyard was such a strategic point. Sioux City was the western terminus of the Illinois Central in Iowa. (Courtesy of the Siouxland Historical Railroad Association.)

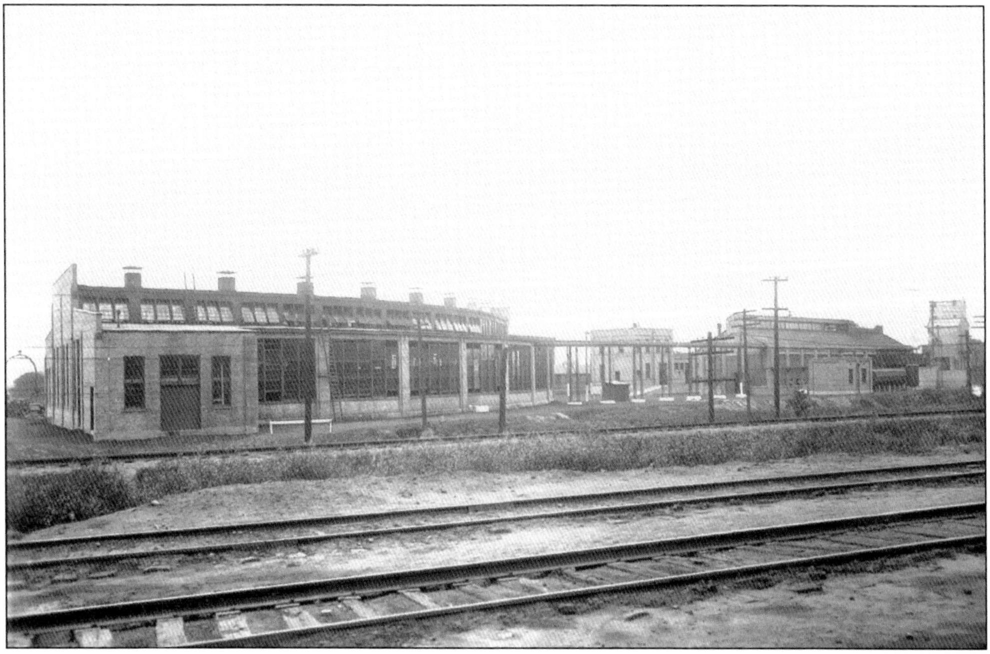

This side view of the Illinois Central complex includes the repair shop. The turntable is noticeable in the far left of the photograph. The railroad had a larger repair facility in Waterloo. (Courtesy of the Sioux City Public Museum.)

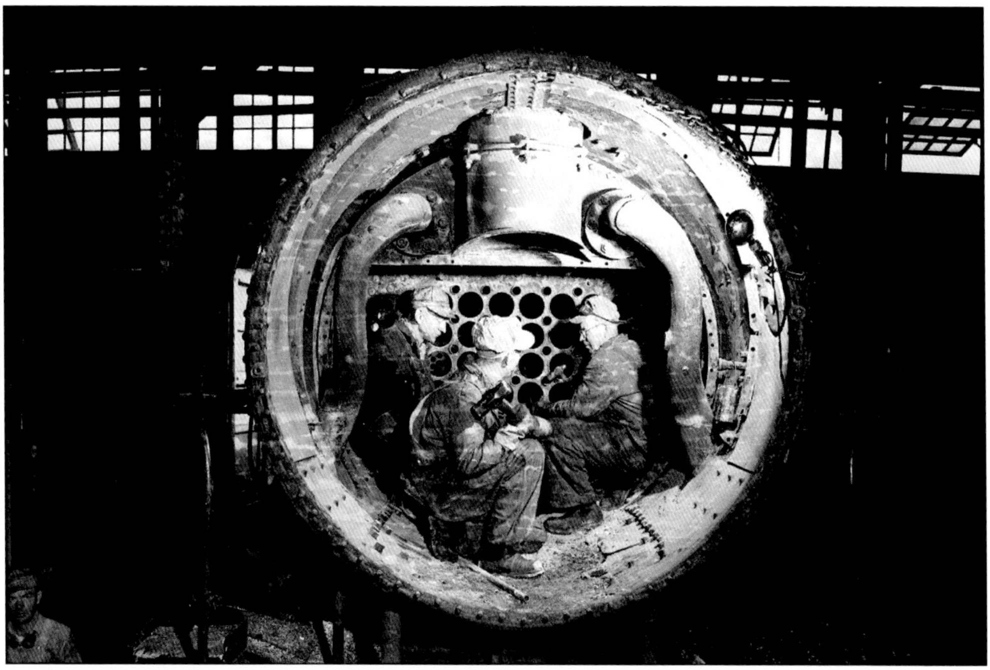

Workers are in a locomotive smoke box and are working on the flues. Flue work was a general maintenance practice on steam locomotives. The flues created the draw on the boiler fire and were part of the chugging sound of a steam engine. (Courtesy of the Sioux City Public Museum, George Newman Collection.)

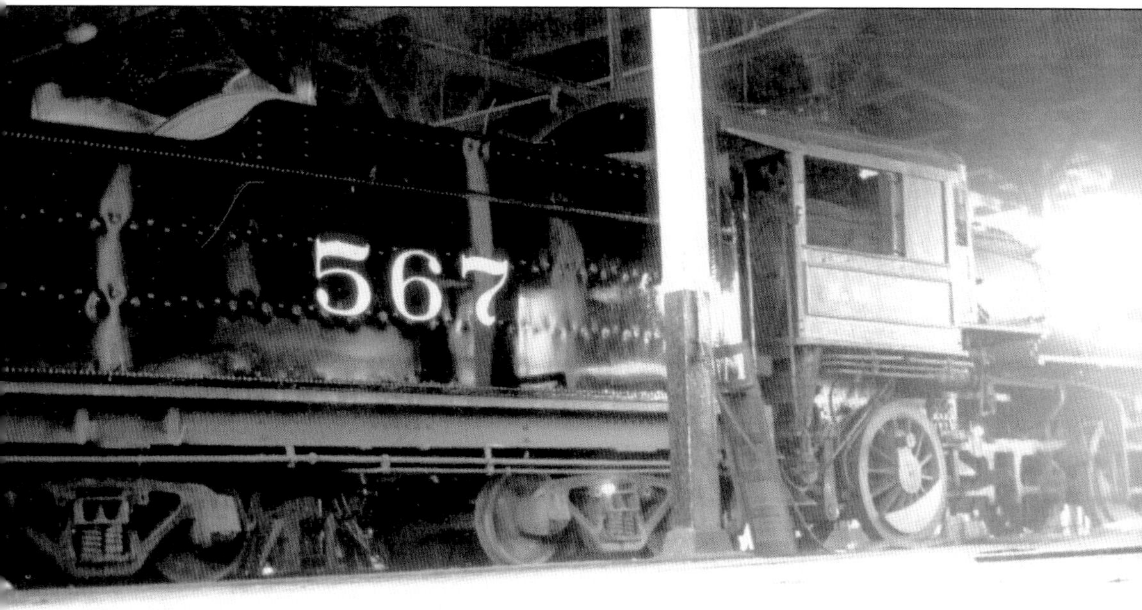

Locomotive No. 567 is undergoing drive wheel repairs. The size of the wheel indicates that it would be a freight engine. Drive wheels, valves, and drive rods were common repair items on steam locomotives. (Courtesy of the Siouxland Historical Railroad Association.)

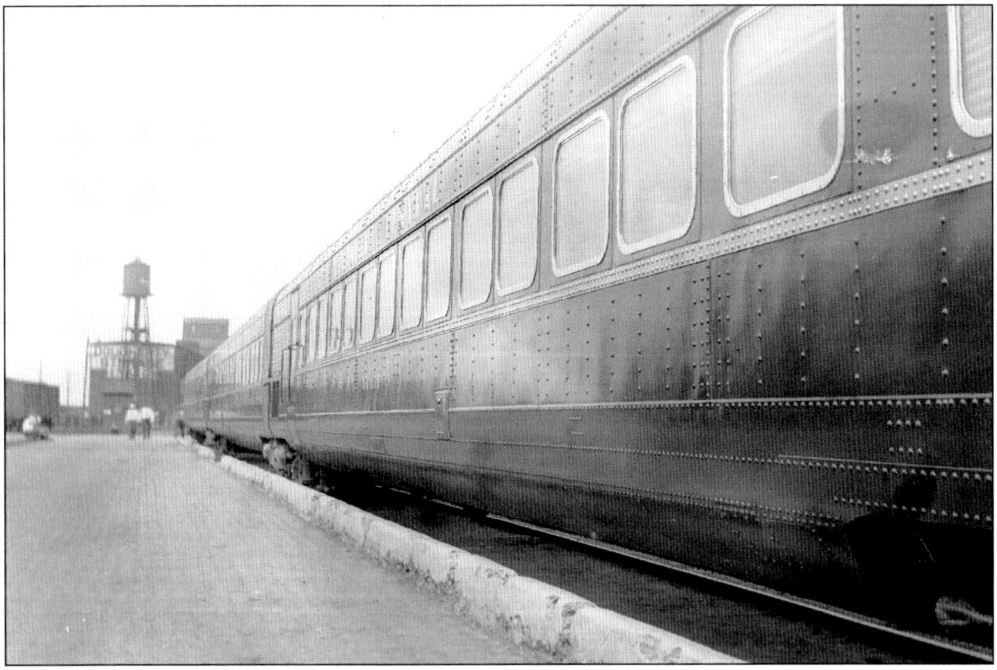

An Illinois Central passenger train is parked at the station in downtown Sioux City. The Dougherty Storage building is in the background. These coaches are of the modern streamline era. (Courtesy of the Siouxland Historical Railroad Association.)

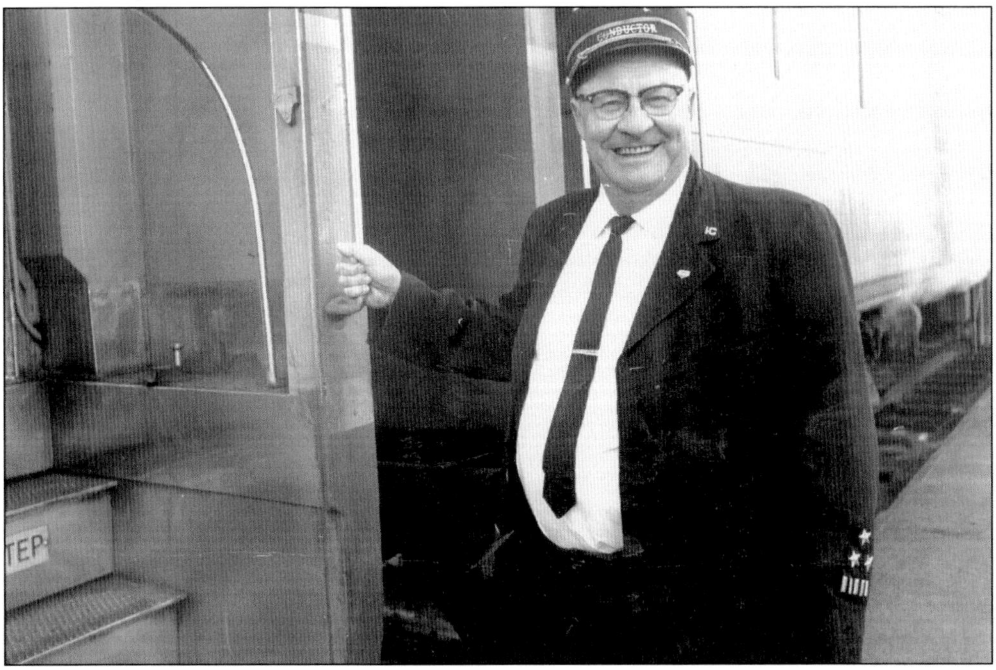

An Illinois Central conductor on the *Land of Corn* prepares to receive passengers in Sioux City. The train was affectionately known as the "pigs and people." It was the last passenger train to arrive and to leave Sioux City before the formation of Amtrak in 1971. (Courtesy of George R. Lindblade.)

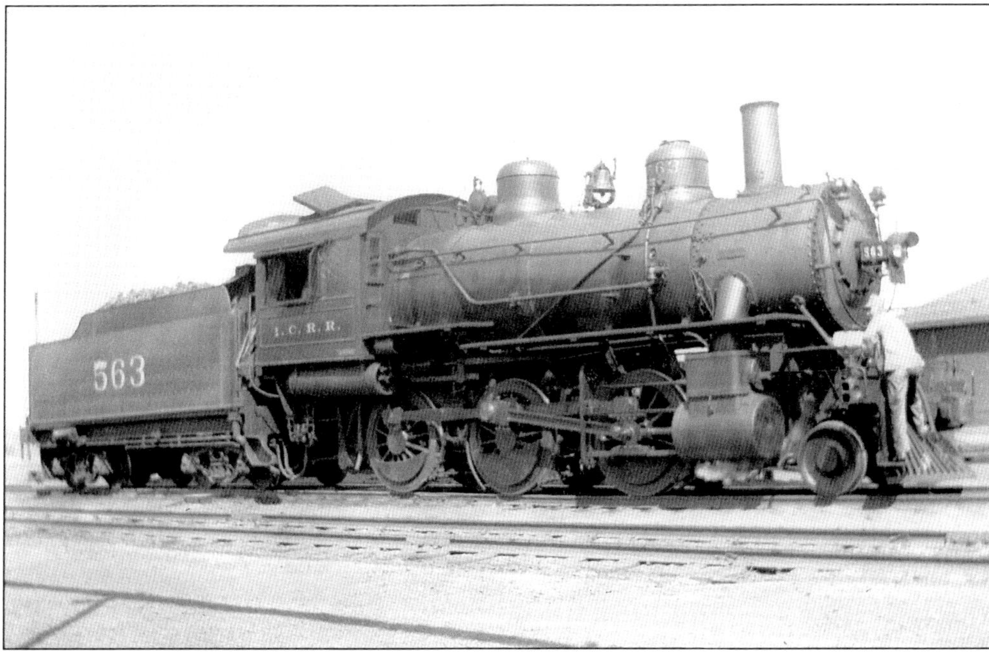

This engineer is following an age-old tradition of checking over his locomotive before a run. Outside the cab he is responsible for the running gear. He is climbing on the front pilot. (Courtesy of the Siouxland Historical Railroad Association.)

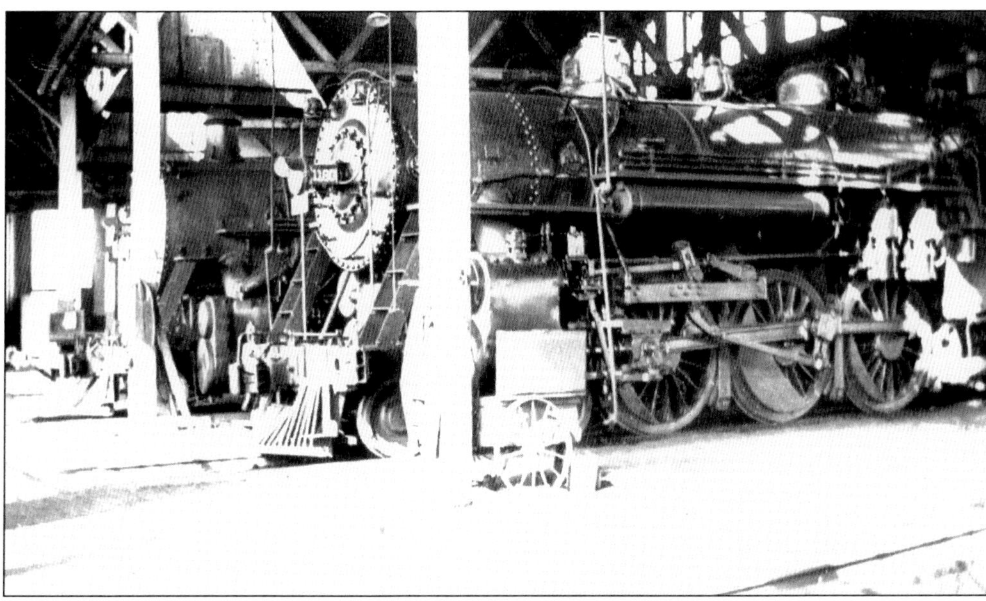

Along with repairs, roundhouses often sheltered locomotives between runs. Roundhouses differed greatly on the type of repairs they were able to carry out. The most complete repairs were made in "backshops." While some of the Sioux City repair facilities were very large, there were no backshops in Sioux City. (Courtesy of the Siouxland Historical Railroad Association.)

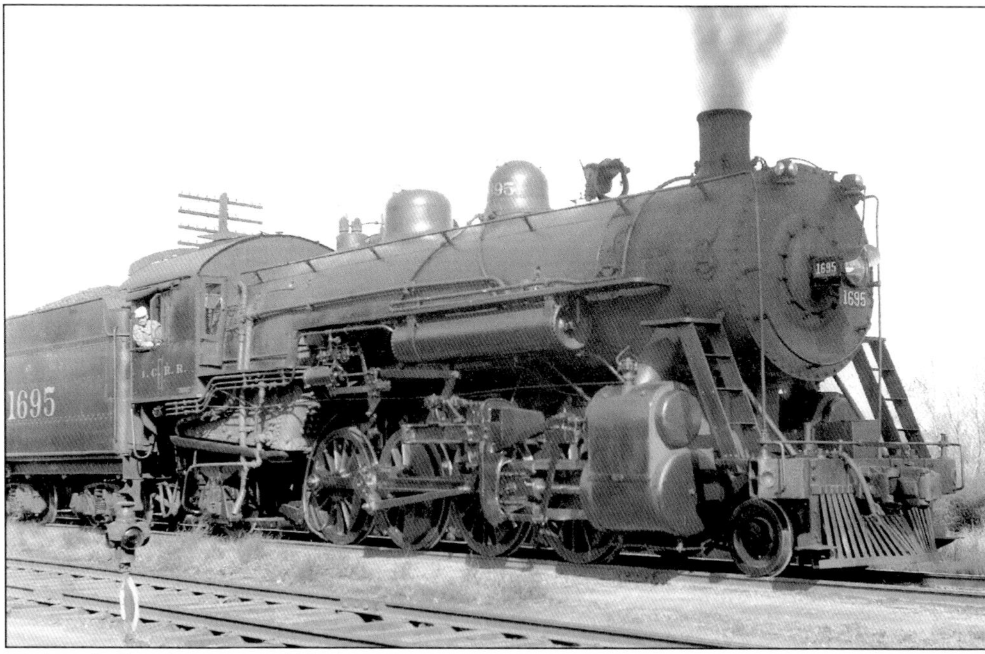

With its bell a-clanging and black coal smoke punched out of the smoke box, No. 1695 is leaving the Illinois Central freight yard. A latter-day "Casey Jones" leans out of the cab window in a classic engineer's pose. Casey Jones was an engineer on the Illinois Central Railroad on the New Orleans run. (Courtesy of the Siouxland Historical Railroad Association.)

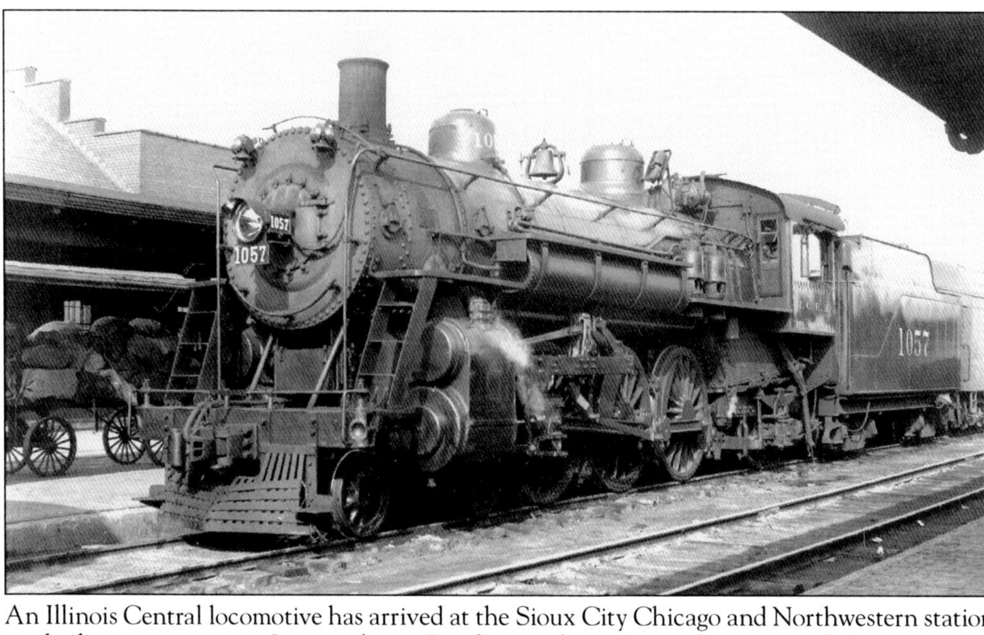

An Illinois Central locomotive has arrived at the Sioux City Chicago and Northwestern station to discharge passengers. It is a classic Pacific-type locomotive. (Courtesy of the Siouxland Historical Railroad Association.)

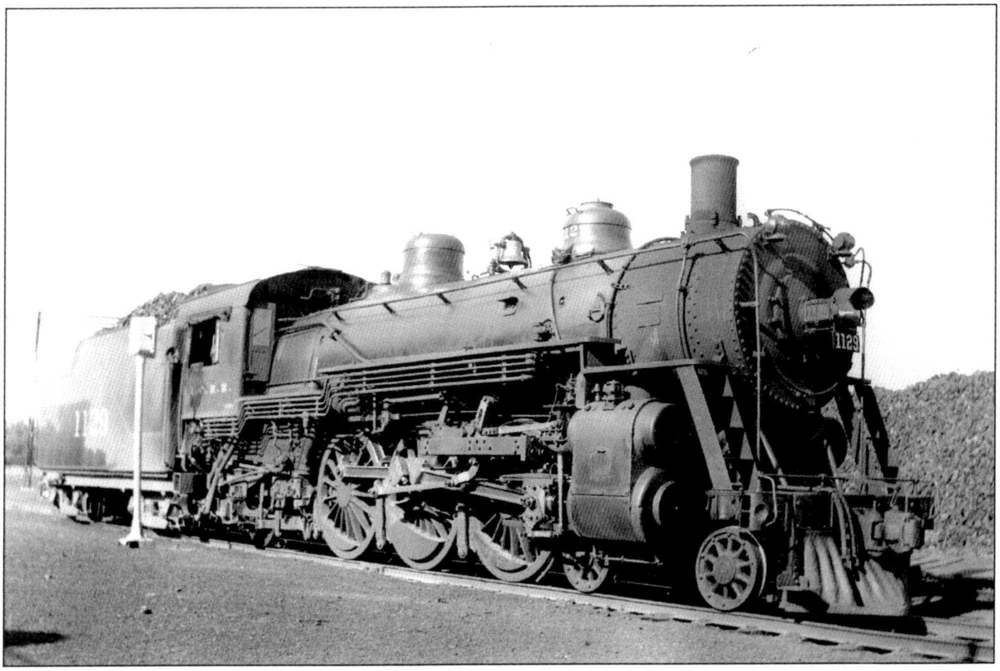

The Illinois Central used these Pacific-type locomotives predominately in passenger service. The No. 1129 is standing near the coal pile in the freight yard, and it has its tender full of the fuel. (Courtesy of the Siouxland Historical Railroad Association.)

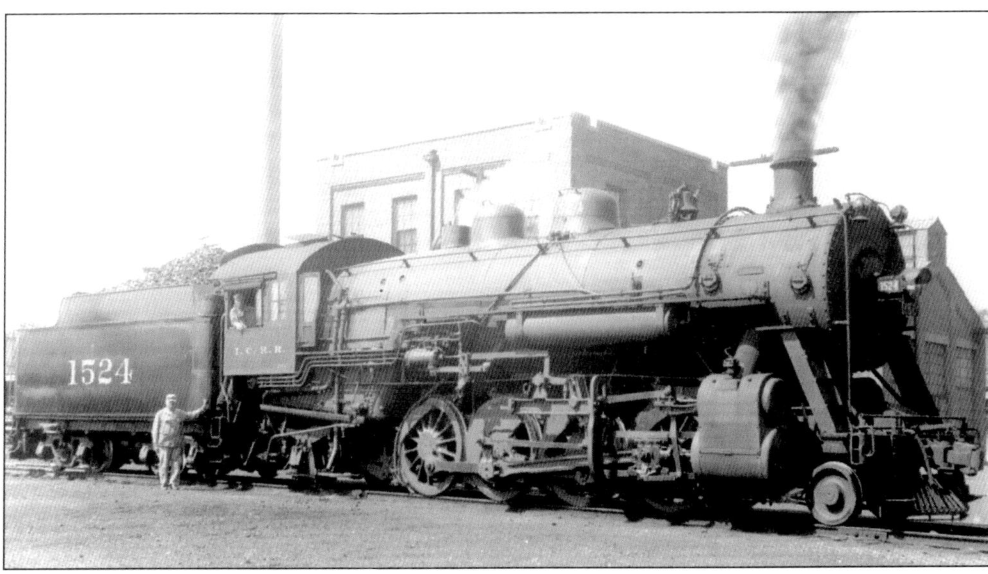

One of Casey Jones's successors is in this photograph at the throttle of this 2-8-2 locomotive in the downtown area of Sioux City. The engineer sat on the right side of the engine cab and the fireman on the left. (Courtesy of the Siouxland Historical Railroad Association.)

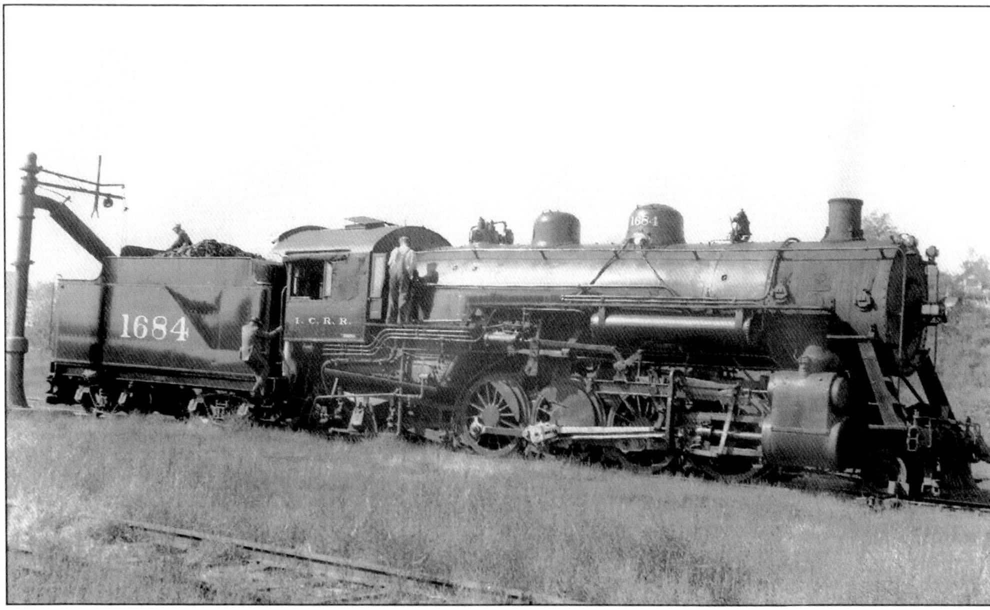

The No. 1684 is taking on a drink of water at the yard tank. Freight locomotives, as this 2-8-2, usually took on water about every 60 miles. It was the lack of water over the boiler crown sheet that caused a boiler explosion. It was the fireman's job to make sure the water level was always above the sheet. (Courtesy of the Siouxland Historical Railroad Association.)

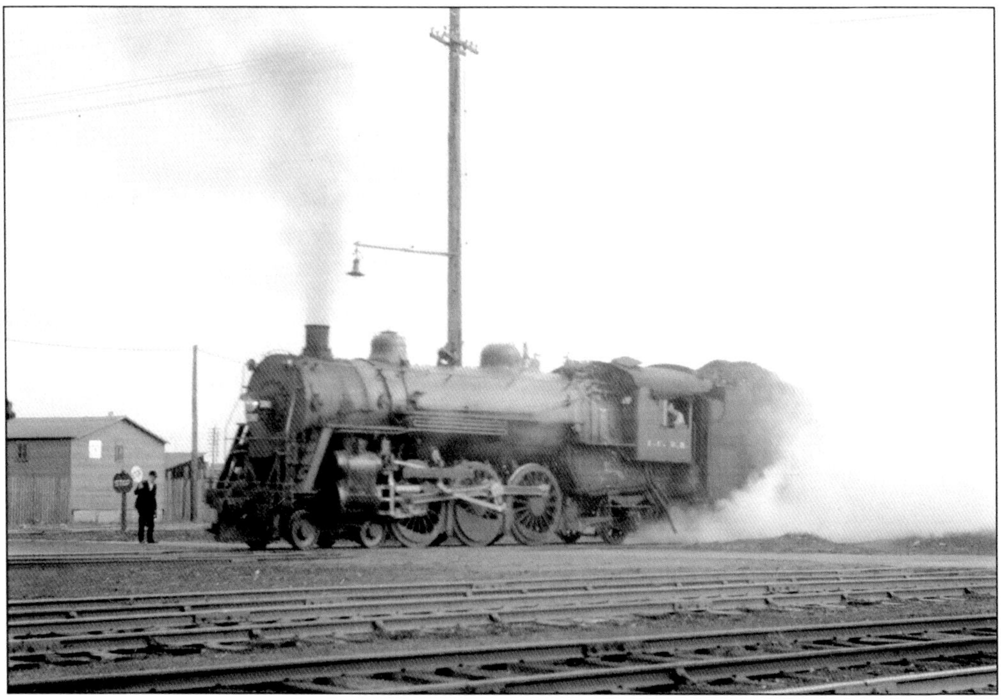

This Illinois Central locomotive is passing through a grade crossing in Sioux City. Notice the crossing attendant holding a stop sign to oncoming automobile traffic. He would be replaced with automatic signals and gates by the 1960s. (Courtesy of the Siouxland Historical Railroad Association.)

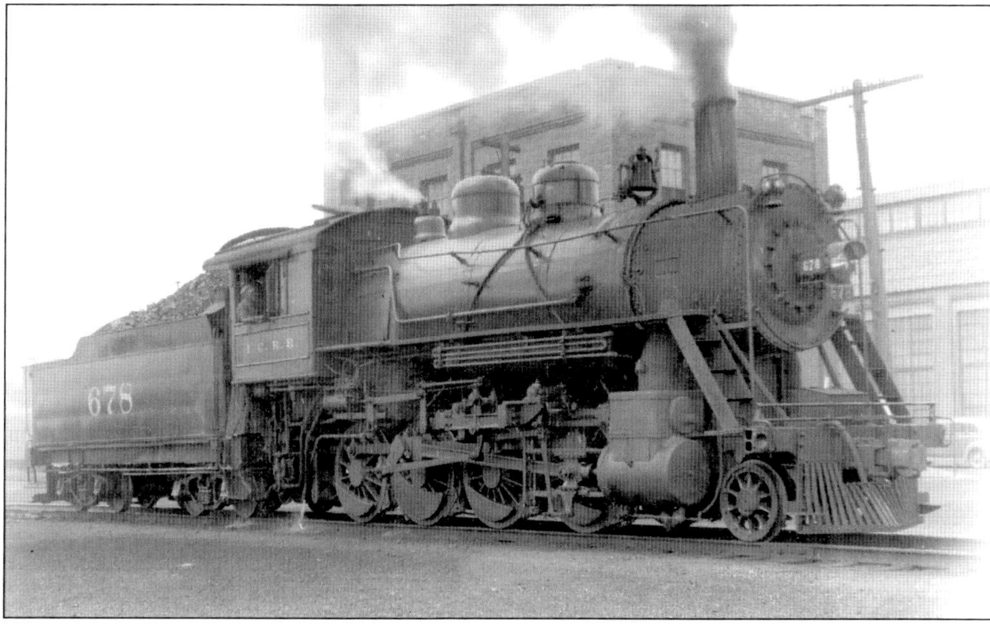

Illinois Central steamer No. 678 is loaded with coal and ready for its assignment. The smaller, white plume of smoke near the cab is from the steam generator. The generator produced electricity for the locomotive and tender lights. (Courtesy of the Siouxland Historical Railroad Association.)

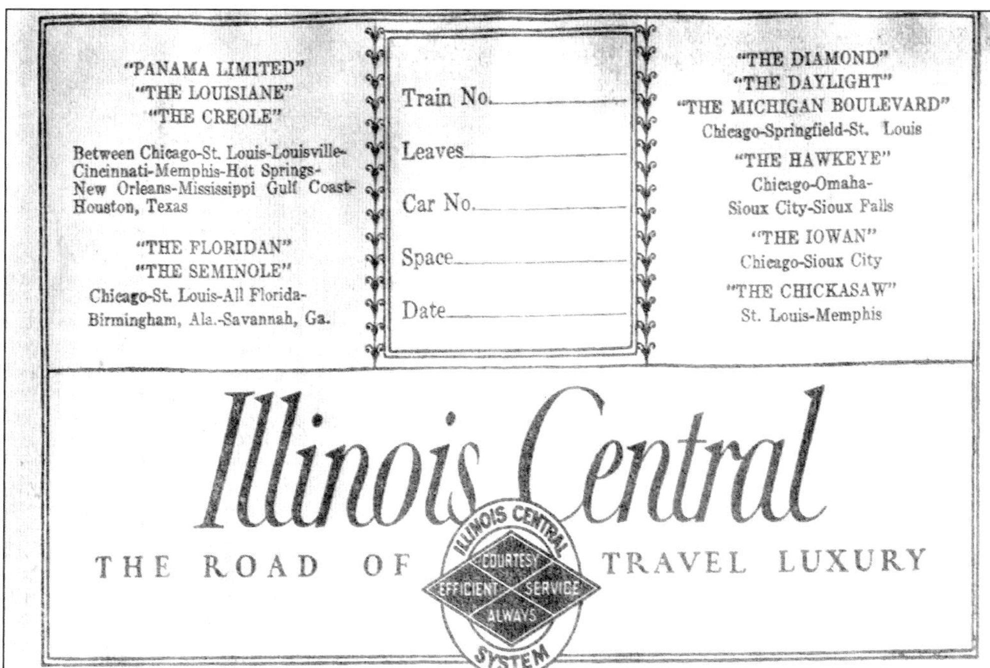

Sioux City has two mentions on this notation-advertisement card for travel on the Illinois Central. The *Hawkeye* and the *Iowan* were prominent trains on the Illinois Central 1940s roster. The card would remind the passenger of his or her seat or berth on the train. (Courtesy of the Siouxland Historical Railroad Association.)

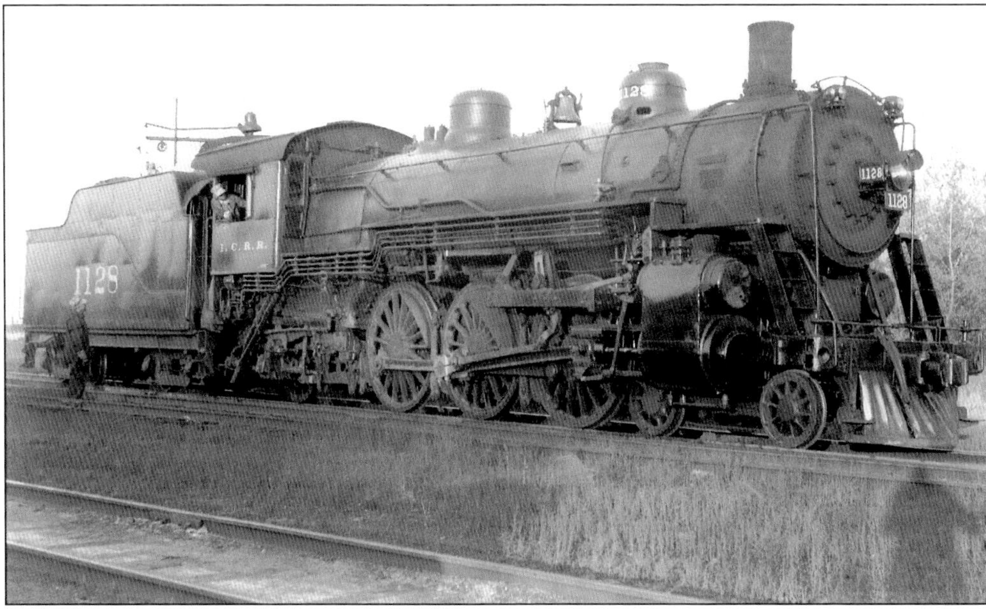

The Illinois Central Pacific-type locomotive is on the ready track to take a passenger train eastward. The Pacifics and later the Hudson locomotives were the heavy consist speedsters of passenger trains for nearly 20 years. (Courtesy of the Siouxland Historical Railroad Association.)

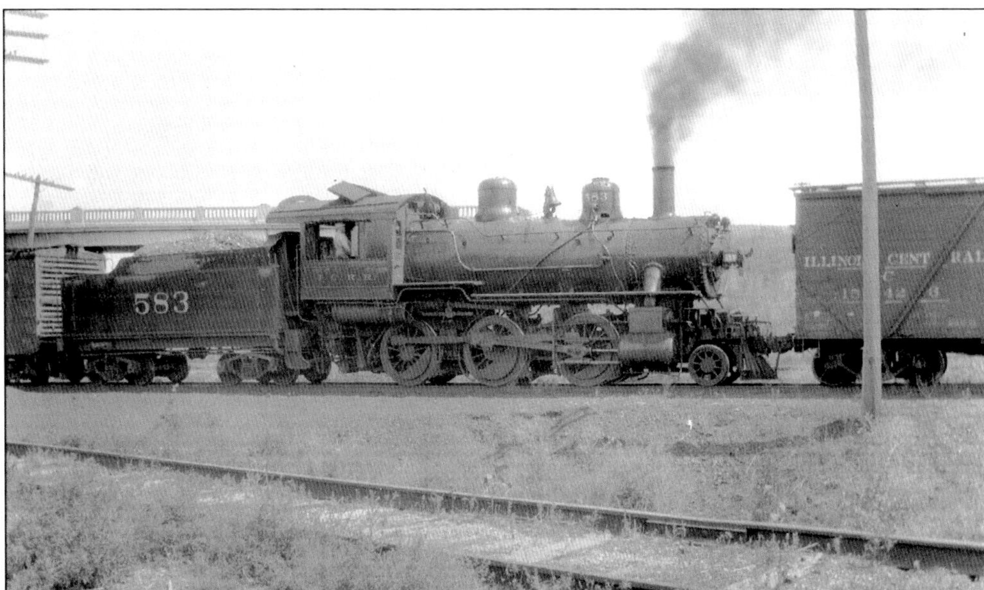

Illinois Central No. 583 is shunting cars in the Leeds area of Sioux City. The bridge above the locomotive and tender is for Highway U.S. 75. The barely visible track behind the locomotive was for the Great Northern Railway. (Courtesy of the Siouxland Historical Railroad Association.)

Streamlined trains were introduced in the 1930s for railroads to compete with automobiles, busses, and air travel. The Illinois Central was not far behind the Union Pacific in the new, light-weight diesel-electric technology. They were sometimes called glow worms. This train set had its own cars and integrated locomotive. They became obsolete when Electro-Motive introduced component E and FA units that could pull any standard passenger car. (Courtesy of the Siouxland Historical Railroad Association.)

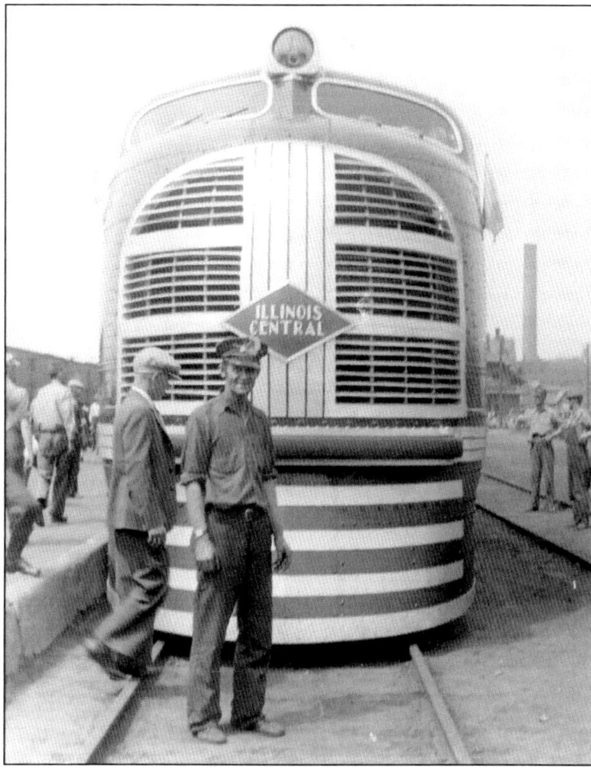

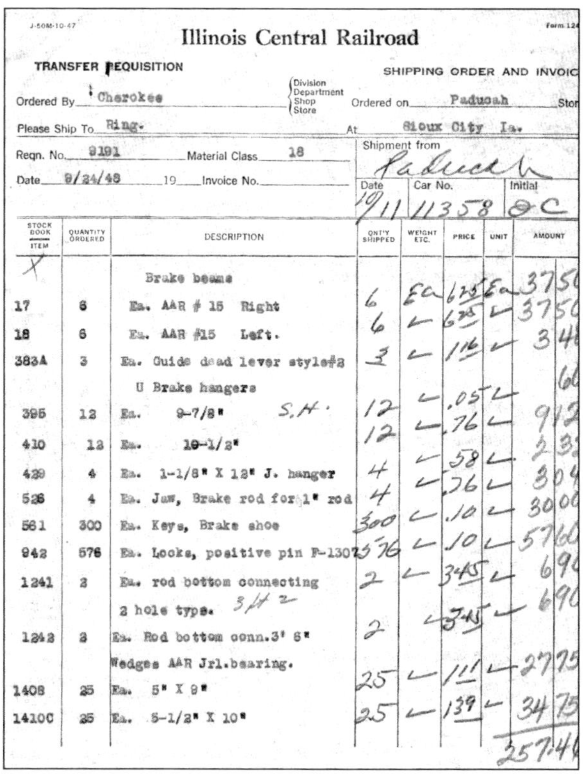

J-50M-10-47 Form 124

Illinois Central Railroad

TRANSFER REQUISITION

SHIPPING ORDER AND INVOIC

Ordered By Cherokee (Division / Department / Shop / Store) Ordered on Paducah Stor

Please Ship To Ring. At Sioux City Ia.

Reqn. No. 9191 Material Class 18

Date 9/24/48 19 Invoice No.

Shipment from Paducah

Date 10/11 Car No. 11358 Initial OC

STOCK BOOK ITEM	QUANTITY ORDERED	DESCRIPTION	QNT'Y SHIPPED	WEIGHT ETC.	PRICE	UNIT	AMOUNT
X		Brake beams					
17	6	Ea. AAR # 15 Right	6	Ea	625	Ea	3750
18	6	Ea. AAR #15 Left.	6		625		3750
383A	3	Ea. Guide dead lever style#2	3		116		348
		U Brake hangers					66
395	12	Ea. 9-7/8" S.H.	12		.05		912
410	12	Ea. 10-1/2"	12		.76		23
429	4	Ea. 1-1/8" X 12" J. hanger	4		.58		304
526	4	Ea. Jaw, Brake rod for 1" rod	4		.76		3000
561	300	Ea. Keys, Brake shoe	300		.10		5760
942	576	Ea. Locks, positive pin F-1307	576		.10		690
1241	2	Ea. rod bottom connecting 2 hole type. 3H 2	2		345		690
1242	2	Ea. Rod bottom conn.3' 6"	2		345		
		Wedges AAR Jrl.bearing.					
1408	25	Ea. 5" X 9"	25		111		2775
1410C	25	Ea. 5-1/2" X 10"	25		139		3475
							257.40

This shipping order contains a list of train car parts—particularly the brake assembly. One of the principle shops of the Illinois Central was in Paducah, Kentucky. The parts were sent to Sioux City to do elementary repairs. (Courtesy of Richard Donaway.)

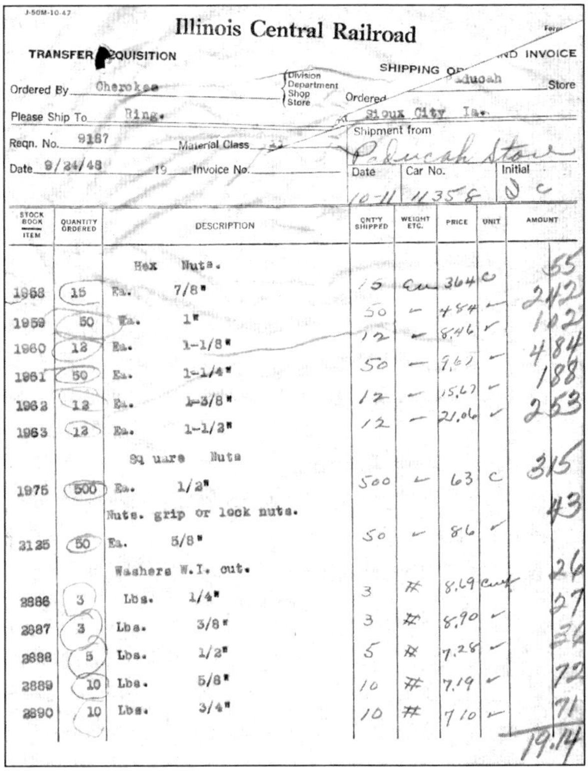

J-50M-10-47

Illinois Central Railroad

TRANSFER REQUISITION ... AND INVOICE

SHIPPING OR...

Ordered By Cherokee {Division Department Shop Store} Ordered ...aducah Store

Please Ship To Ring. At Sioux City Ia.

Reqn. No. 9187 Material Class ...

Date 9/24/48 19__ Invoice No.

Shipment from Paducah Store

Date	Car No.	Initial
10-11	11358	J C

STOCK BOOK ITEM	QUANTITY ORDERED	DESCRIPTION	QNT'Y SHIPPED	WEIGHT ETC.	PRICE	UNIT	AMOUNT
		Hex Nuts.					55
1958	15	Ea. 7/8"	15	Ea	364	c	242
1959	50	Ea. 1"	50		484		102
1960	12	Ea. 1-1/8"	12		8.46		484
1961	50	Ea. 1-1/4"	50		9.67		188
1962	12	Ea. 1-3/8"	12		15.67		253
1963	12	Ea. 1-1/2"	12		21.06		
		Square Nuts					315
1975	500	Ea. 1/2"	500		63	c	
		Nuts. grip or lock nuts.					43
3125	50	Ea. 5/8"	50		86		
		Washers W.I. cut.					26
2886	3	Lbs. 1/4"	3	#	8.69	cwt	27
2887	3	Lbs. 3/8"	3	#	8.90		[illegible]
2888	5	Lbs. 1/2"	5	#	7.28		72
2889	10	Lbs. 5/8"	10	#	7.19		72
2890	10	Lbs. 3/4"	10	#	7.10		71
							19.14

The Illinois Central Transfer Requisition orders a variety of hex nuts from Paducah, Kentucky. This order traveled from the easternmost to the westernmost points of the Illinois Central system. (Courtesy of George R. Lindblade.)

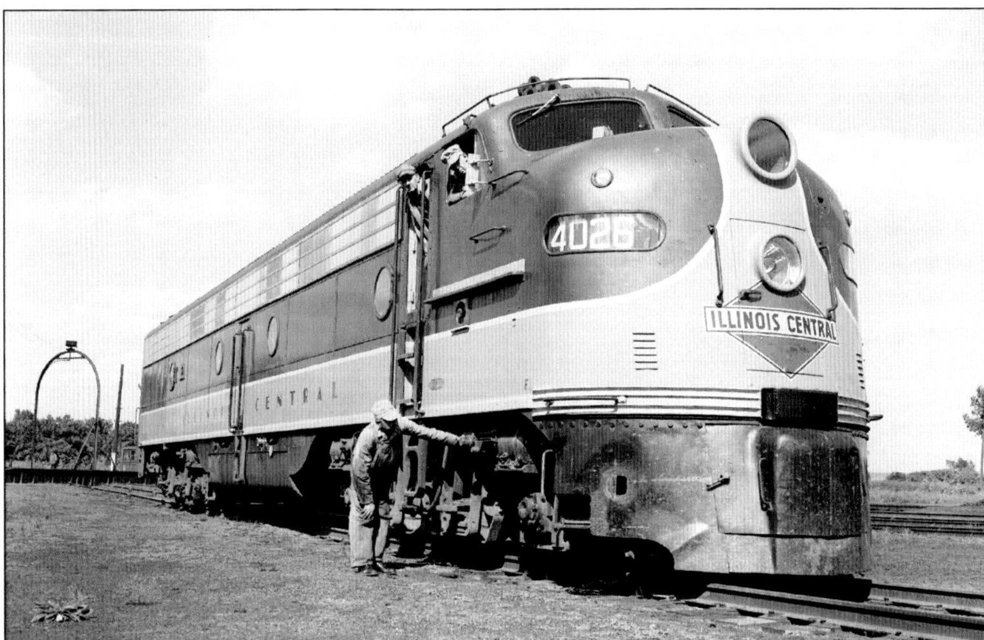

An Illinois Central F unit is undergoing a brief inspection before leaving the yard. The turntable is at the left. As with steam locomotives, this first generation of road diesels, often called covered wagons, had to be turned to face the traveling direction. (Courtesy of the Sioux City Public Museum, George Newman Collection.)

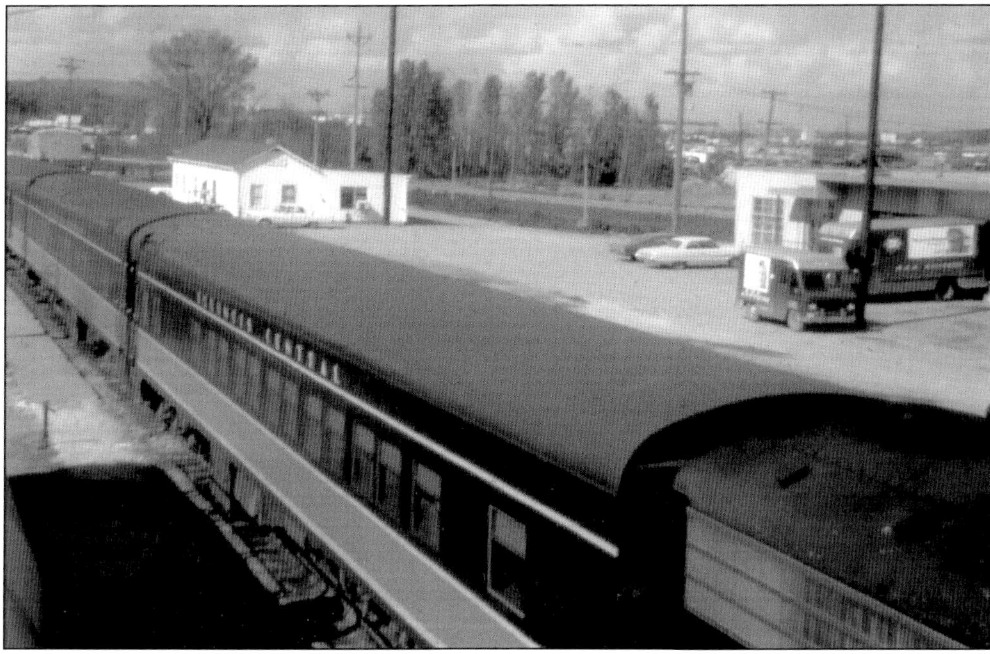

These Illinois Central passenger cars are parked and ready to take on passengers. The trucks in the background belong to the Railway Express Agency, which was the predominant package carrying service until the 1960s. (Courtesy of the Siouxland Historical Railroad Association.)

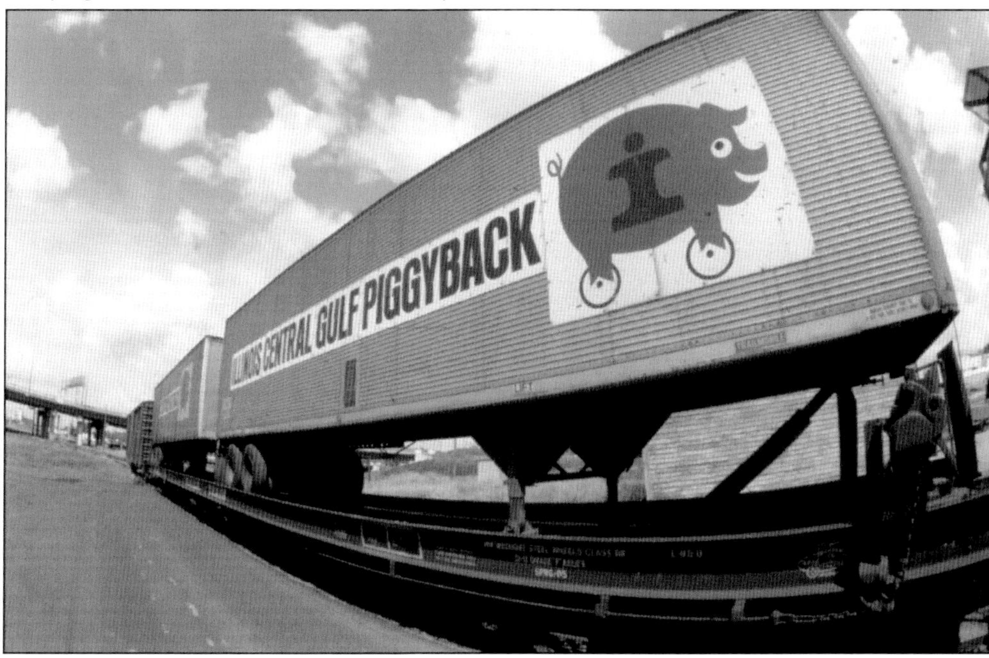

The pig on wheels symbol represented trailer-on-flatcar service offered by the railroads since the midyears of the 20th century. It was commonly called piggyback, most appropriately. This photograph was taken in the then Illinois Central Gulf yard near Sixth Street in Sioux City. The Illinois Central merged with the Gulf, Mobile, and Ohio Railroad in 1971. (Courtesy of George R. Lindblade.)

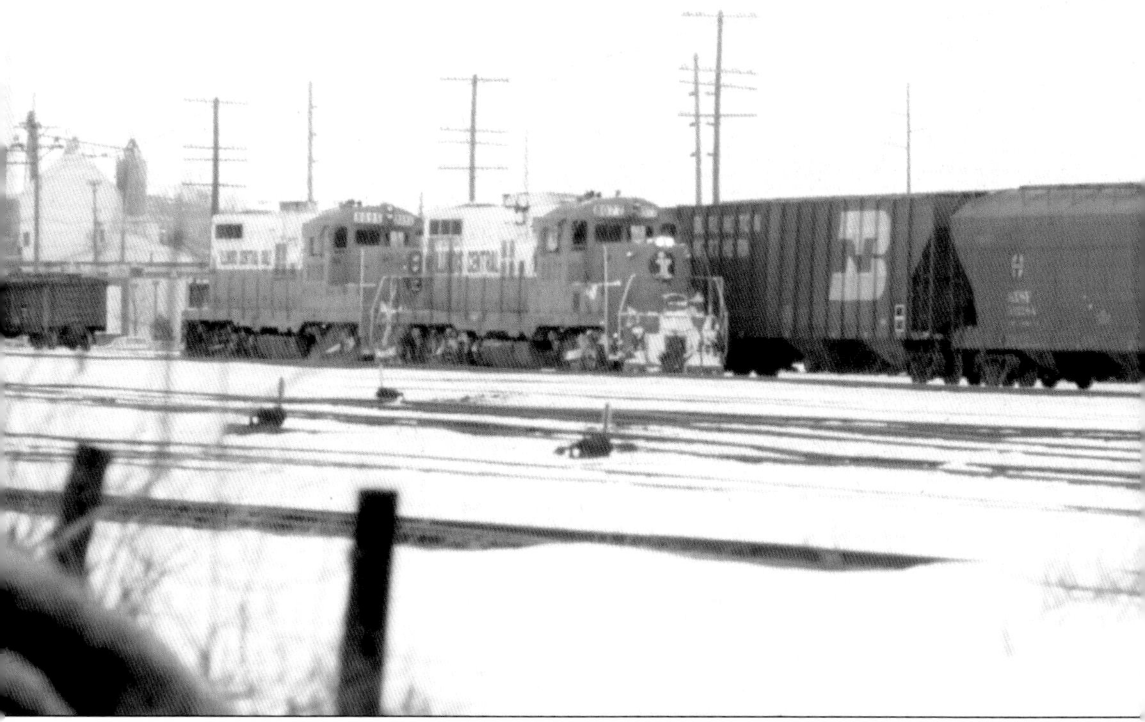

Two Illinois Central Gulf locomotives await their eastern run in the freight yard. Illinois Central Gulf ran mostly geeps (pronounced jeep) into Sioux City until its takeover by the Canadian National Railway in 1999. The railroad reconditioned and turbo-charged its older geeps to make them more efficient. (Courtesy of George R. Lindblade.)

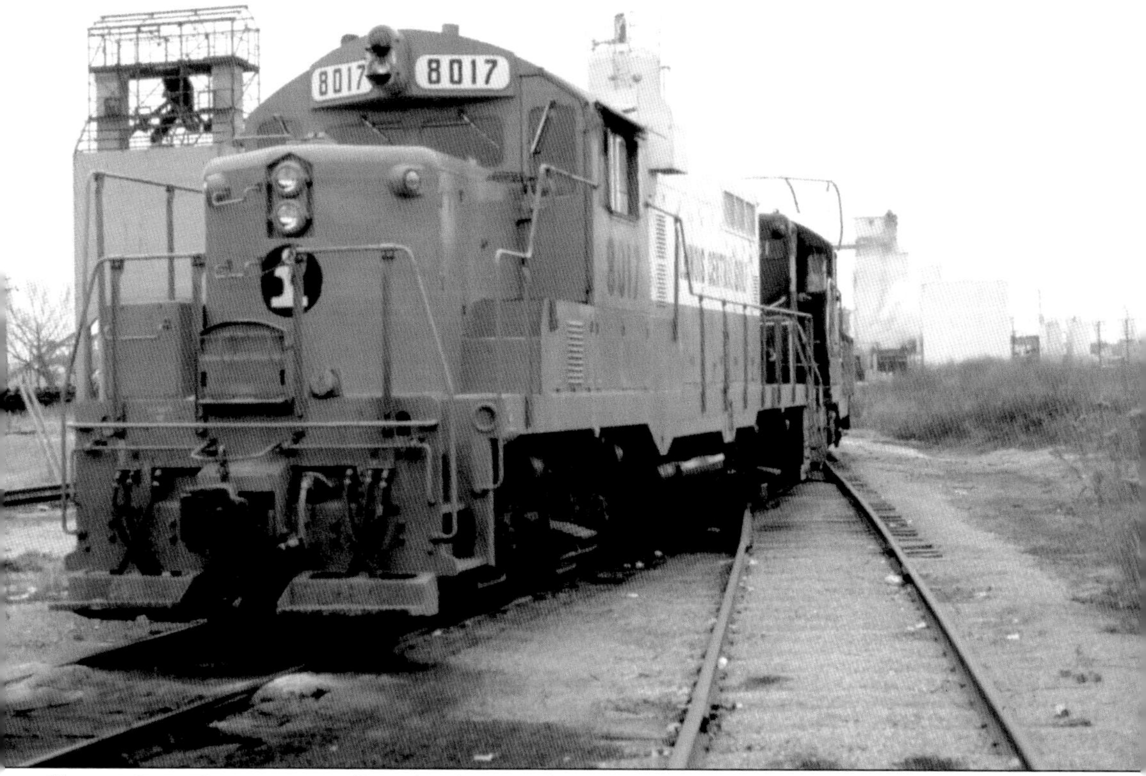

Illinois Central geeps are pulling freight out of Sioux City. After the merger with the Gulf, Mobile, and Ohio, the railroad sold off its western line to Sioux City to the Chicago Central Railroad Company in 1985. After an Illinois Central repurchase in 1996, the entire system was sold to Canadian National Railway. (Courtesy of George R. Lindblade.)

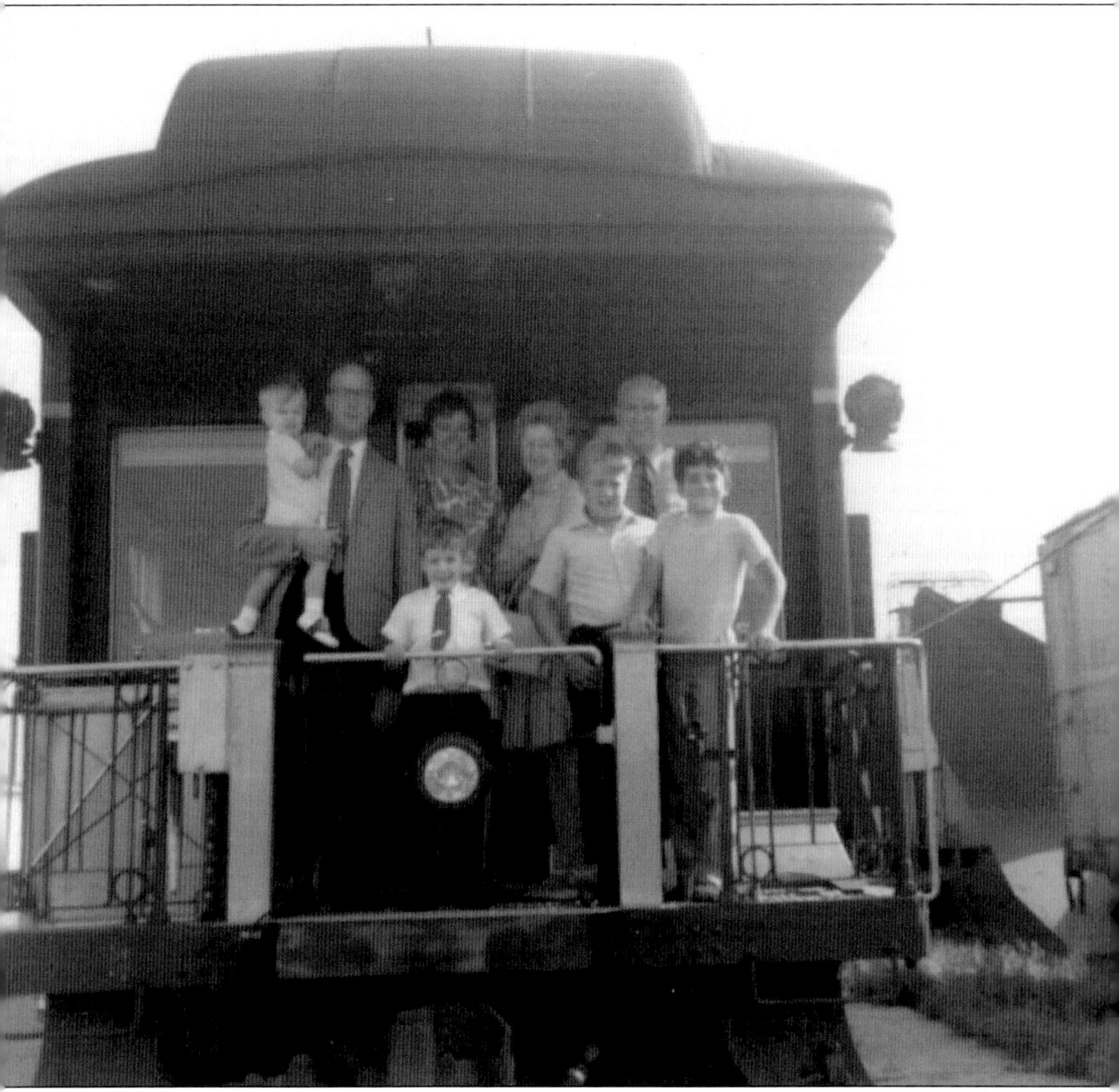

The Sibley and Reistrup families of Sioux City are standing on the open platform of Illinois Central business car No. 9. Business cars were usually placed at the end of a train. They were rolling houses with sometimes even more amenities than at home. They were rented to dignitaries and often used by railroad company executives when traveling. (Courtesy of Paul H. Reistrup)

Four

THE MILWAUKEE ROAD

It can be argued that the Chicago, Milwaukee, St. Paul and Pacific Railway had more unique passenger features than any other railroad in the country. The Milwaukee Road, as it became known in the 1920s, was the favorite of many Sioux Citians traveling to the Pacific coast and to Chicago. The Tip Top Tap lounge, smooth riding and comfortable coaches, and speeding Hiawatha locomotives were the main attractions.

Even though the Milwaukee was chartered to build to Sioux City as early as 1856, it veered its trackage to the north to cross the Big Sioux River and to enter Dakota Territory at Canton in the 1870s. It took over the Sioux City and Pembina, the Sioux City and Dakota, and the Dakota Southern Railroads to enter Sioux City from the west. Given the growth of the meatpacking industry in the 1880s, the Milwaukee Road constructed tracks to Manilla to connect Sioux City with its southern main line to Chicago and to Omaha.

The Chicago, Milwaukee, and St. Paul Railway constructed its own tracks to the Pacific Northwest and began operation as a transcontinental railroad in 1911. The Milwaukee Road, therefore, operated coaches out of Chicago through Sioux City with connecting trains to Seattle and other Pacific coast cities. There were also similar freight advantages on the Milwaukee. It thereby added the word Pacific to its name in the 1920s: Chicago, Milwaukee, St. Paul and Pacific Railway.

The Milwaukee also had the advantage of two main lines across the state of Iowa. A traveler from Sioux City could arrive at many more communities across the state in comparison with any other railroad. It also had a station stop at Perry, just north of the state capital of Des Moines.

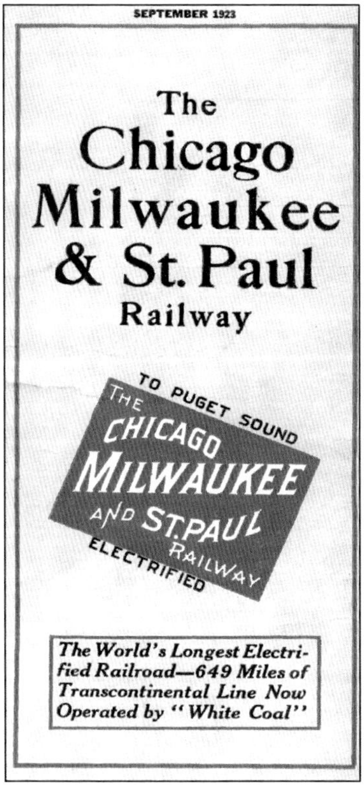

The Chicago, Milwaukee and St. Paul Railway was a favorite of many Sioux City travelers during its years of passenger service. The word *Pacific* was added in the late 1920s. The timetable cover had a yellow background with black and red print. The railroad was a true transcontinental, and it was the only United States railroad that had tracks and facilities in four continental time zones. This edition is from 1923. (Author's collection.)

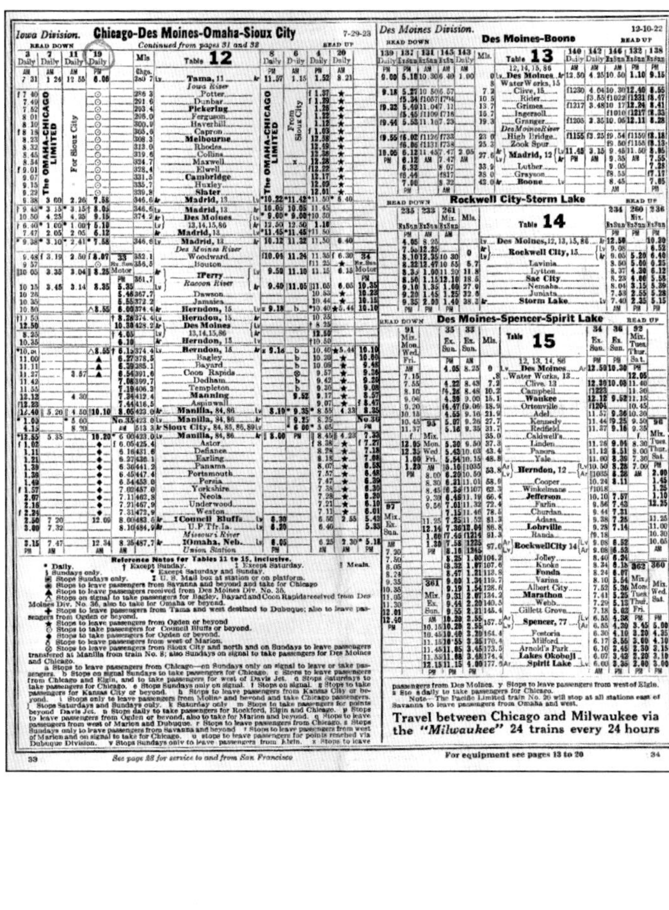

The Chicago to Sioux City Milwaukee Road passenger trains left the southern line east–west main track at Manila. It was a short jaunt from Manilla both to Sioux City and to Omaha. Passengers would enjoy such amenities as the Tip Top Tap lounge. (Author's collection.)

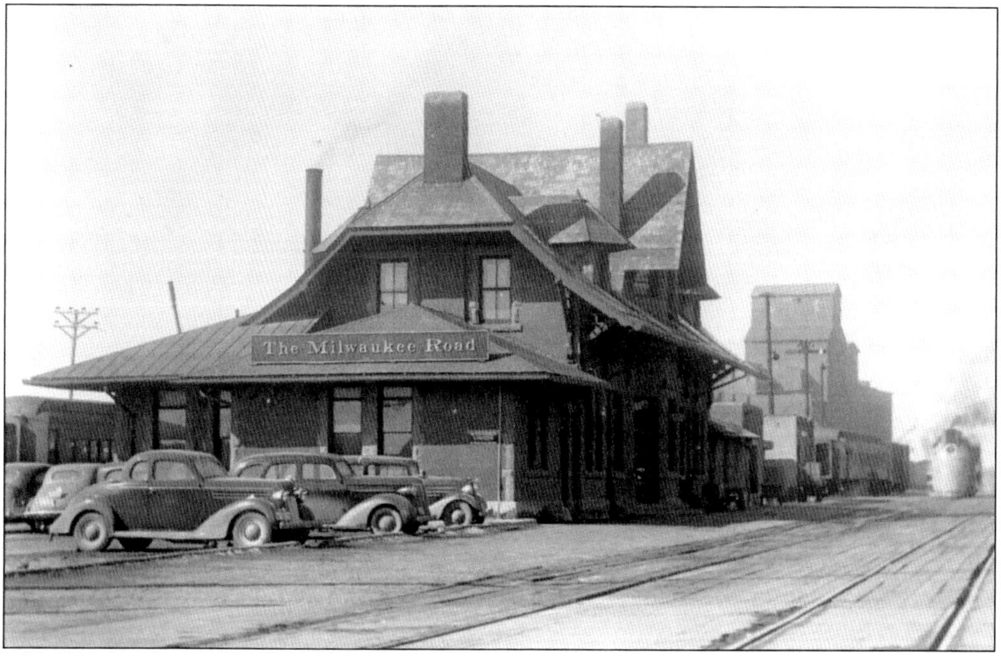

The old or original Milwaukee Road railroad station was located in downtown Sioux City just to the west of Pierce Street. There is a streamlined Hiawatha steam locomotive approaching in the distance. A new brick station was built in the 1950s. (Courtesy of the Sioux City Public Museum.)

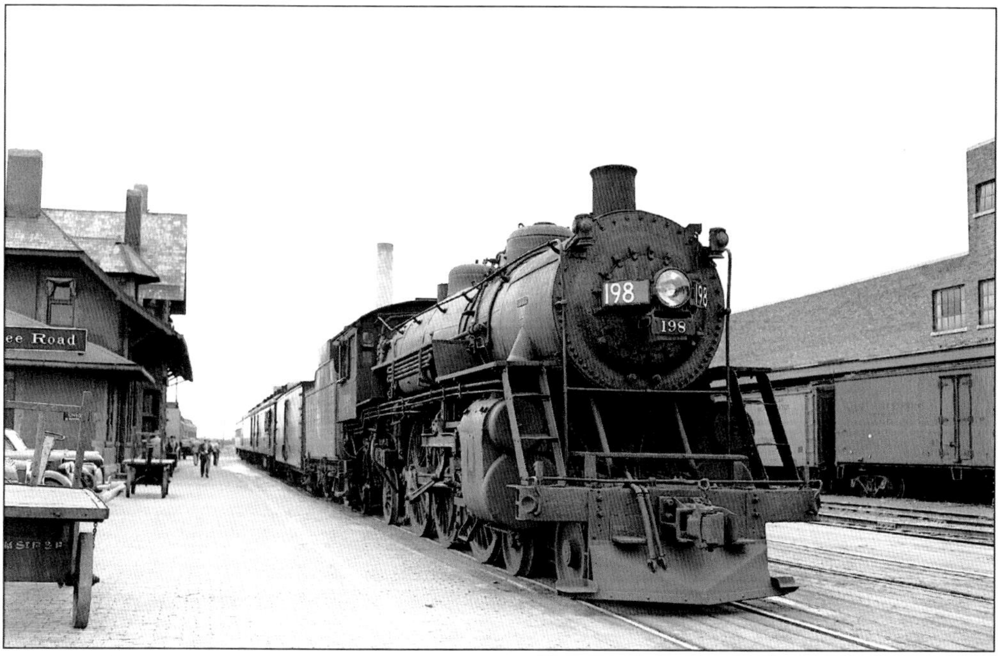

A Milwaukee Road passenger locomotive pauses to let off and to take on passengers at the Sioux City station. It is a local in all probability, since it lacks name train streamlining. The building across the tracks was a food wholesale warehouse. (Courtesy of the Sioux City Public Museum, George Newman Collection.)

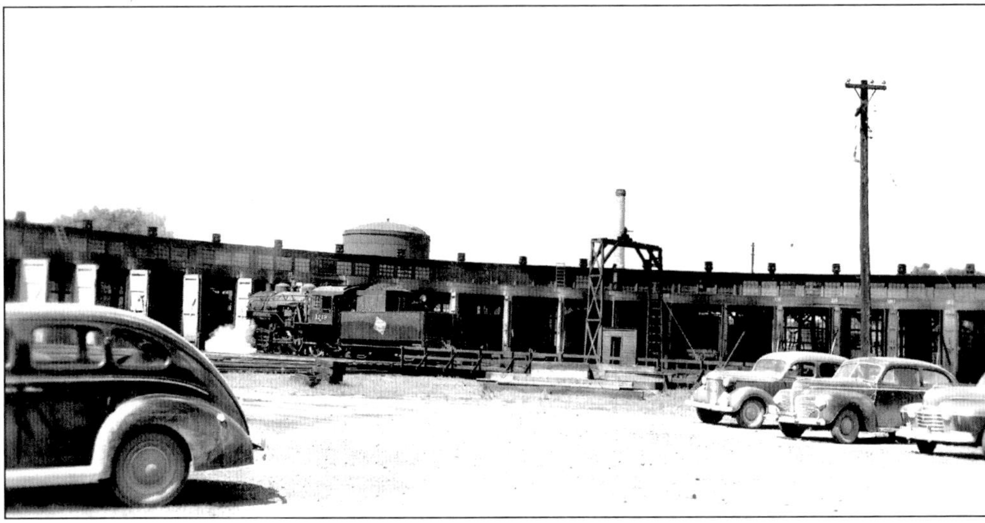

In a scene probably from the 1940s, a Milwaukee Road steam switch locomotive is entering (or leaving) the turntable. This action would take place dozens of times each day to service locomotives in the roundhouse. (Courtesy of the Sioux City Public Museum.)

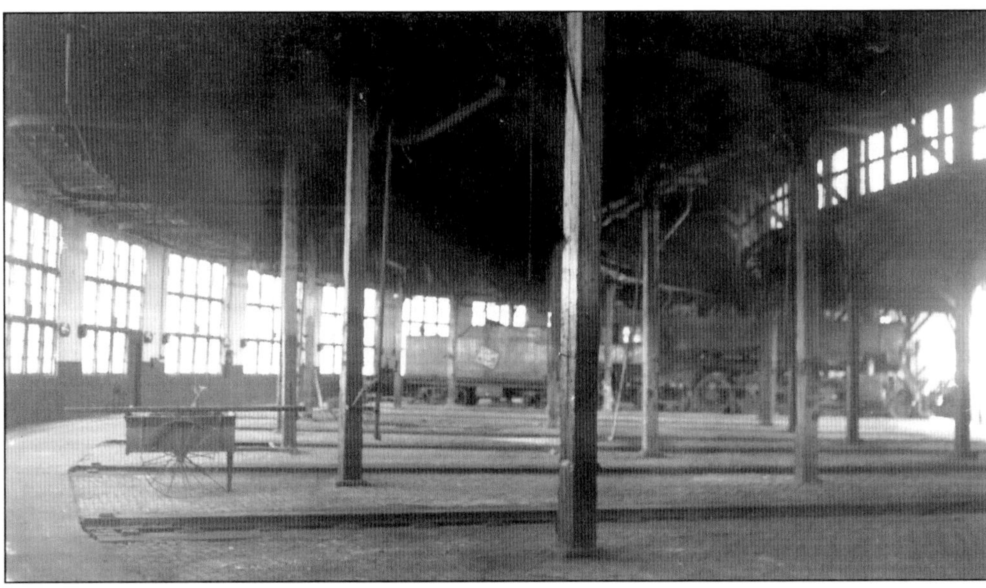

A steam locomotive occupies a track in the Milwaukee Road roundhouse. Major work took place at the roundhouse including replacing "tires" on steam locomotives. Locomotive tires were steel rims fired on the drive wheels. The facility has been turned into a museum operated by the Siouxland Historical Railroad Association. (Courtesy of the Sioux City Public Museum.)

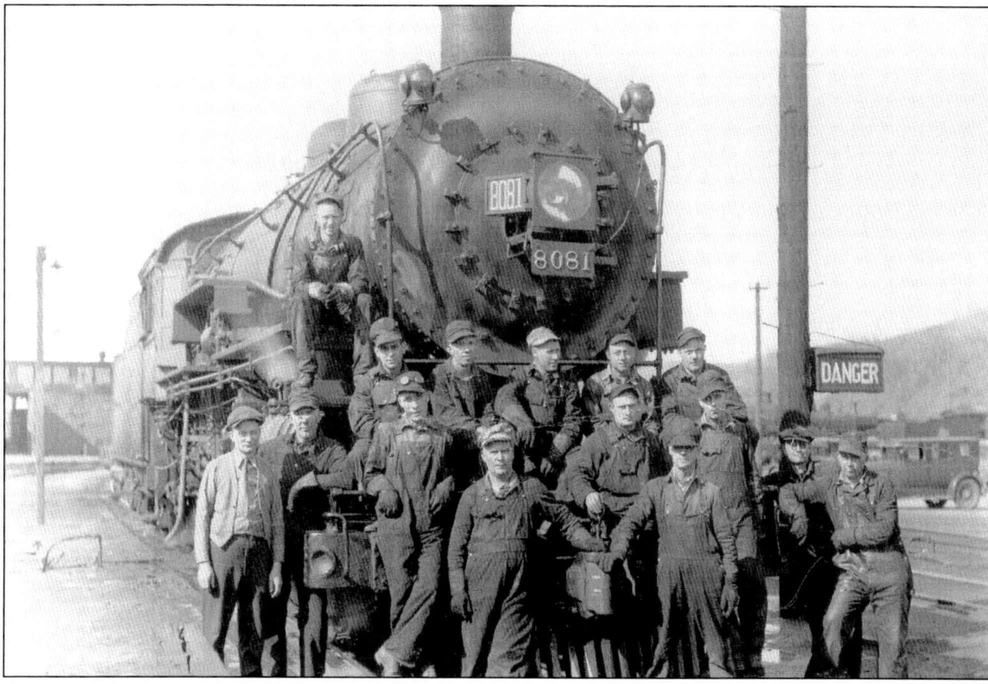

A 14-member crew worked the second shift at the Milwaukee Road roundhouse in the Riverside part of Sioux City. They were expert craftsmen. A machinist could often tell the valves he worked on by sound alone! The photograph is from 1932. (Courtesy of the Siouxland Historical Railroad Association.)

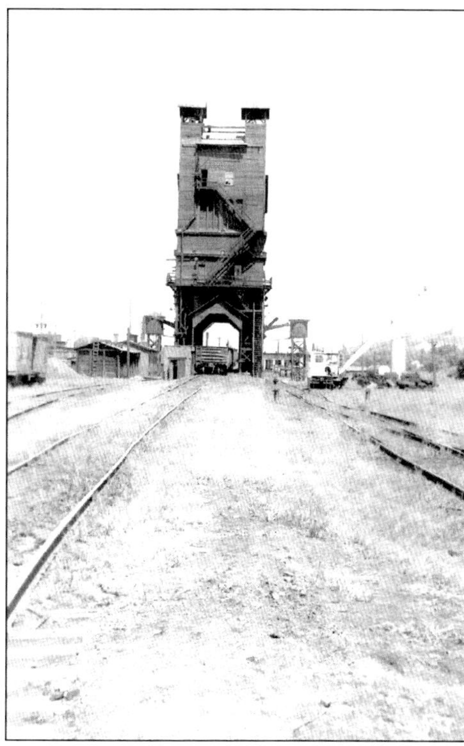

Coal towers stood in the larger railroad yards. Trains would pass under this one to receive their fuel. They were far less attractive and had less attention than the familiar water tower with its pull-down spigot. Sand towers flank the coaling station in the background. (Courtesy of George Berkstresser.)

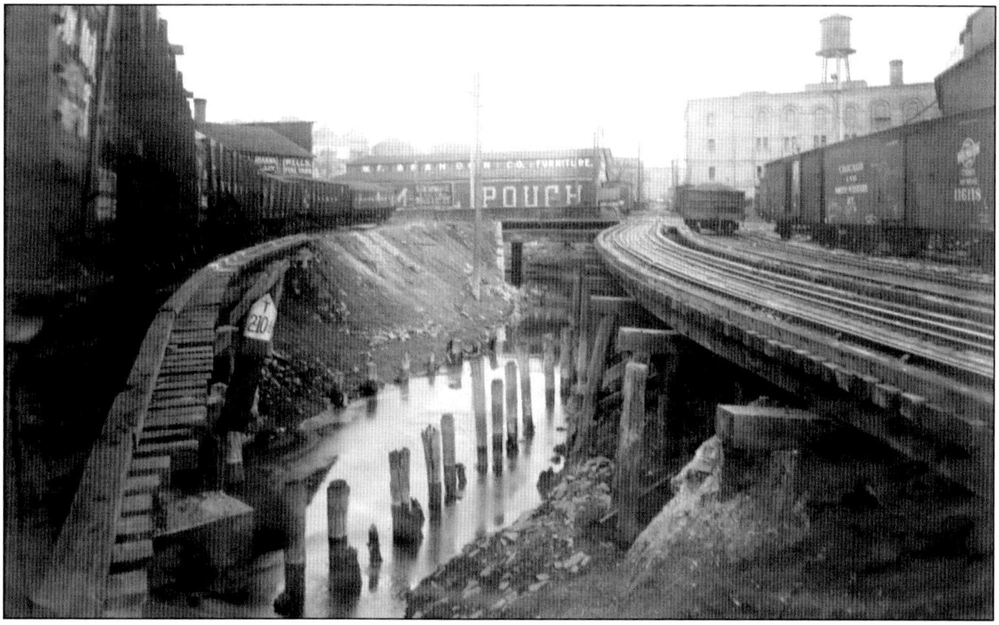

The curved trestle track supporting the freight cars follows along Perry Creek in Sioux City. The pylons in the foreground bear witness to former trestles in the area that were destroyed due to flooding. Perry Creek often flooded after a heavy rainfall. The structure in the background with the water tank is referred to as the "battery building" because it manufactured batteries during World War II. (Courtesy of George R. Lindblade.)

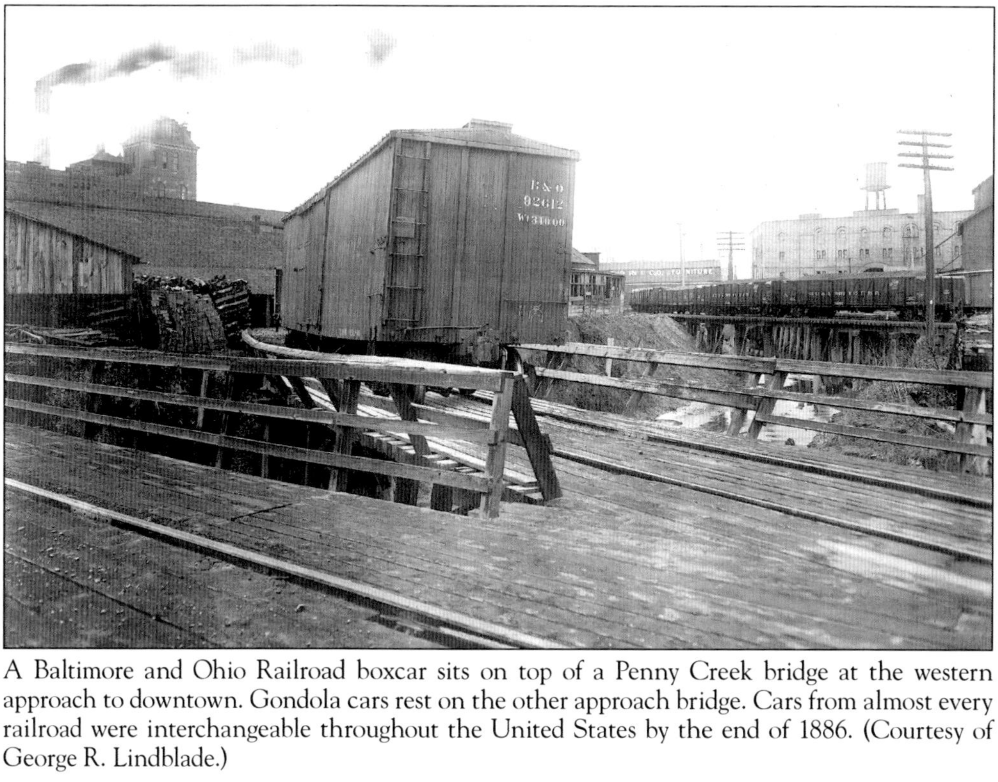

A Baltimore and Ohio Railroad boxcar sits on top of a Penny Creek bridge at the western approach to downtown. Gondola cars rest on the other approach bridge. Cars from almost every railroad were interchangeable throughout the United States by the end of 1886. (Courtesy of George R. Lindblade.)

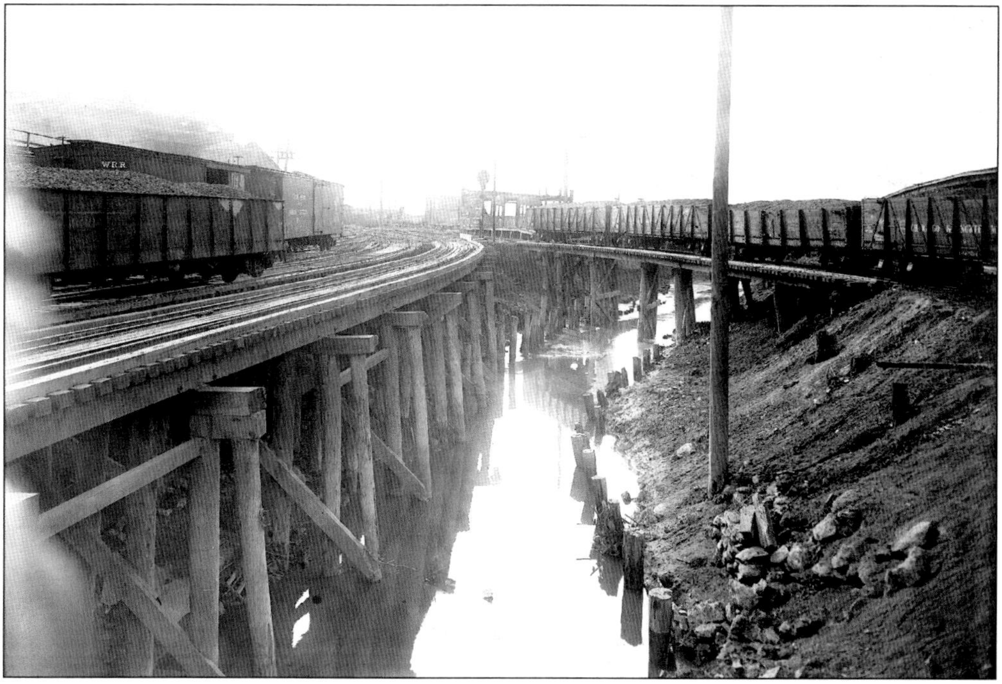

Coal cars and boxcars wait to be moved on the bridge approaches to the stockyards and downtown Sioux City. The stockyards approach area was a hub of railroad activity until the midyears of the 20th century. (Courtesy of the Sioux City Public Museum.)

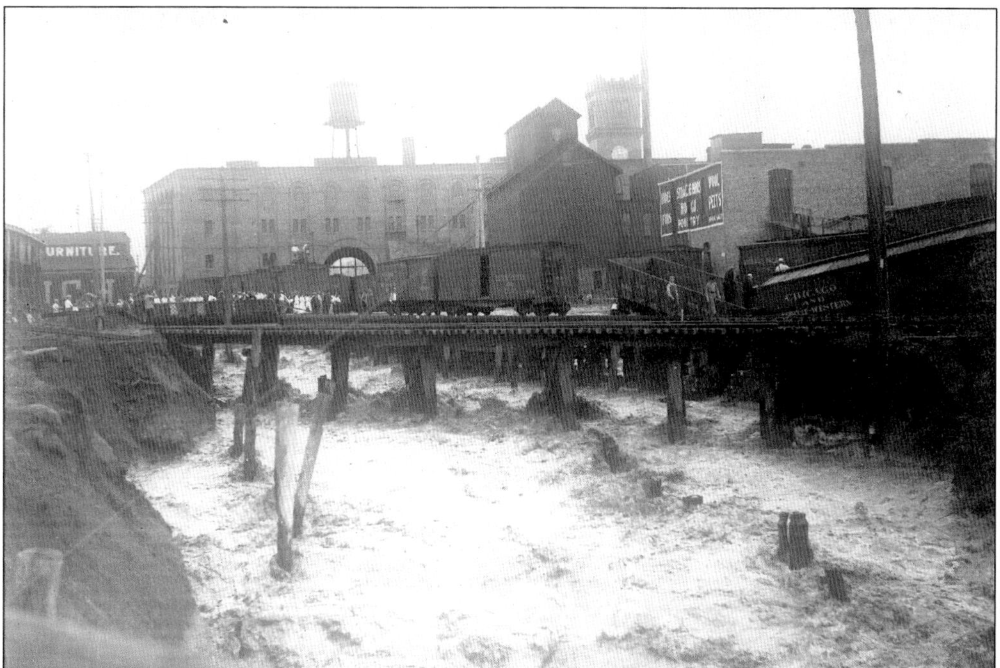

The Perry Creek flood of the summer of 1902 damaged the Milwaukee Road bridge. The water swept several freight cars into the creek and damaged those that remained on the bridge. (Courtesy of the Sioux City Public Museum.)

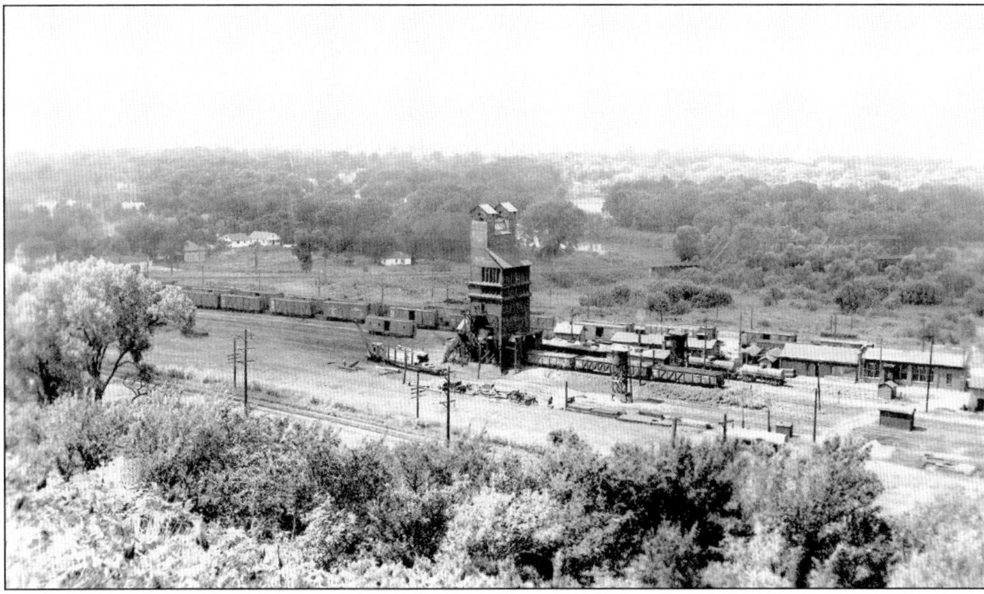

Coal is being lifted into the coaling tower. Steam locomotive tenders will be driven underneath. The tower will provide quick and easy replenishment for the locomotives. They were driven in one end and out the other. (Courtesy of George Berkstresser.)

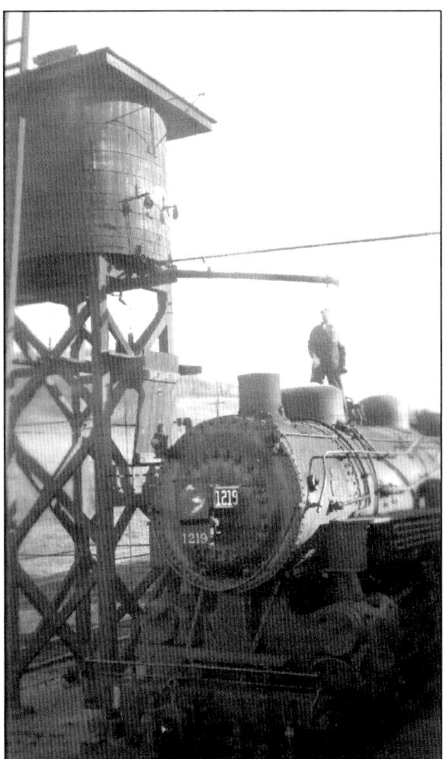

Locomotive No. 1219 sits below a sand tower. Steam locomotives—and diesel-electric locomotives today—use sand to place on tracks in slippery conditions and particularly when starting. The sand was stored in one of the domes atop the steam locomotive boiler. (Courtesy of George Berkstresser.)

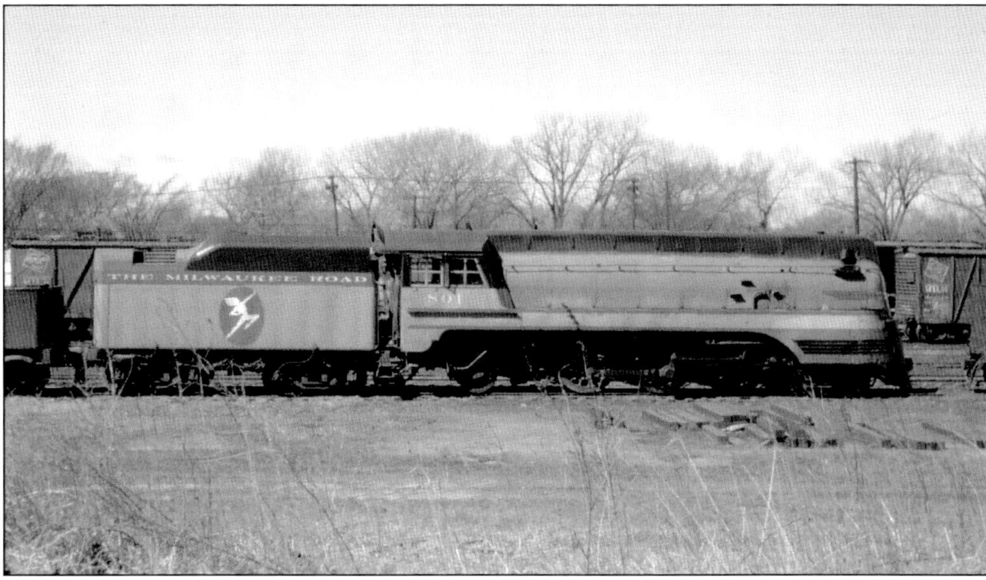

A streamlined Hiawatha rests in the yard before its next assignment out of Sioux City. Legend states that the Native American archer Hiawatha could run so swiftly that he could catch an arrow he had just shot from his bow. These Milwaukee Road locomotives could easily cruise over 90 miles an hour. (Courtesy of George Berkstresser.)

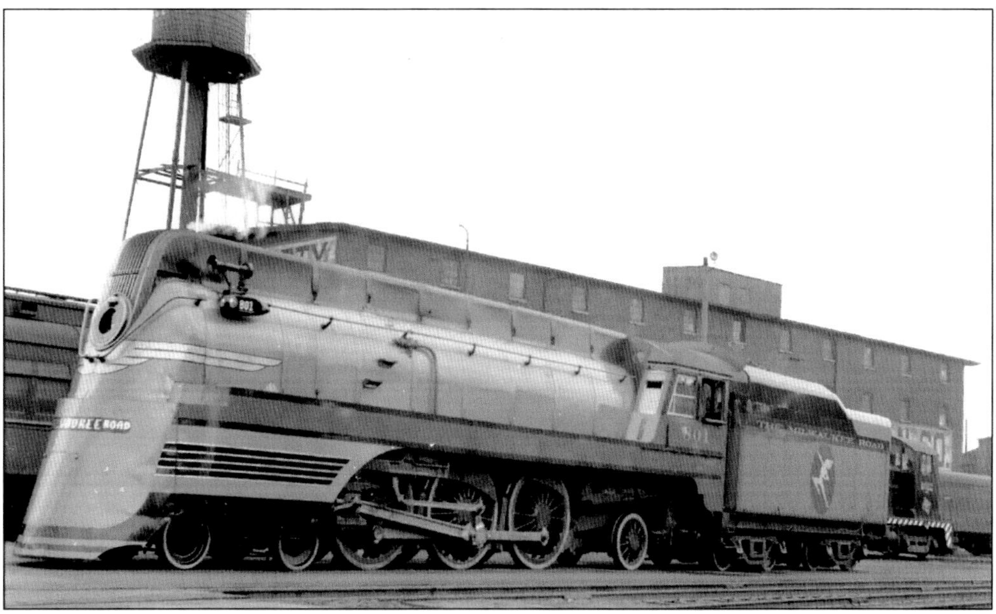

A closer, diagonal view of the Hiawatha-type locomotive shows its scoop nose and top spoiler, which was designed to lift the smoke higher off the locomotive. These locomotives pulled the *Arrow* and *Midwest Hiawatha* through Sioux City for many years. (Courtesy of the Siouxland Historical Railroad Association.)

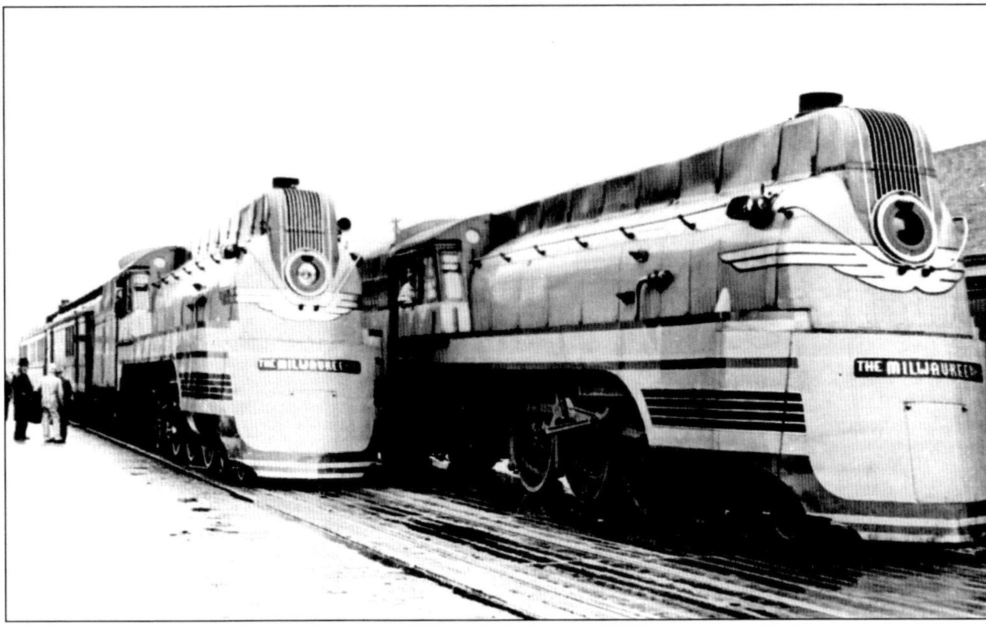

Two classic Milwaukee Road streamlined locomotives stand ready to pull their passenger cars. They glisten after a rain storm. The 1930s art deco styling was recognizable throughout the entire country. An early form of this styling was used in luggage advertisements during World War II. (Courtesy of the Sioux City Public Museum.)

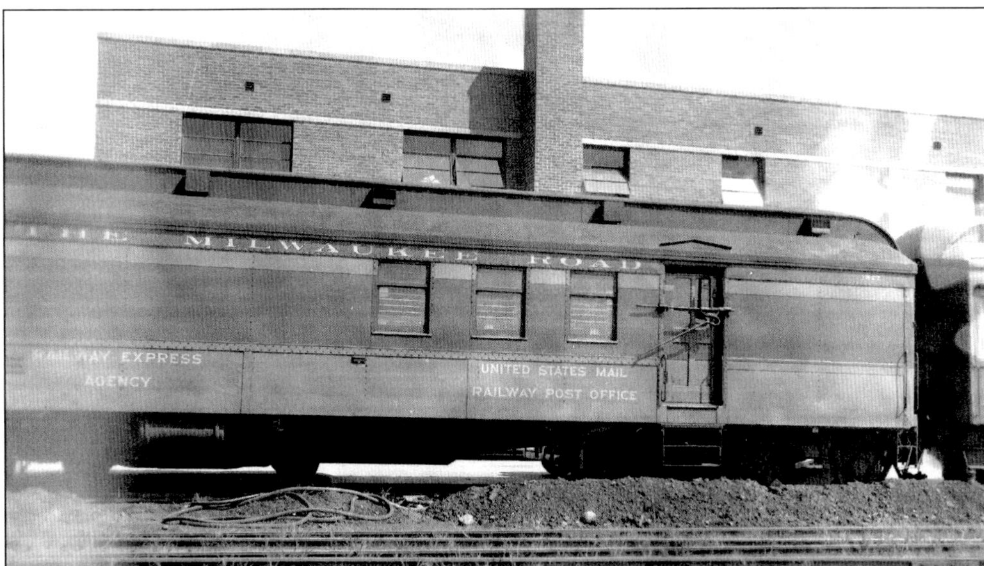

This Milwaukee Road railway post office car is standing at the downtown Sioux City passenger station. The bar with a hook across the large door was to catch mail bags with the train on the run. The bags were placed on a post on the station platform. They would be snapped up by the bar with the train running at speed. The men in the car would throw the incoming mail bag on the station platform. This process was usually performed by an express train for small towns along its route. (Courtesy of George Berkstresser.)

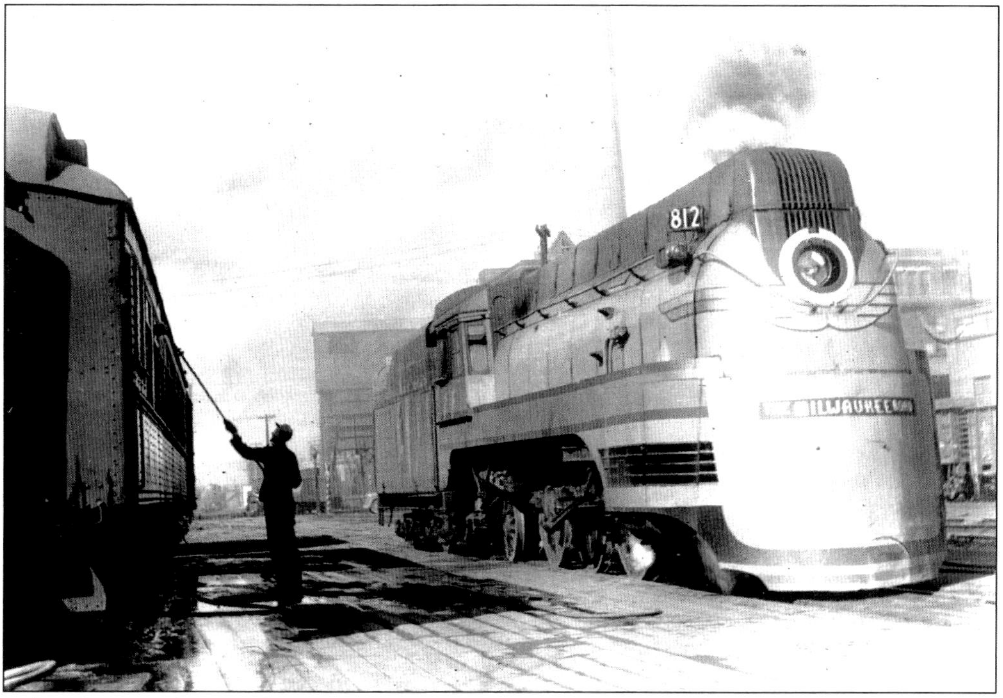

Milwaukee Road Hiawatha No. 812 stands in downtown Sioux City. On the adjacent track a worker washes the windows of a passenger car. Watching the scenery pass by from a moving train was a rare experience after the 1960s. When looking out the window, it appeared as if the scenery was moving, and the train was standing still. Those Milwaukee cars gave a velvet-smooth ride. (Courtesy of the Siouxland Historical Railroad Association.)

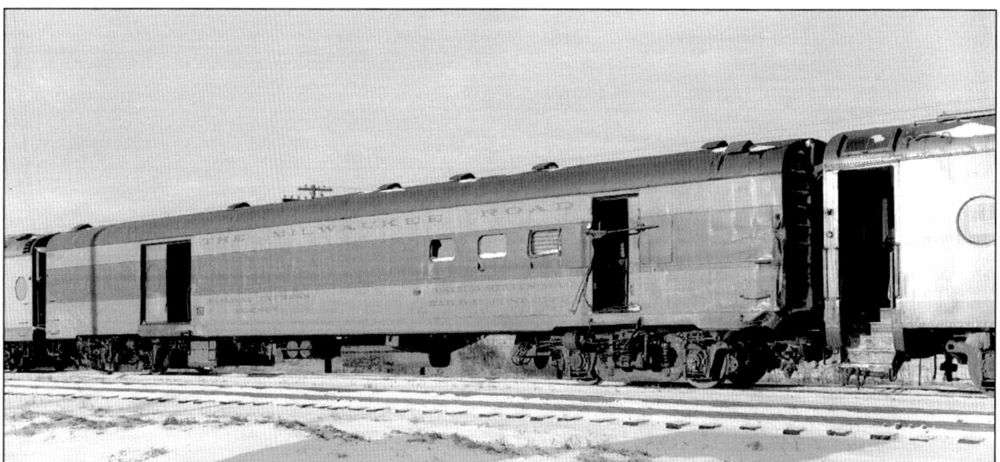

The baggage car combined with the railway post office car was a familiar sight on every long-distance passenger train. Some railroads ran trains that consisted of only mail cars. They were often referred as the "fast mail." On some train schedules, a letter mailed from Chicago early in the morning could arrive in Sioux City by evening. (Courtesy of George R. Lindblade.)

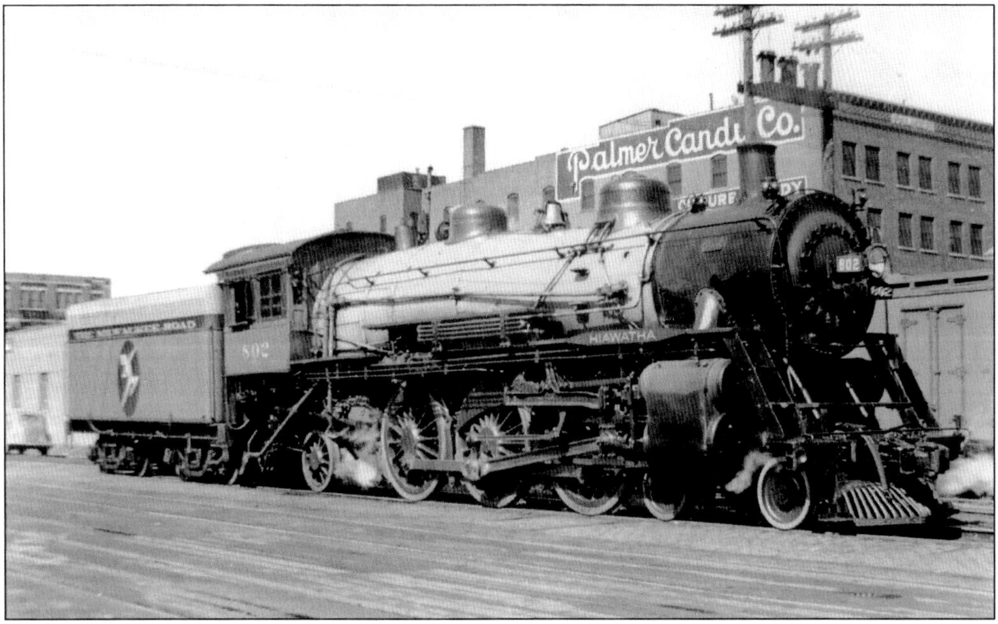

A Milwaukee Road Pacific locomotive without streamlining stands in downtown Sioux City with a streamlined Hiawatha tender. Although some railroads used tenders from one type of locomotive to another, this combination was not usual at the height of the streamlined era. (Courtesy of the Siouxland Historical Railroad Association.)

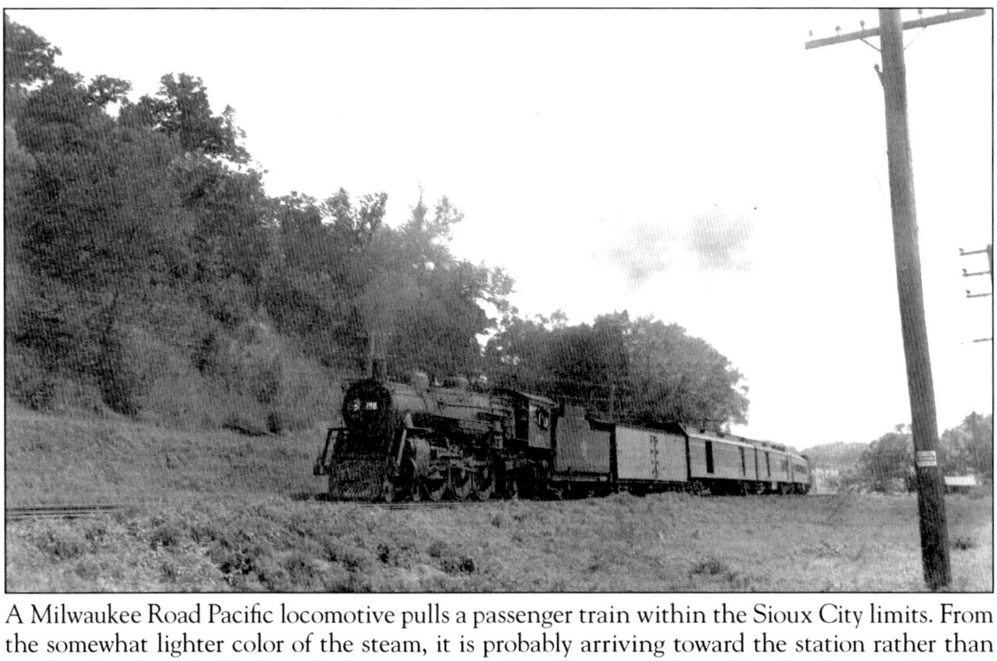

A Milwaukee Road Pacific locomotive pulls a passenger train within the Sioux City limits. From the somewhat lighter color of the steam, it is probably arriving toward the station rather than accelerating from it. Black or dark steam means that the engine is working hard or accelerating. (Courtesy of George Berkstresser.)

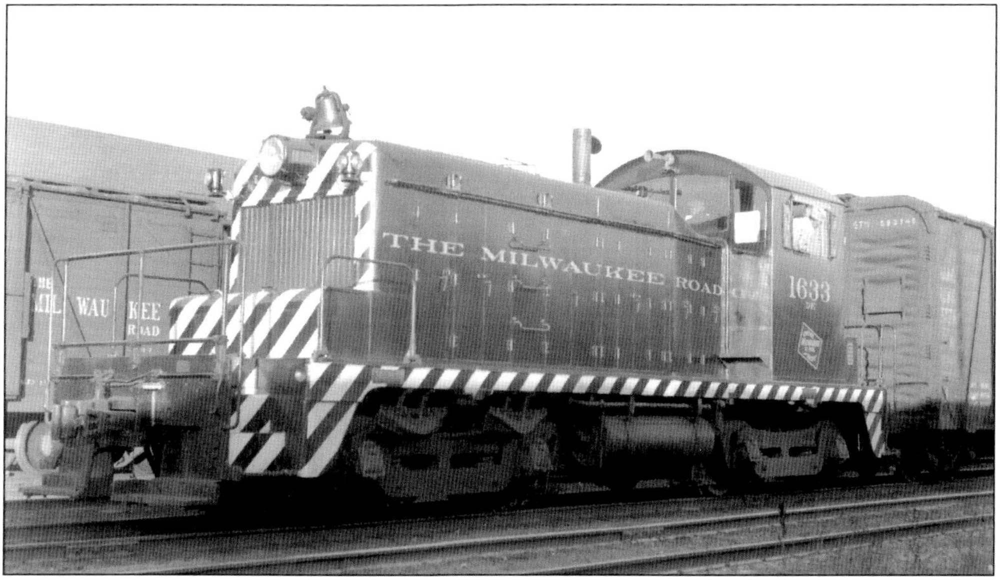

The Chicago, Milwaukee, St. Paul, and Pacific Railway had a number of switch locomotives in Sioux City. The No. 1633 was its own version of the Electro-Motive SW800. The SW stands for switcher, and the numbers stand for horsepower. (Courtesy of the Siouxland Historical Railroad Association.)

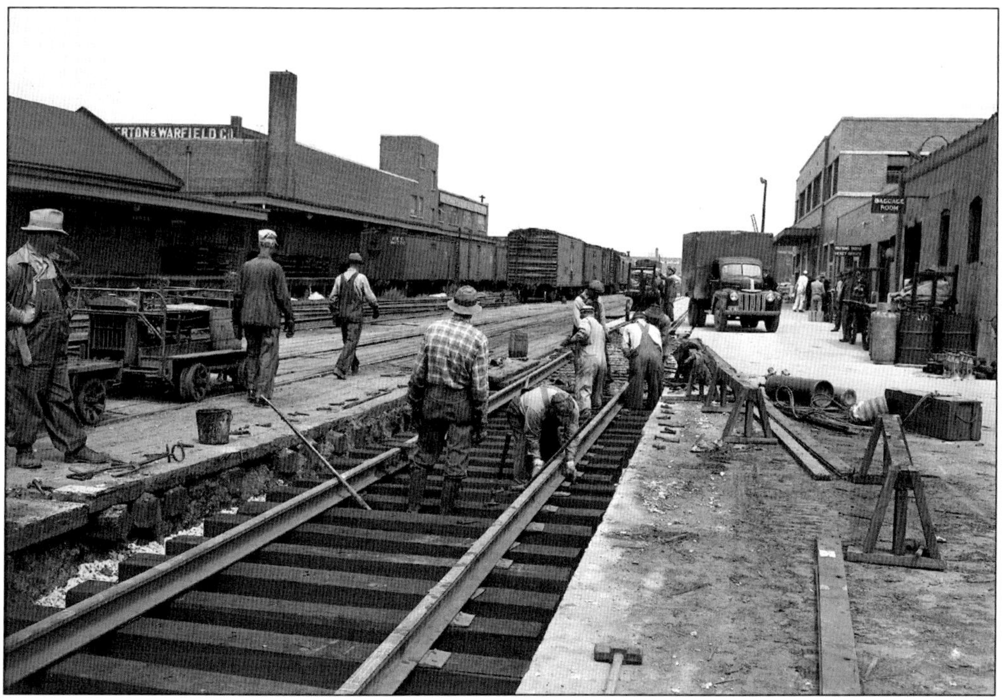

A crew is repairing tracks near the Milwaukee Road station in the downtown. Track crews were often referred to as gandy dancers. It seems that they appeared to be doing an off-beat dance when viewed from a distance. The term goes back to sometime during the 19th century. (Courtesy of the Sioux City Public Museum, George Newman Collection.)

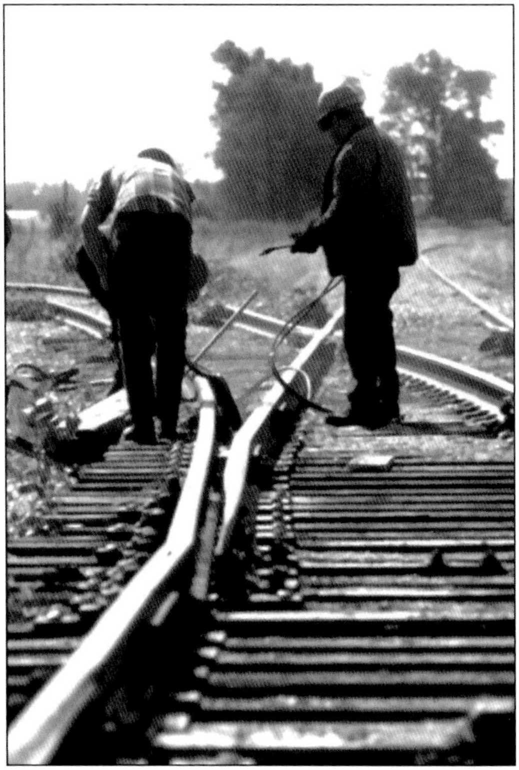

Two railroad track repair crewman are working on a switch. Switch tracks and diamonds need more attention as they wear out more quickly than straight road rail. They are also more prone to derailments. (Courtesy of George R. Lindblade.)

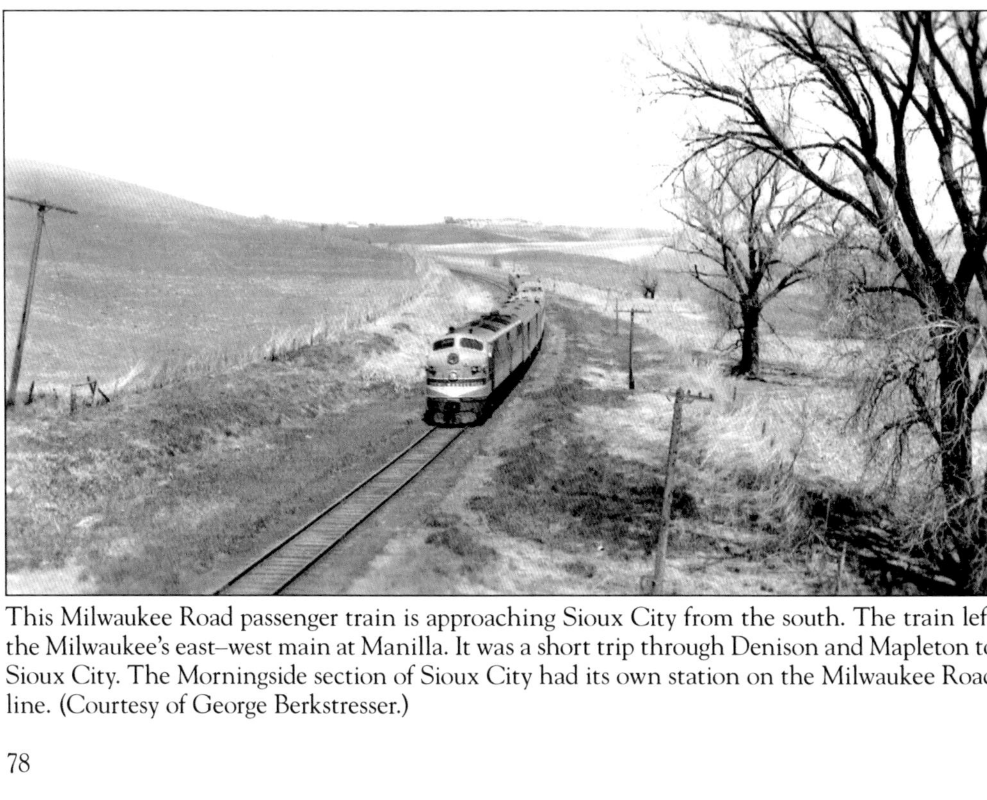

This Milwaukee Road passenger train is approaching Sioux City from the south. The train left the Milwaukee's east–west main at Manilla. It was a short trip through Denison and Mapleton to Sioux City. The Morningside section of Sioux City had its own station on the Milwaukee Road line. (Courtesy of George Berkstresser.)

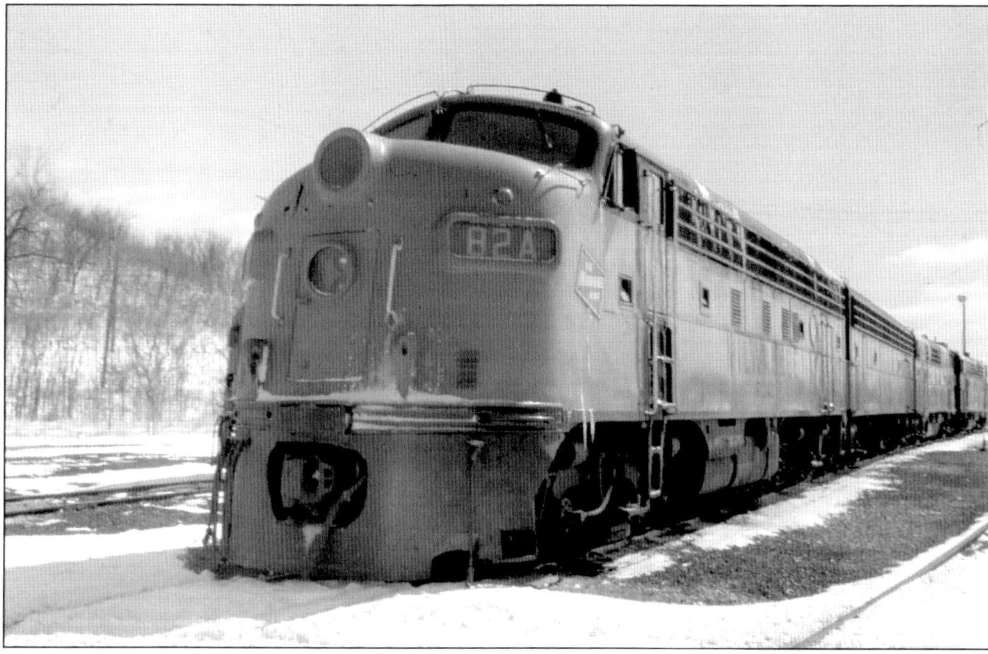

This elegant "covered wagon" leads a four-section group of F unit locomotives. The snow on the ground will not deter this lash-up from its task. It waits only for its green light signal. (Courtesy of George Berkstresser.)

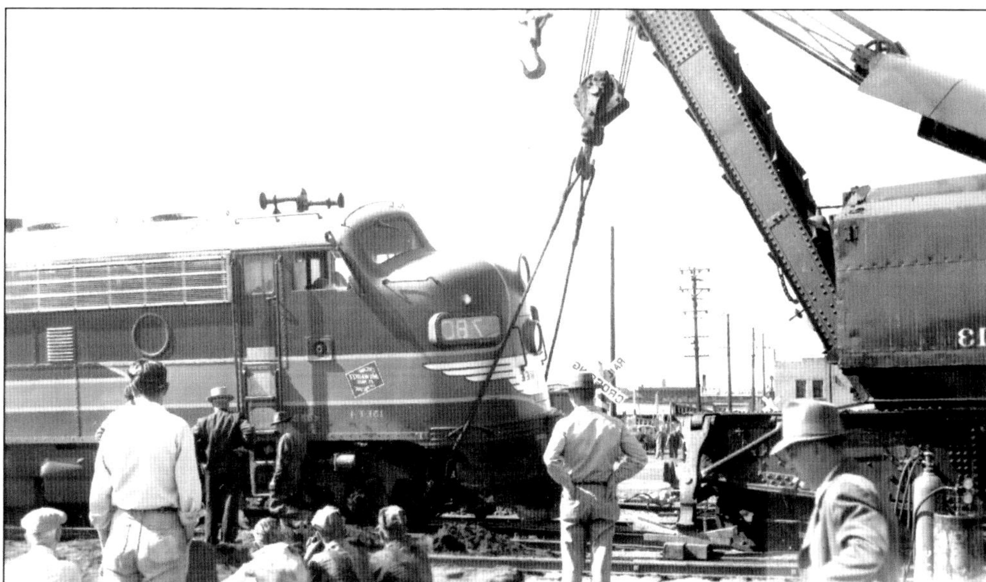

A railroad crane lifts a Milwaukee Road F unit onto its tracks after a derailment. The scene appears to be from the 1950s in downtown Sioux City. If a derailment is only slight, or one or two feet from the track, workers could use special ramps called frogs to rerail the locomotive or cars. (Courtesy of George Berkstresser.)

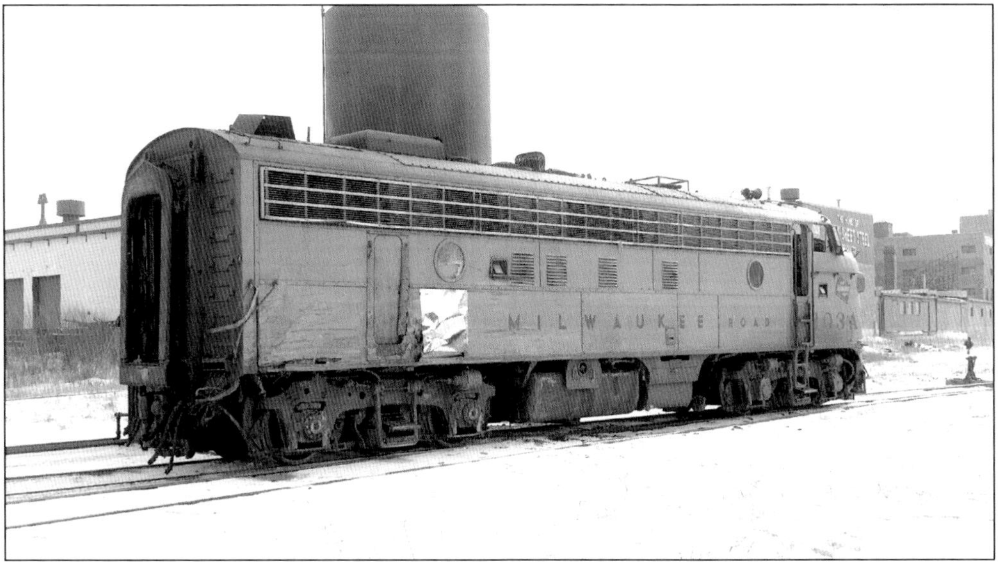

A lone Milwaukee Road FP 7 unit awaits assignment in downtown Sioux City. These units represent the first practical road or distance diesel-electric locomotives. Some F units were a bit longer to accommodate a steam generator and water supply. These items were necessary to pull passenger trains in winter. Only 40 such units were built. (Courtesy of George R. Lindblade.)

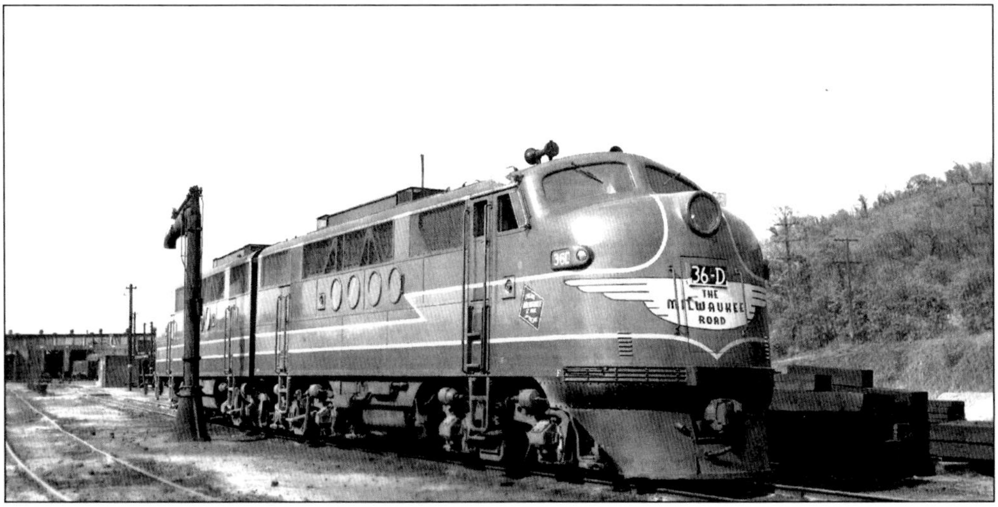

This set of beautiful F units stands alongside a then already antiquated water pipe for steam locomotives. These two A-type units back to back were ready to run in any direction. (Courtesy of George Berkstresser.)

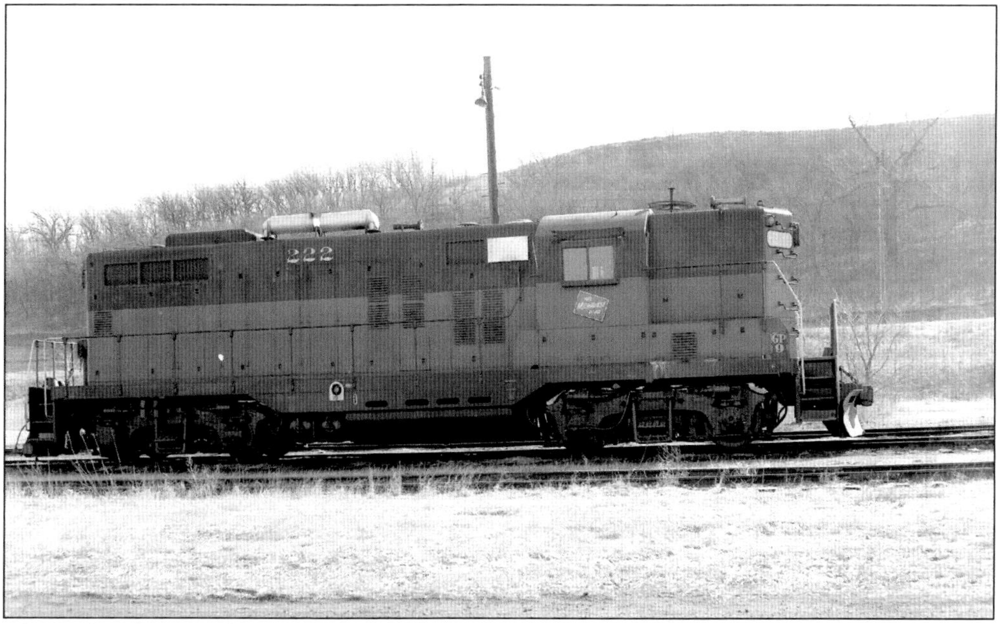

This Milwaukee Road geep or general purpose locomotive was painted orange and black. They were used primarily in freight service. This one is standing near the yards in the Riverside area of Sioux City. (Courtesy of George R. Lindblade.)

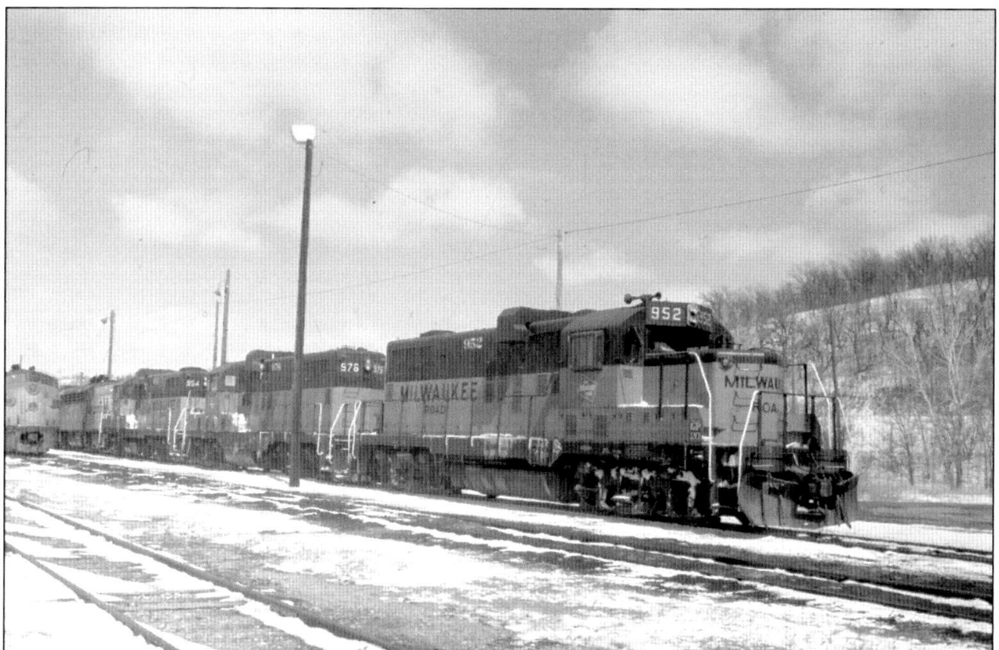

Four geeps stand in the Milwaukee Riverside yard. This lash up is ready to pull a freight train of Sioux City products to somewhere in the nation. The front nose of an F or E unit appears to the far left of the photograph. (Courtesy of George Berkstresser.)

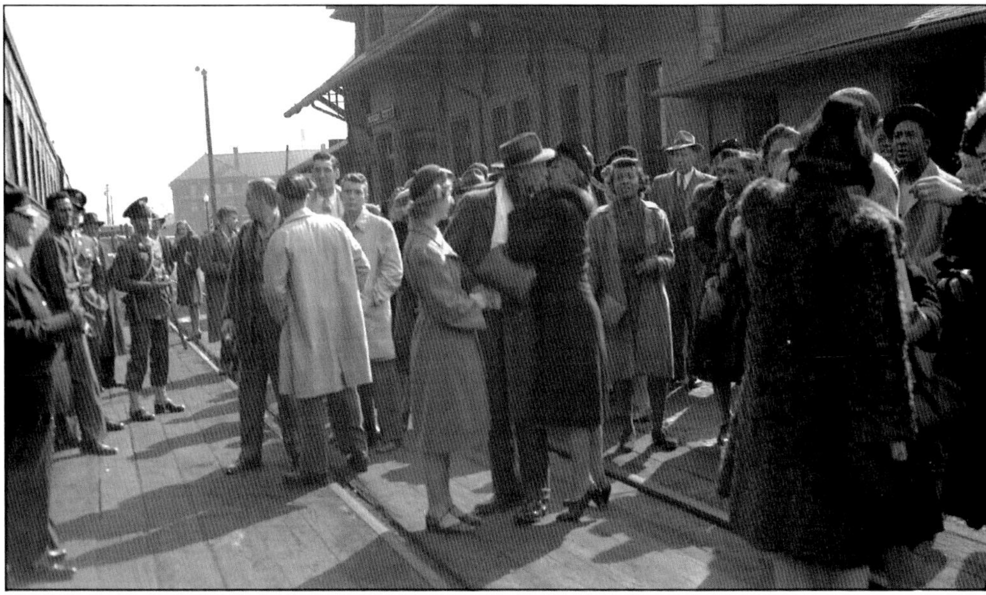

A group of people gather at the Milwaukee Road station in the 1940s during World War II. These scenes were common during the war. Soldiers left for camp and returned home on leave by train. In fact, given gasoline rationing and the impossibility of purchasing new tires, over 80 percent of everything moved by rail. (Courtesy of George Berkstresser.)

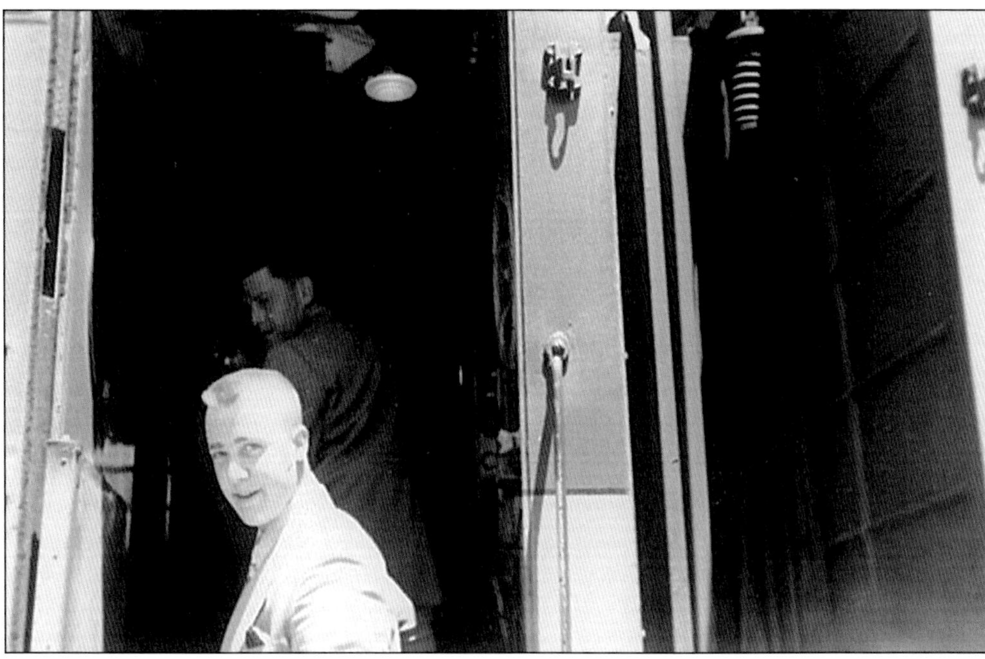

Paul H. Reistrup is boarding the Milwaukee Road's *Midwest Hiawatha* in Sioux City in June 1950. He is leaving to attend West Point Military Academy. Reistrup later became the second president of the National Rail Passenger Corporation or Amtrak. During that time, he modernized and reinvigorated Amtrak by purchasing new equipment. His interest in trains started in Sioux City, and he fondly remembers the trip to West Point. (Courtesy of Paul H. Reistrup.)

Five

THE SIOUX CITY EL

When it was in operation during the 1890s the Sioux City Rapid Transit Company's elevated railway was considered "Iowa's most distinctive engineering glory." This reputation was earned without question. Sioux City's el was the third successful elevated railroad in the world. (The first construction of the New York and Erie Railroad was on a series of trestles for over 100 miles, but it was never functional.) Chicago sent representatives to Sioux City to view its el construction. The famous Chicago El is modeled after the earlier one in Sioux City.

With the growth of the meatpacking industry, Sioux City expanded first northward from the Missouri River. It had a cable car along Jackson Street. Further extension in that direction, however, encountered numerous hills. At that point, some businessmen intended to expand the rapidly growing town to the east—to a plateau that would come to be known as Morning Side (Morningside). If they wanted to have people purchase that land, they knew they had to furnish efficient and relatively inexpensive transportation. The problems were a swamp, packing companies and their accompanying odors, and 84 railroad crossings to reach the downtown. According to tradition, A. S. Garretson, E. C. Peters, J. F. Booge, and A. M. Jackson finished a poker game by throwing $1,000 each into a pot to create an elevated railway.

Poor financial management along with the panic of 1893, ended the plan. The managers gave the Morningside residents a year of free rides without being able to keep track of who was entitled to the privilege. People simply did not pay the fare. In order to take advantage of efficiencies, the el changed from steam locomotives to electricity in 1892. The Sioux City El then became the first electrical elevated railway in the world.

The el ceased operation entirely in 1899, and it was subsequently dismantled. In some ways, the el represented Sioux City's economic successes, ambitions, and frustrations at the end of the 19th century. Setbacks aside, Sioux City continued to grow and to make its mark on the world economy. Morningside became a modern suburb and had its own railroad station on the Milwaukee Road. All of this growth was the chief reason for the el. More specifically, the el was due to Sioux City's many railroad connections and tracks that led to every part of the nation.

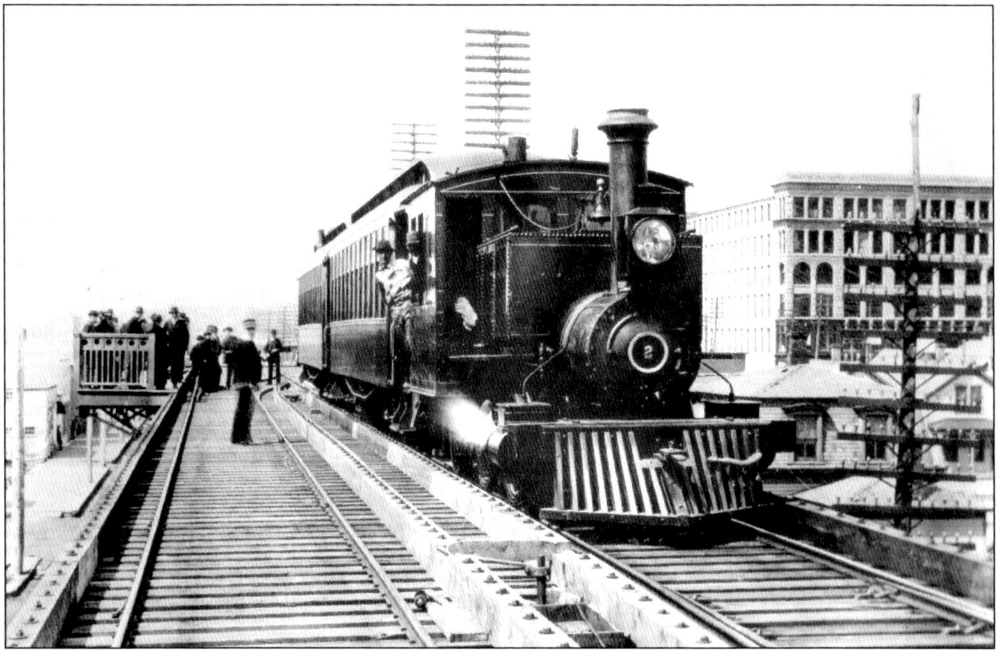

The steam-driven Sioux City El stops to take on passengers on an elevated portion of the railway. The engineer, fireman, and conductor can be seen clearly in this late-19th-century photograph. The train is headed east toward the Morningside area of Sioux City. (Courtesy of the Sioux City Public Museum.)

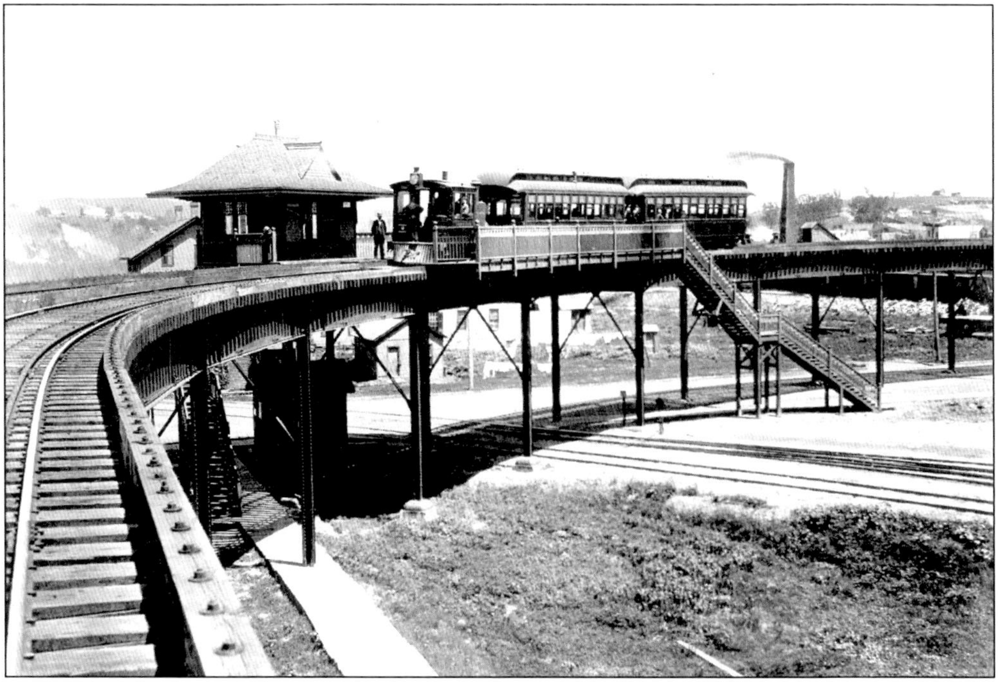

One of the two Sioux City El steam-operated train sets pauses to take on passengers at its main station at Third and Jones Streets. The tracks leading to the stockyards are beneath the station to the east. (Courtesy of the Sioux City Public Museum.)

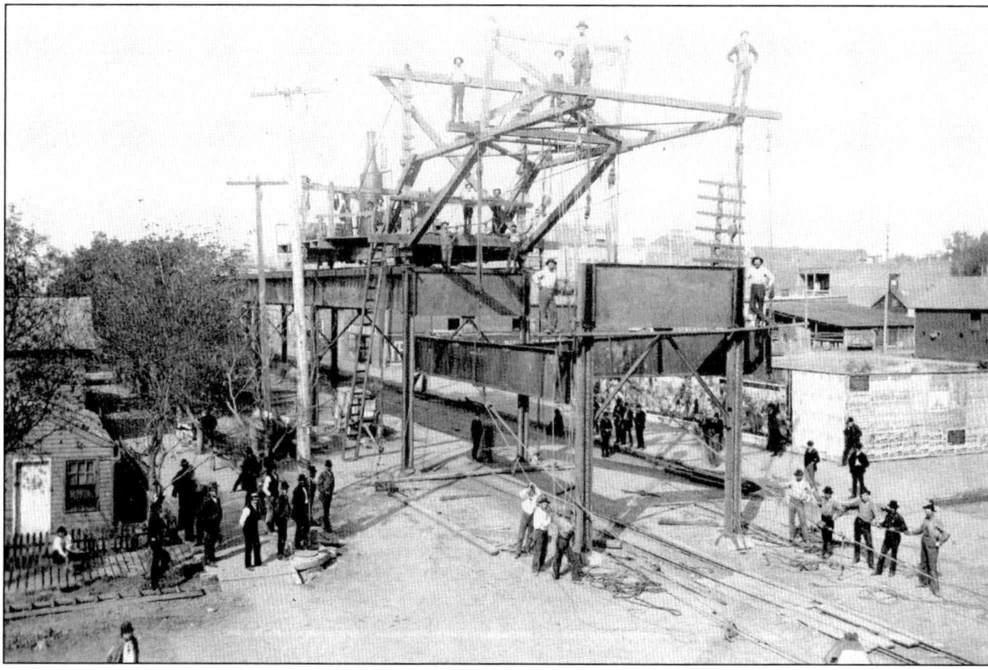

The Sioux City Rapid Transit Company, which was the proper name for the Sioux City El, had two miles of elevated double track. This construction scene is at Third and Virginia Streets. The 1890 Corn Palace is in the background. A steam loader lifted the beams above the street level. (Courtesy of the Sioux City Public Museum.)

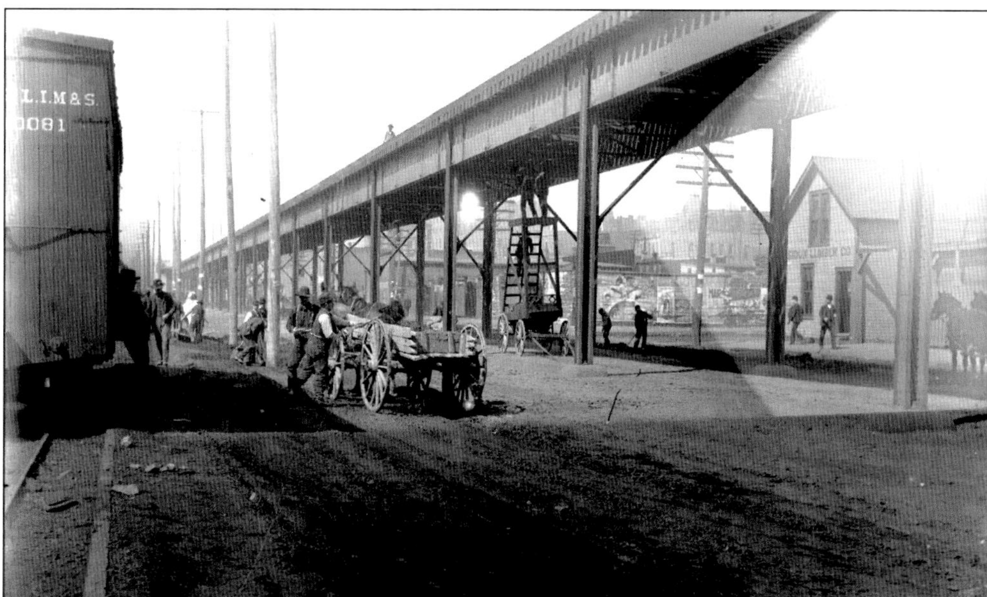

Workers from the King Bridge and Iron Company of Cleveland, Ohio, constructed the elevated portion of the Sioux City Rapid Transit Company. The elevated portion of the tracks was in the downtown area to traverse the myriad of train tracks below. (Courtesy of the Sioux City Public Museum.)

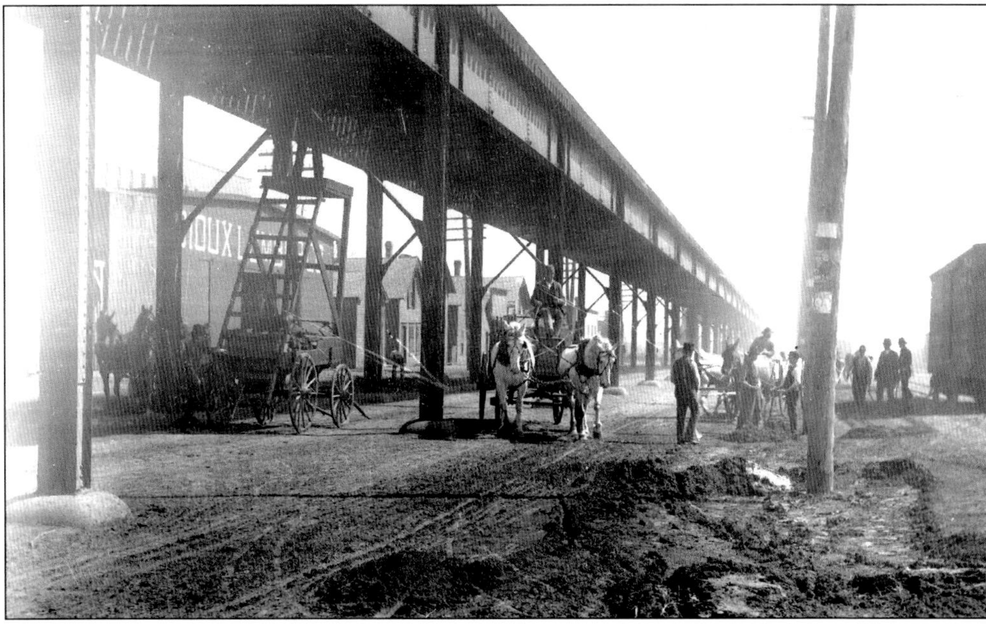

Materials for the elevated railway were brought to Sioux City by train. While local businessmen had the idea for the project, most of the financing came from eastern investors. The cost was over $500,000 in 1890 dollars.

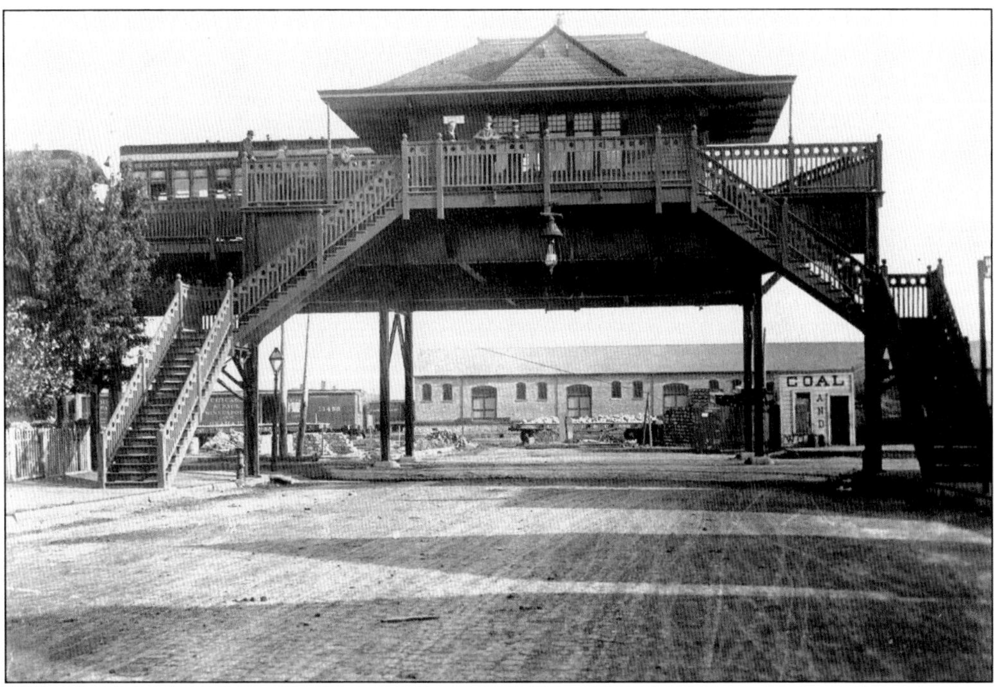

The business office of the Sioux City El was located at its Third and Jones Street station. Steps ascended from both sides of Jones Street. During the daytime, trains ran every 30 minutes between the downtown and Morningside. (Courtesy of the Sioux City Public Museum.)

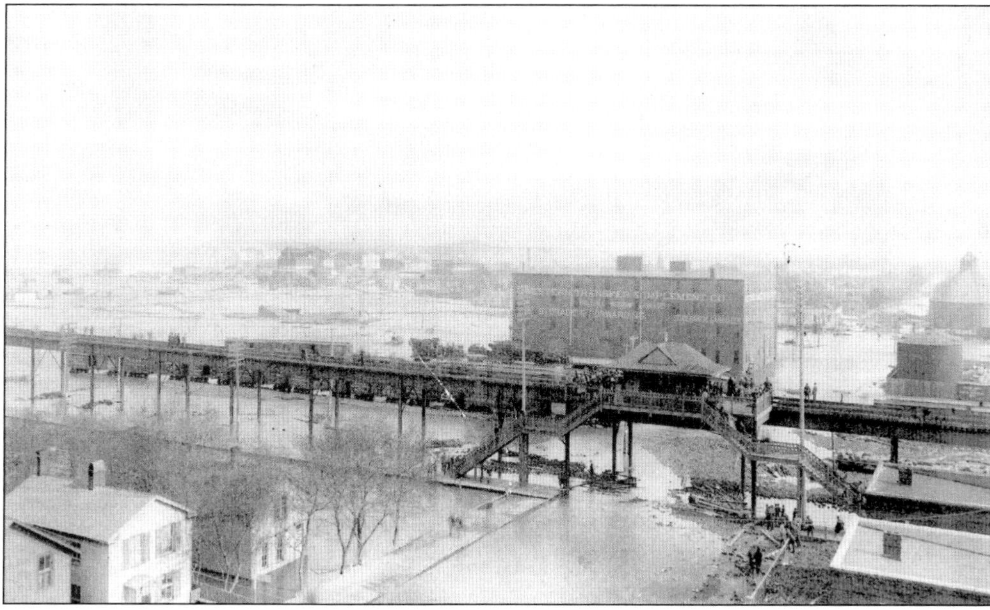

During the Floyd River flood of 1892, people gathered on the Sioux City El platform, steps, and tracks to escape the rising water. Ten persons died in the flood and thousands were left homeless. The el saved hundreds of lives that day. (Courtesy of the Sioux City Public Museum.)

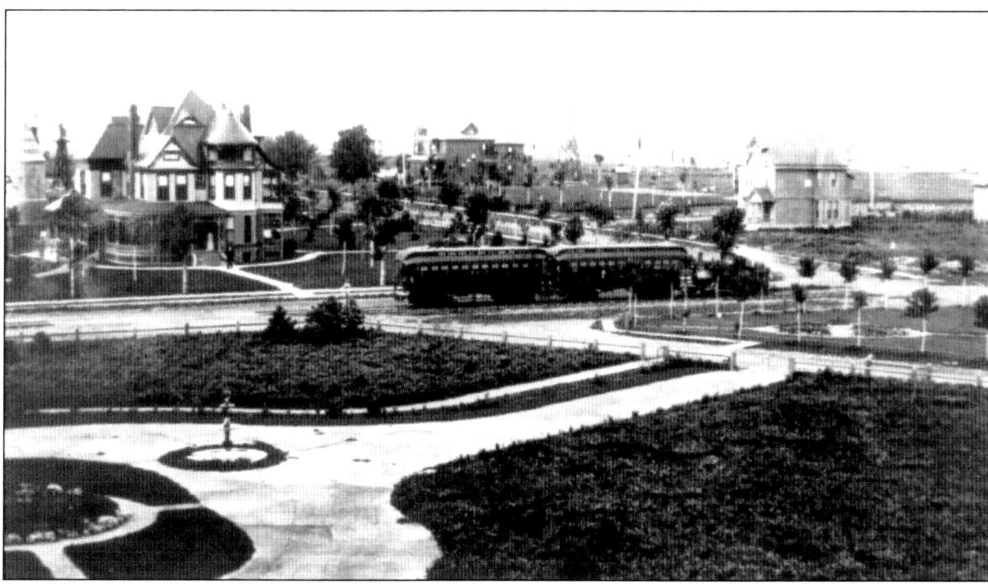

The Sioux City El's eastern station stop was in the Peters Park location in the Morningside development of Sioux City. Tracks reached the area in 1891. Fares were only a nickel to ride the entire distance. The el permitted the suburb of Morningside to flourish. (Courtesy of the Sioux City Public Museum.)

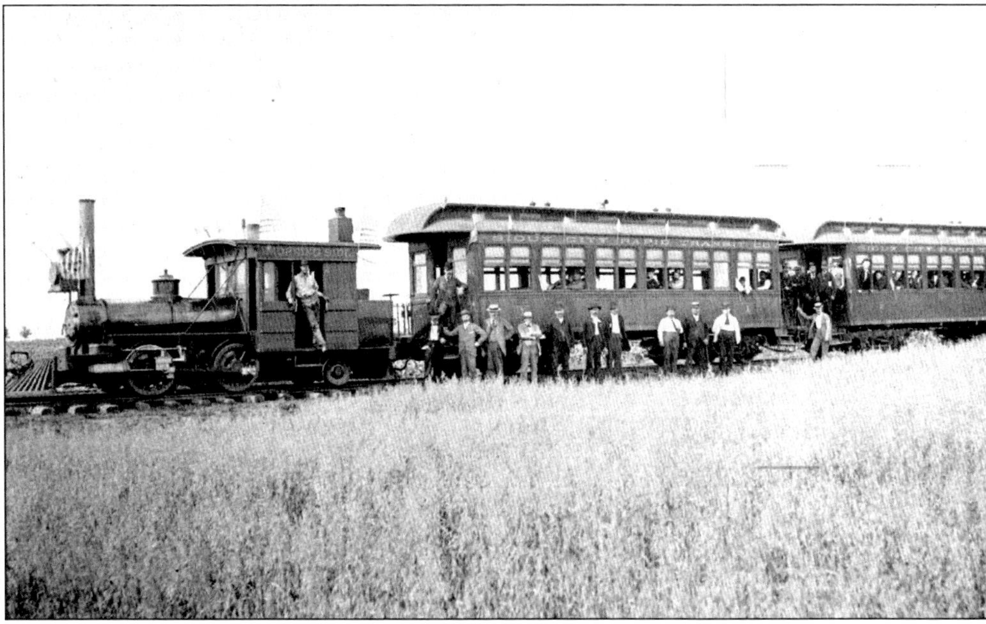

Plans were made to expand the Sioux City El all the way to Sargeant Bluff. It was hoped that the Morningside area would expand to the east and south. A celebratory gathering occurred in the field east of the Morningside development. There is every possibility that this photograph chronicles the event. (Courtesy of the Sioux City Public Museum.)

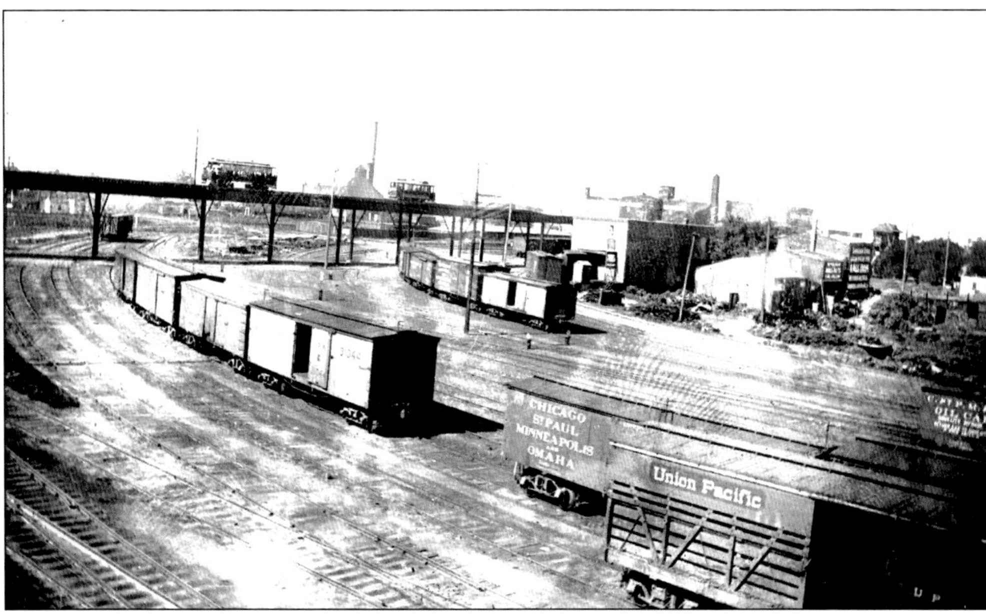

Within two years, the Sioux City El changed from steam to electric power. The Sioux City elevated railway was the third such form of transportation in the nation. It was, however, the first to use electricity to power its cars. Two of the electric-powered cars can be seen above and behind the freight cars on the curve leading to downtown Sioux City. (Courtesy of the Sioux City Public Museum.)

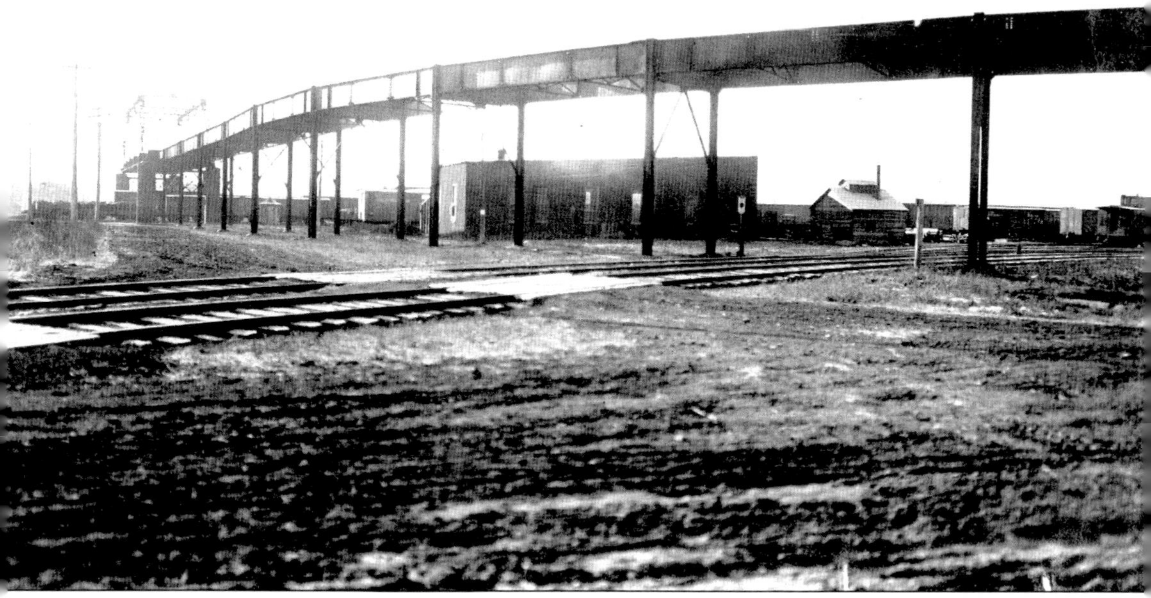

The main reason that the Sioux City Rapid Transit Company chose to build elevated tracks was to go above the tracks of the railroad companies entering the downtown. A person then could travel east or west of the downtown without rail traffic interference. (Courtesy of the Sioux City Public Museum.)

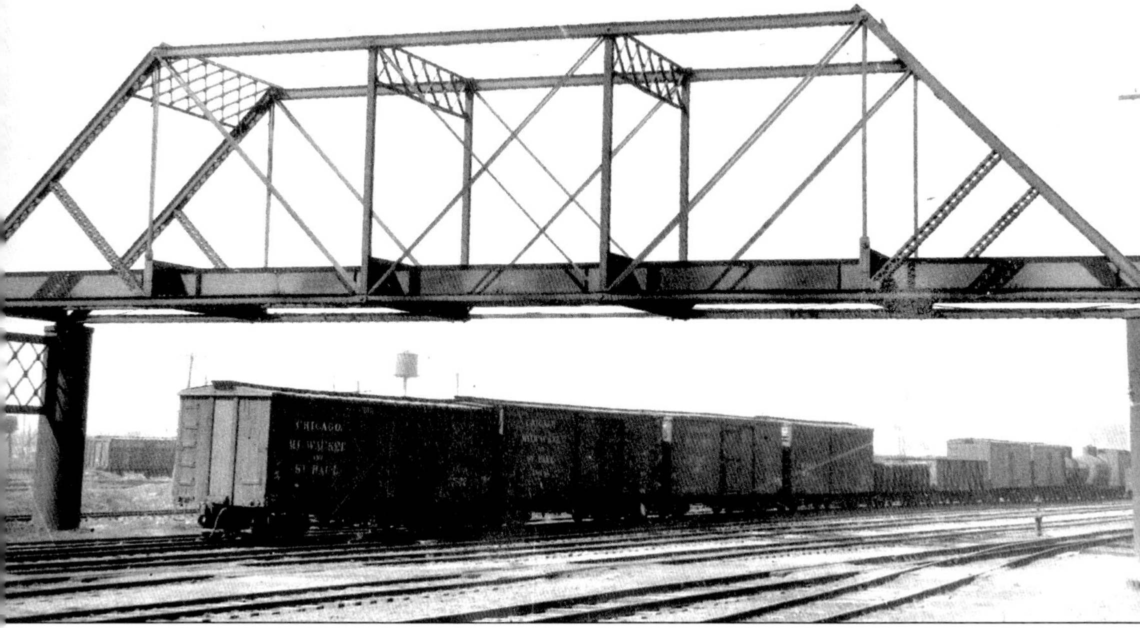

The railcars spotted beneath the elevated railway tracks bear witness to the necessity of the trestle. Rail traffic increased in the 1880s and 1890s due to the growth of the meatpacking industry in Sioux City. (Courtesy of the Sioux City Public Museum.)

Six

The Sioux City Terminal Railway

Several Midwest cities had terminal railroads to move cars to and from local industries. They also shunted cars from one railroad company's track to another. Sioux City's own terminal railway takes its place among those in Chicago, St. Louis, and Kansas City. With the growth of rail traffic by the end of the 19th century, entrepreneurs created the Sioux City Terminal and Warehouse Company Railroad in 1899. All of its investors were Sioux Citians, and it was created primarily to serve the stockyards and the meatpacking companies.

The Sioux City Terminal and Warehouse Company Railroad originally consisted of 17 blocks and tracks for a distance of 1,400 feet. When further expansion was considered in 1907, entrepreneurs reconstituted the tracks and rolling stock as the Sioux City Terminal Railway. Its president was A. S. Garretson, who was a longtime Sioux City businessman. It operated on one square mile of roadbed and as many as 25 tracks. By the 1920s, the Sioux City Terminal Railway had 11 steam locomotives, and it moved an average of 600 cars a day. Most of the products moved were cattle and hogs, feed, fertilizers, processed meats, grains, and coal.

The Sioux City Terminal Railway dieselized in 1951, as did many United States railroads. The movement of cattle and other products by train, however, declined in the mid-20th century in favor of the trucking industry. Farmers now drove their cattle in trucks to the stockyards rather than ride with them to Sioux City in a caboose. Shortly thereafter, farmers began to sell their animals directly to the processing plants rather than through auction at the stockyards.

The Sioux City Terminal Railway ceased operation in 1971. The Burlington Northern Railway served the stockyard area for a short period of time. The stockyards and many nearby meat processing plants closed or moved by the end of the 20th century.

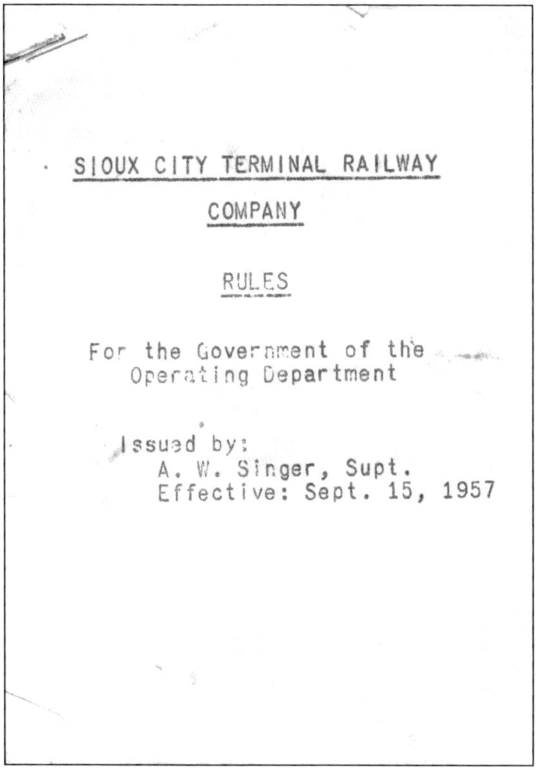

SIOUX CITY TERMINAL RAILWAY COMPANY

RULES

For the Government of the Operating Department

Issued by:
A. W. Singer, Supt.
Effective: Sept. 15, 1957

Every railroad company had a book of operating rules, and the Sioux City Terminal Railway was no exception. Most companies listed all of the subsidiaries. The Sioux City Terminal Railway uniquely stood alone. The book was more of pamphlet size, and it was copied from a simple typescript. (Courtesy of Richard Donaway.)

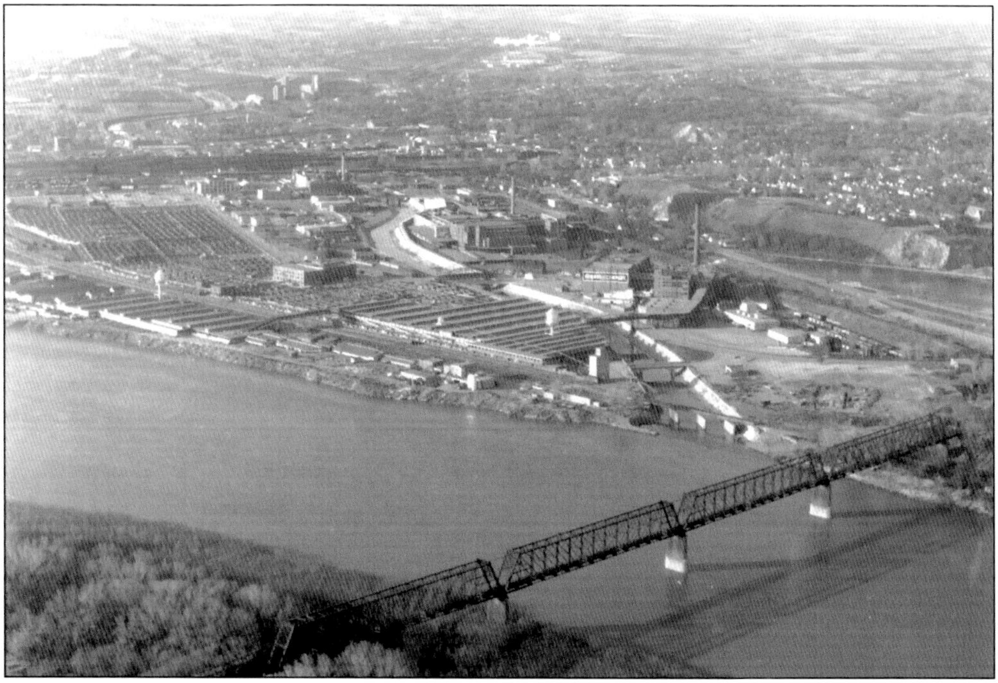

The original channel of the Floyd River and the Chicago, St. Paul, Minneapolis, and Omaha Railway bridge is highly visible in the pre-1960 scene. The packinghouses and stockyards can be easily viewed in this aerial photograph. (Courtesy of the Sioux City Public Museum.)

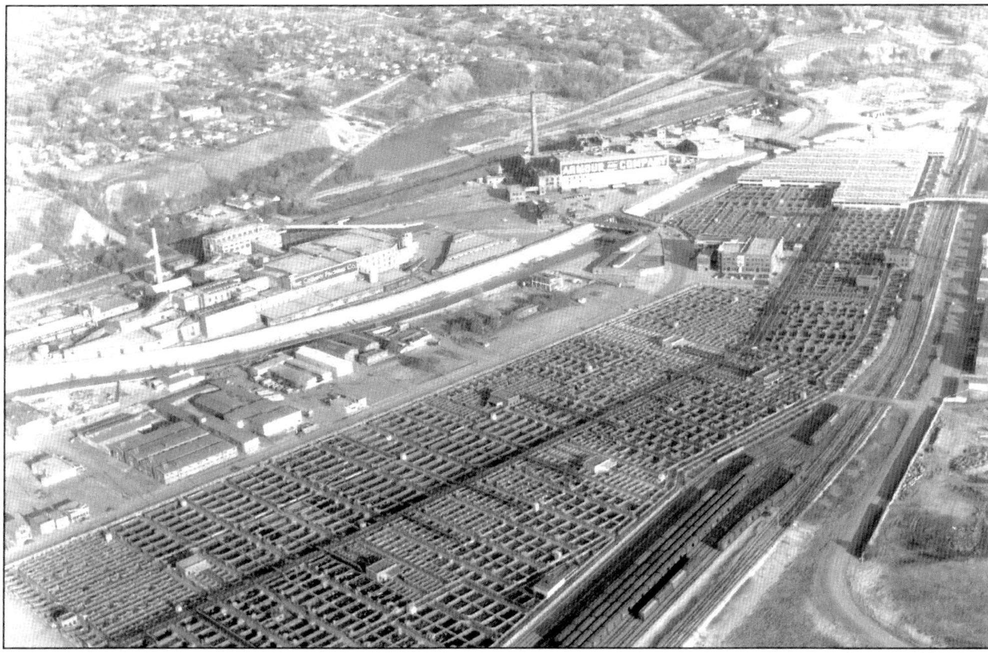

This aerial photograph of the stockyards area shows the complex in its entirety. The animal pens are in the center with the meatpacking plants in the background. The rail yard with cars is in the foreground. The Chicago and Northwestern through tracks are to the right in the photograph. (Courtesy of the Sioux City Public Museum.)

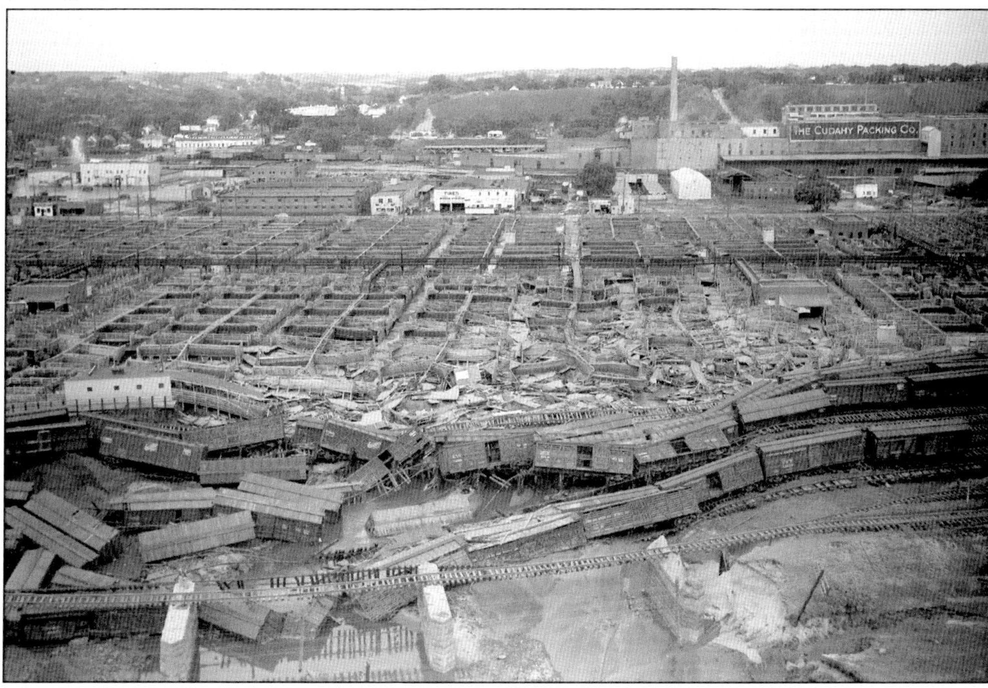

The Floyd River flooded the stockyards area and freight yard in 1953. The tracks suspended in the air in the foreground are the main line of the Chicago and Northwestern Railway. Many livestock died in the flooding. (Courtesy of the Sioux City Public Museum.)

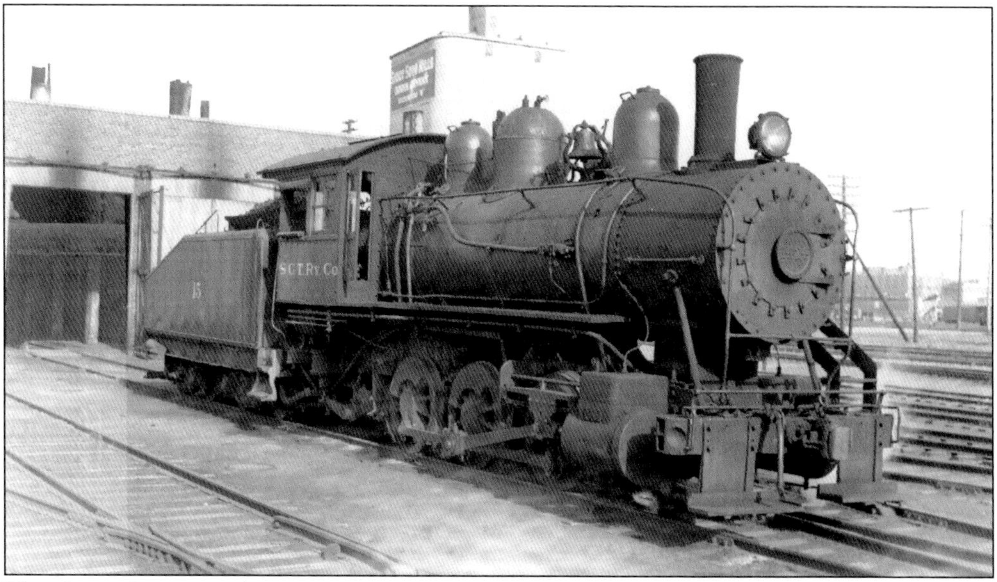

This Sioux City steam locomotive No. 15 stands just outside its barn. The Sioux City Terminal Railway did not have a true roundhouse as did the other Sioux City railroads. The barn, however, did house the locomotives and permit the most elementary maintenance. (Courtesy of George Berkstresser.)

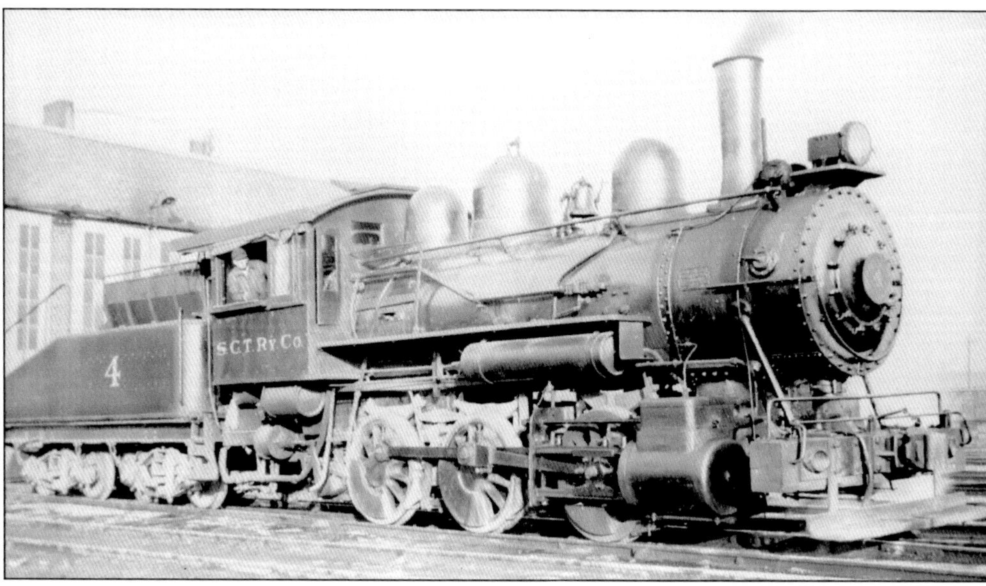

Switch engine No. 4 stands a classic pose. It has a typical 0-6-0 wheel arrangement, which makes it both powerful and agile over curves and switches in rail yards. (Courtesy of the Sioux City Public Museum.)

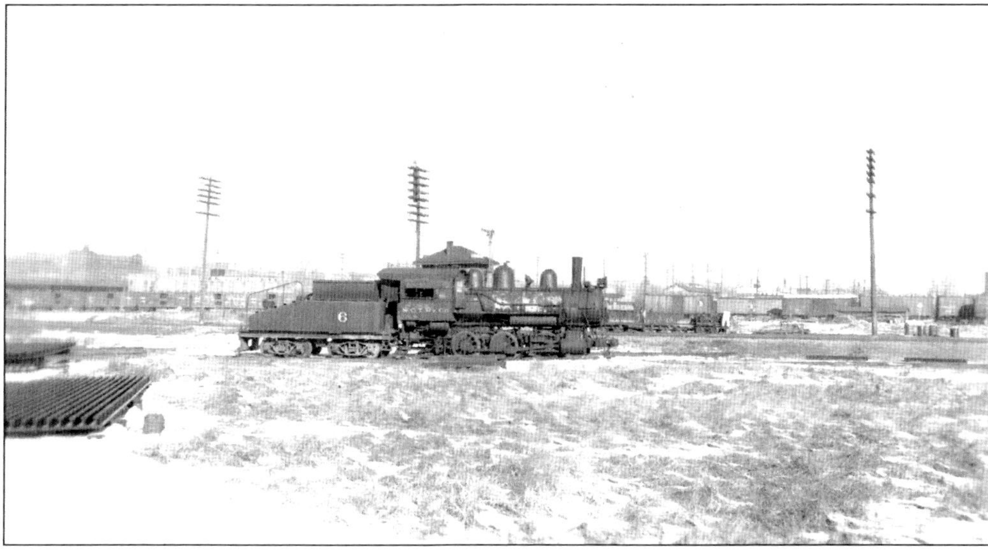

A Sioux City Terminal Railway switch engine is running on the outer track of the freight yard. It is probably running from the north yard into the immediate stockyards area. (Courtesy of George Berkstresser.)

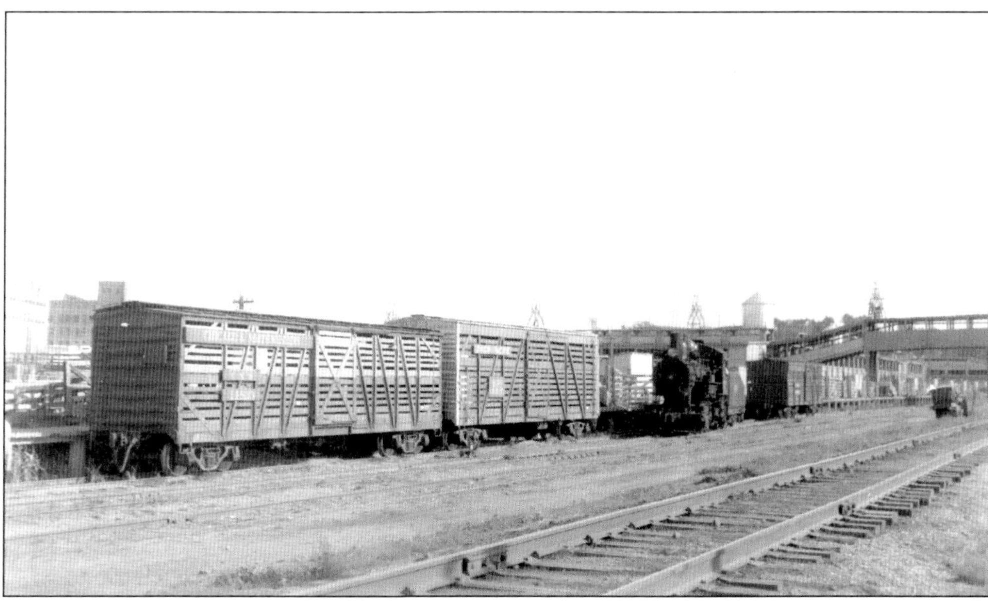

A Sioux City Terminal Railway steam locomotive has just deposited a cattle car on a yard track. Other unloaded cattle cars are on another track. They are signed Chicago and Northwestern Railway and Union Pacific. Stockyards movement was the most frequent switching of the Sioux City Terminal Railway. (Courtesy of the Sioux City Public Museum.)

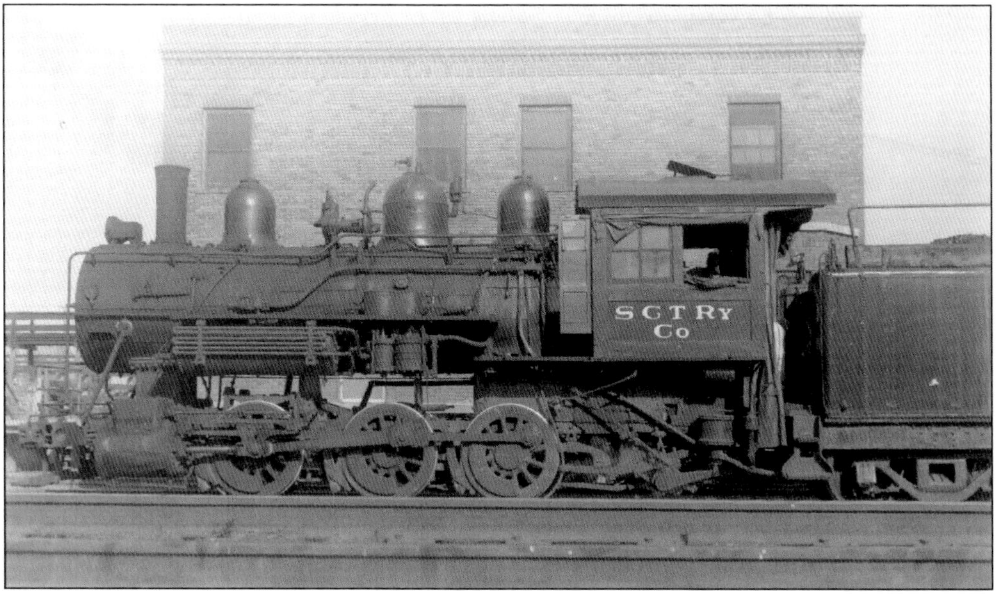

This is an excellent side view of a Sioux City Terminal Railway locomotive. The 0-6-0 wheel arrangement and valve casings are clearly visible. (Courtesy of George Berkstresser.)

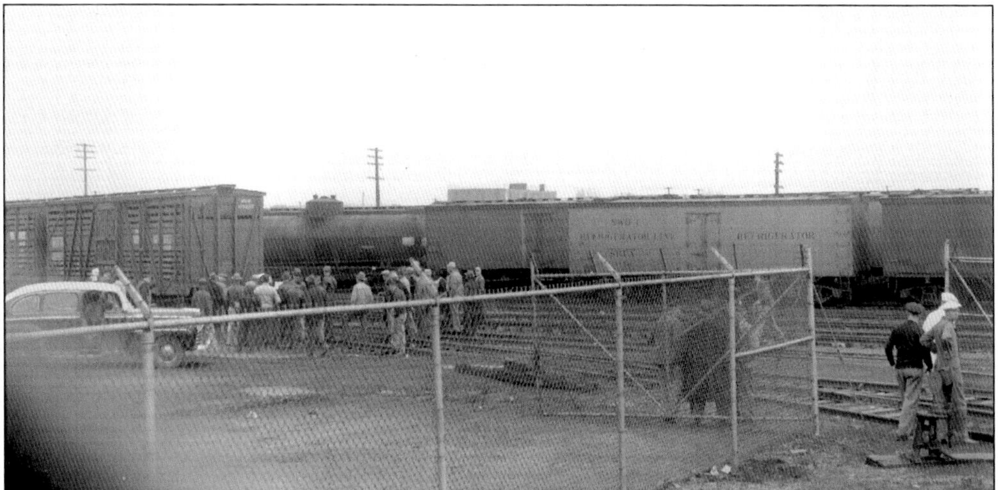

A group of strikers gathers at the stockyards in the 1930s. This photograph illustrates the three chief types of railcars used in the meat-processing industry at that time: cattle (transport) car, refrigerator car, and a tank car for liquid by-products. (Courtesy of Sioux City Lewis and Clark Interpretive Center Association.)

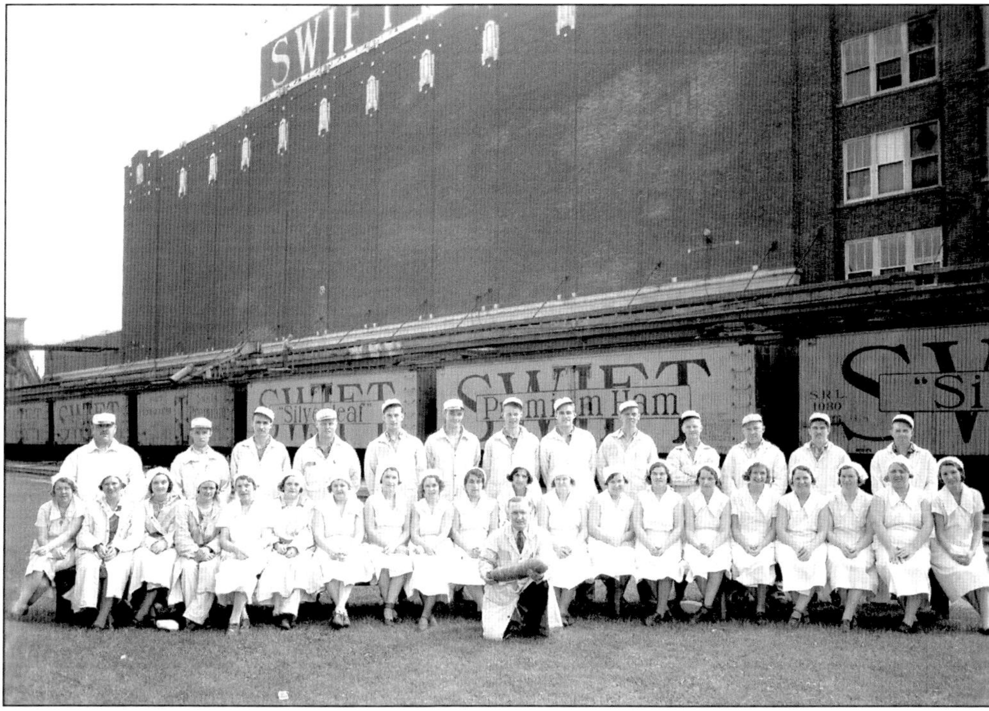

Meatpacking workers at the Swift plant pause for a photograph. Swift had its own refrigerator cars that were, of course, moving billboards for the company throughout the entire country. Sioux City's meatpacking industry fed the nation and the world. (Courtesy of the Sioux City Public Museum.)

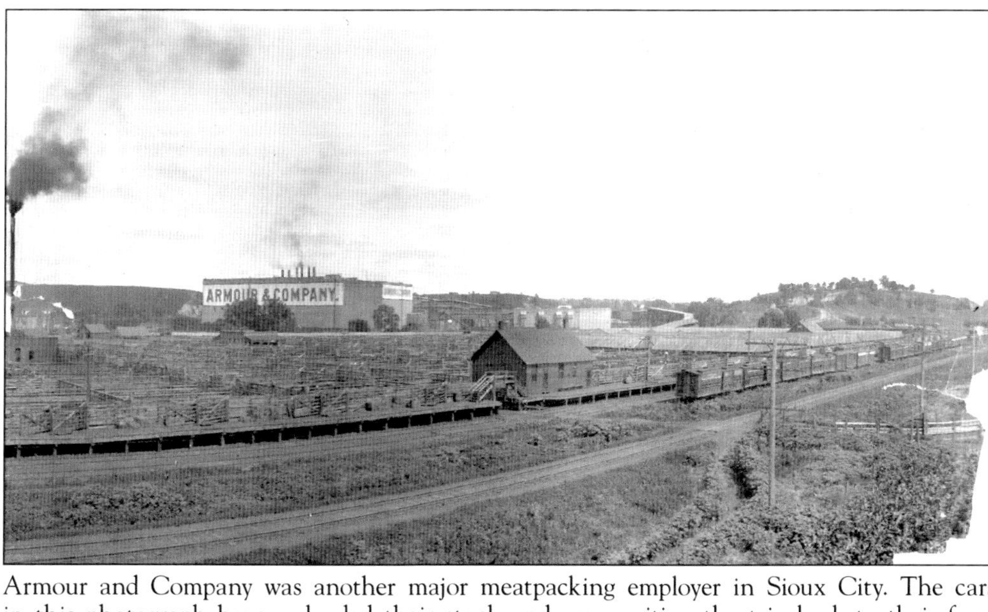

Armour and Company was another major meatpacking employer in Sioux City. The cars in this photograph have unloaded their stock and are awaiting the trip back to their farm origins. Armour was so influential that Union Pacific painted its passenger cars "Armour yellow." Yellow was the herald color of the Armour and Company. (Courtesy of the Sioux City Public Museum.)

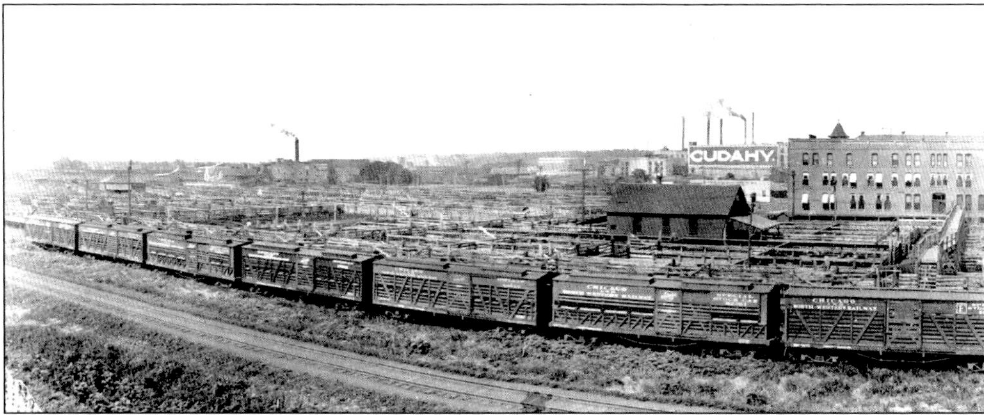

Cattle cars stand before the stockyards pens. The Cudahy plant was one of the main packinghouses of the nation. Cattle were loaded off the train cars directly into the pens. The cars visible in this photograph bear the Chicago and Northwestern signature. (Courtesy of the Sioux City Public Museum.)

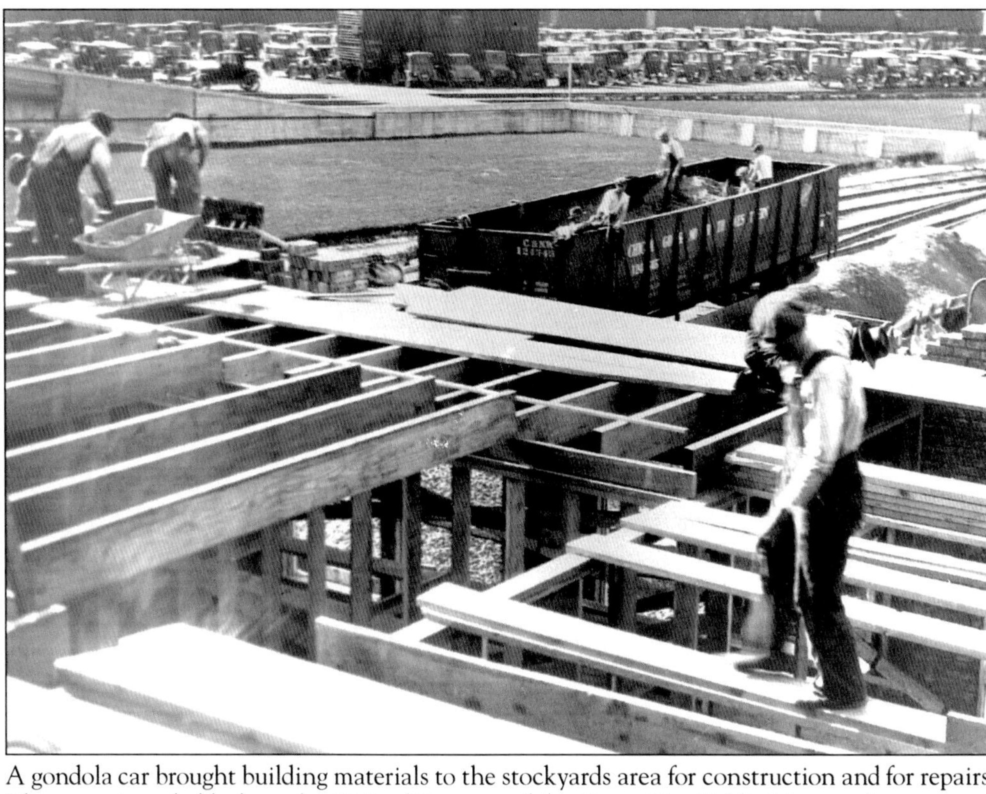

A gondola car brought building materials to the stockyards area for construction and for repairs. The scene is probably from the 1920s. (Courtesy of the Sioux City Public Museum.)

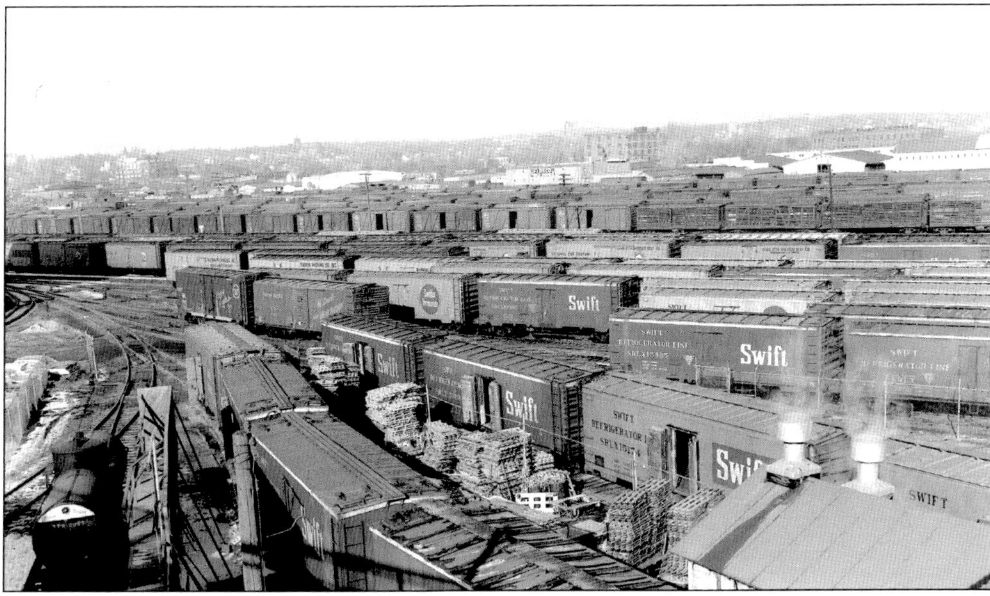

This excellent view overlooks the Sioux City Terminal Railway's north yard, to the east of the immediate downtown area. Company cars for finished products are in the foreground while the empty cattle cars await their return assignment. Some buildings of the downtown can be seen in the background. (Courtesy of George R. Lindblade.)

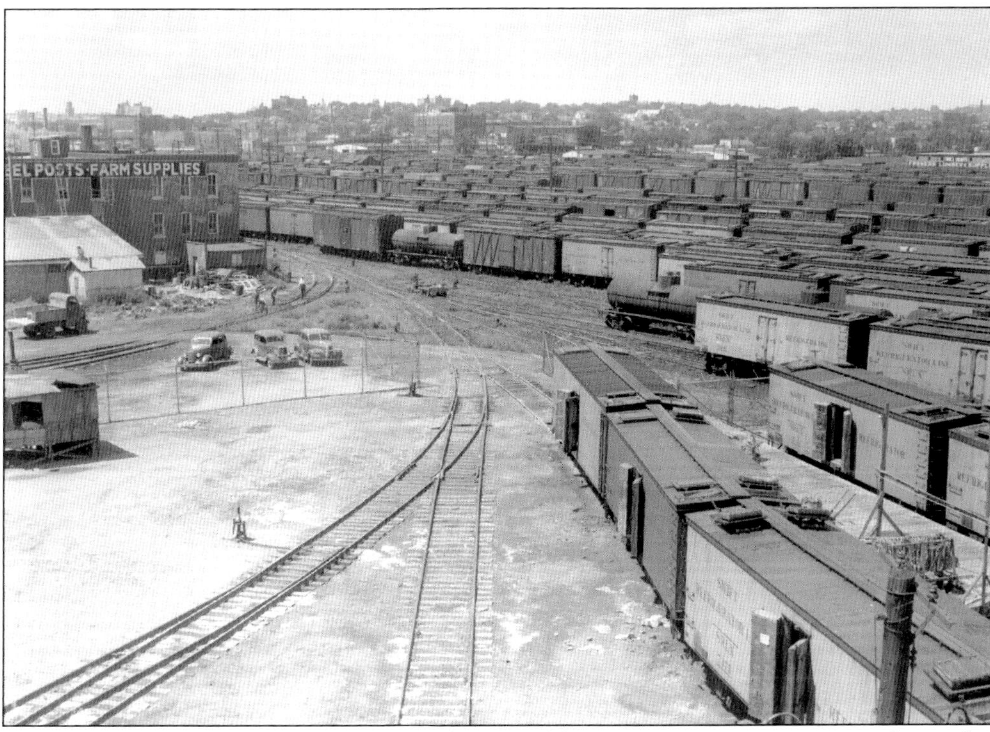

This view of the Sioux City Terminal Railway yard features iced refrigerator cars, often called "reefers," in the foreground. Until modern times, they used ice to keep the contents cold. There were icing stations at various points to replenish the supply. (Courtesy of George R. Lindblade.)

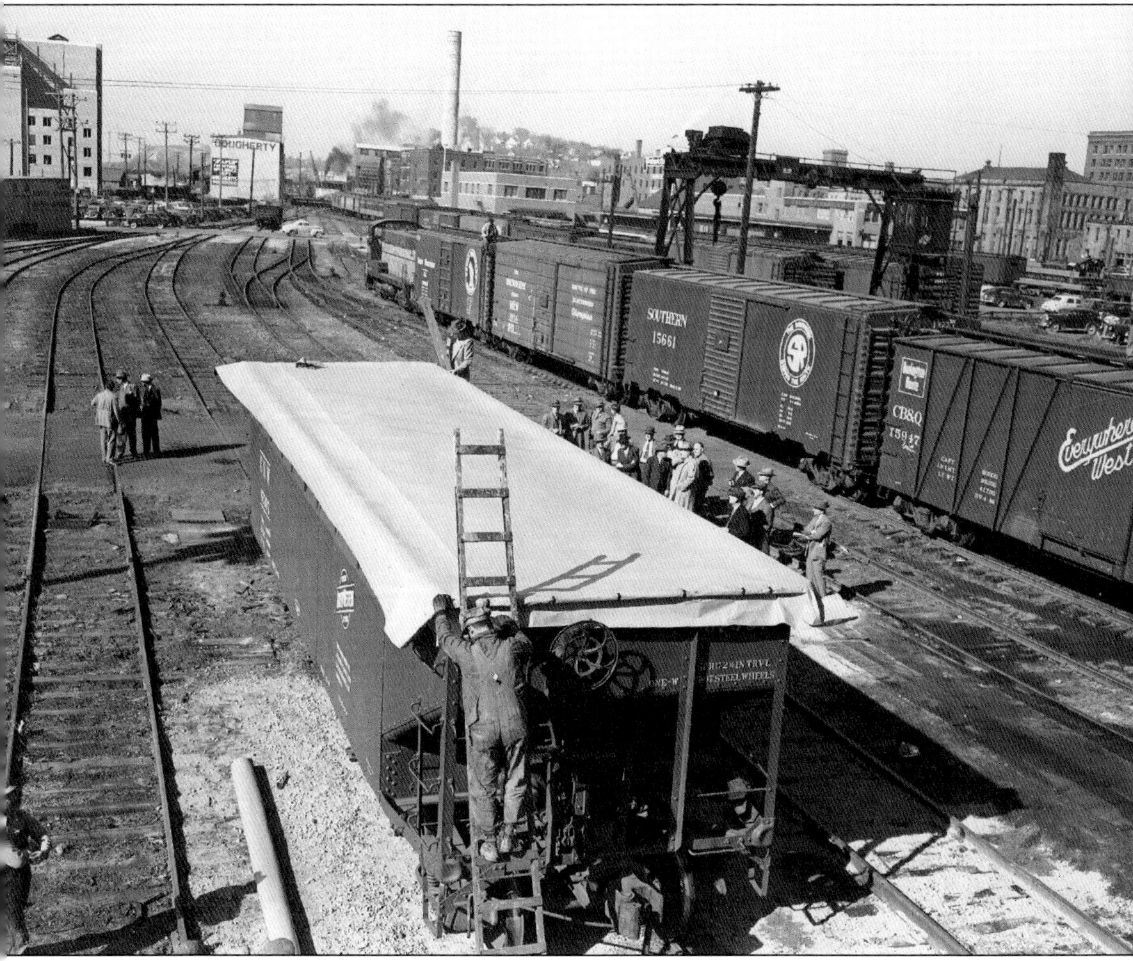

Workers are placing a tarp on an open hopper car. Another is walking on top of a boxcar. This activity is taking place in the Sioux City Terminal Railway north yard. Buildings of the eastern side downtown are seen in the background. (Courtesy of the Sioux City Public Museum, George Newman Collection.)

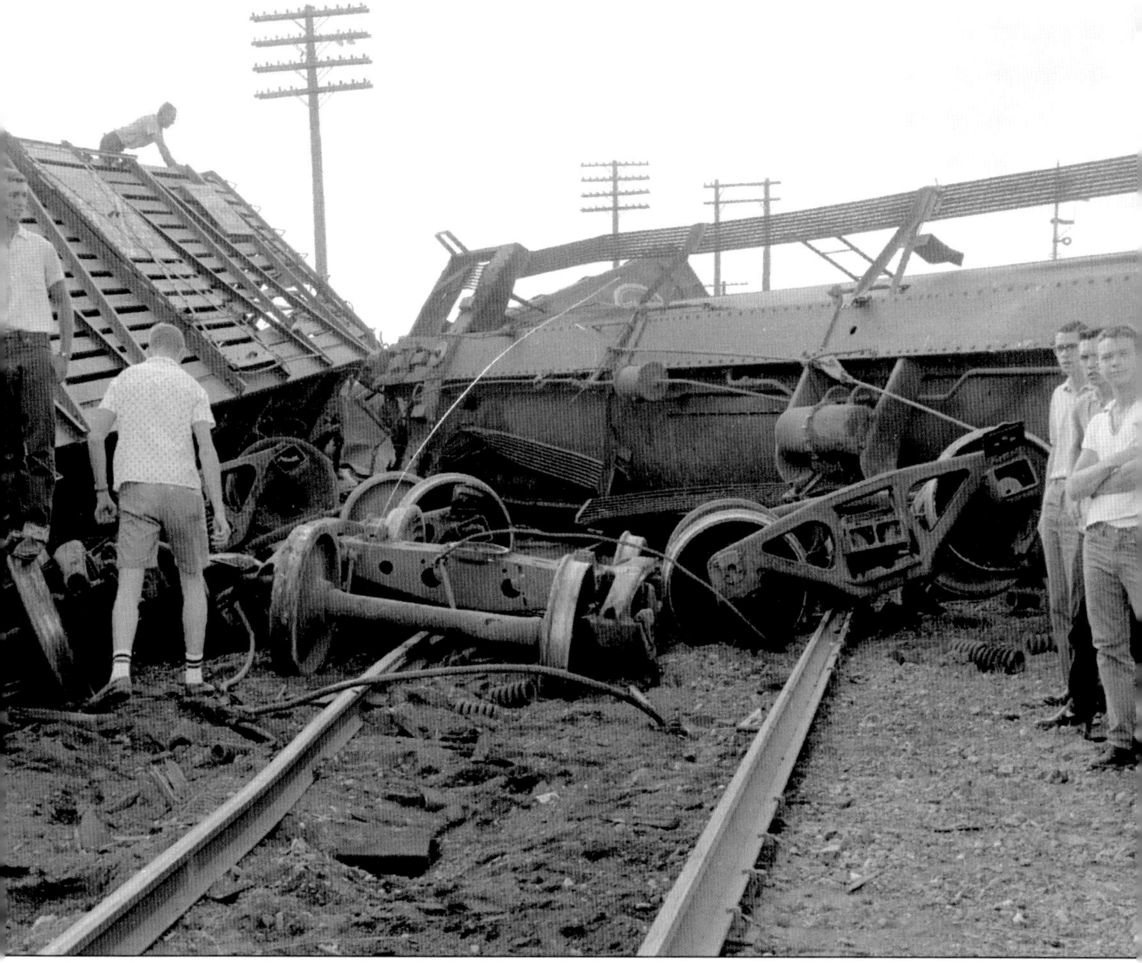

This collision was between a cattle car and another freight car in the yards. It had to have occurred prior to 1971 and was most likely in the stockyards rail yard. These types of accidents in yards were usually cause by switches left often from one track to another. (Courtesy of George R. Lindblade.)

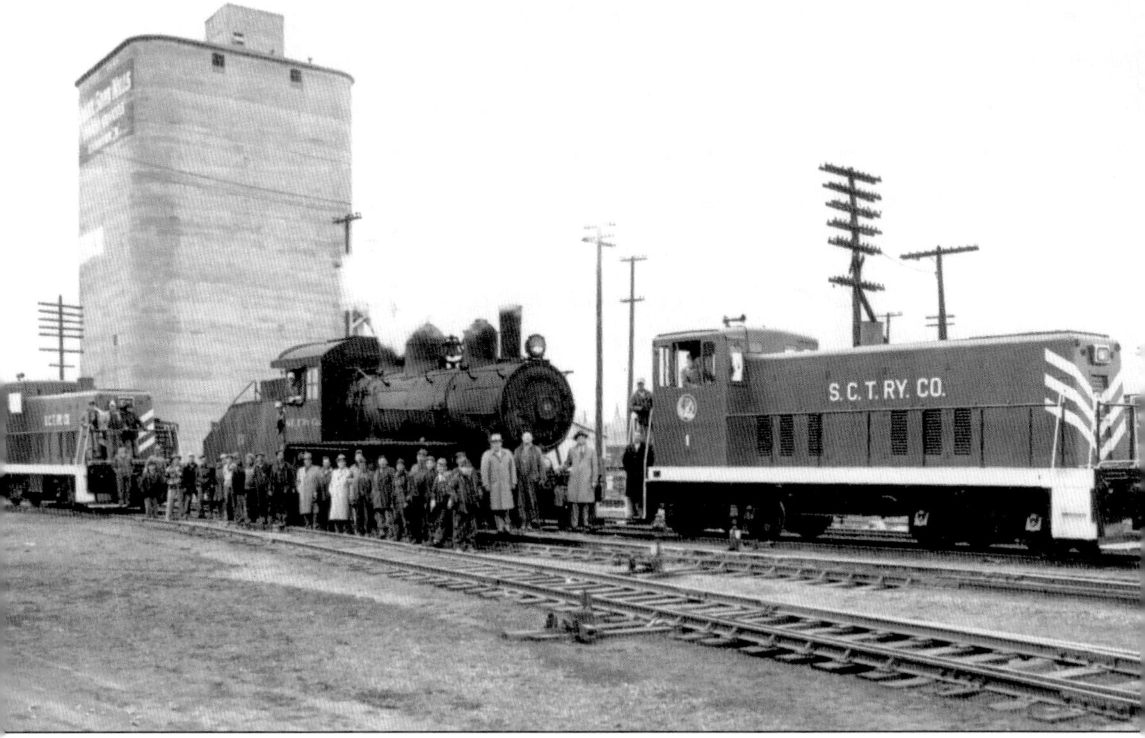

The Sioux City Terminal Railway's first diesel-electric locomotives were purchased in 1951. Railroad officials and workers pose for this photograph to celebrate the occasion. The new locomotives flank old steamer No. 13. The steam era is near an end, and the end is also near for the Sioux City Terminal Railway—within two decades. (Courtesy of the Sioux City Public Museum.)

Seven

The Hill Railroads

Sioux City played a prominent role in perfecting the railroad network created by James J. Hill. Four large railroad companies worked in tandem to increase traffic and to maximize revenue: the Chicago, Burlington and Quincy Railway, or Burlington Route; the Great Northern Railway; Northern Pacific Railway; and the Spokane, Portland and Seattle Railway. Cotton and other agricultural products were shipped from the Burlington Route area to the Pacific northwest. The Great Northern and Northern Pacific carried lumber and other products from the Orient to the plains states and to the south. During the 1890s, Hill made several attempts to merge these railroads into one company. His efforts, however, were stopped by the courts.

Even if the mergers had taken place, the network had only two connecting points: through Chicago and Billings, Montana. It needed a third somewhere in the center of the system, and Sioux City provided that opportunity. In light of Sioux City's growing economy toward the end of the 19th century, A. S. Garretson, John Pierce, and James Booge invested their money to build a railroad to Duluth, Minnesota. They wanted to bypass Chicago and send Sioux City products directly to the East Coast and Europe via the Great Lakes. Their Sioux City and Northern Railroad experienced financial difficulties during the panic of 1893, and it was able to build tracks only as far as Garretson, Minnesota. The Great Northern purchased the Sioux City and Northern Railroad and joined the tracks of its east–west main line at Willmar, Minnesota. Sioux City then had its second transcontinental railroad company in town.

The arrival of the Chicago, Burlington and Quincy Railway was a two-part operation. The Burlington Route operated a separate branch line from O'Neill, Nebraska, to Sioux City. The Chicago, Burlington, and Quincy, or "Q" as it was commonly called, completed track construction from its main line at Lincoln, Nebraska, to Sioux City in 1916. The Burlington Route, thereby, could compete with the Omaha Road in eastern Nebraska. More important, however, was its connection with the Great Northern in Sioux City. The empire of the Great Northern; Chicago, Burlington, and Quincy; Northern Pacific; and Spokane, Portland, and Seattle now had a strategic meeting point at its center—Sioux City.

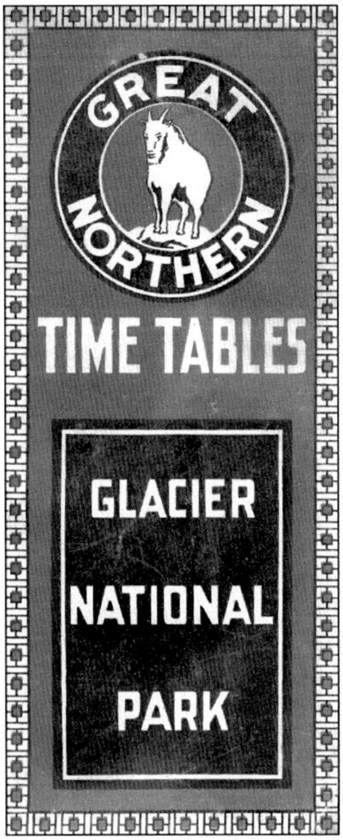

This Great Northern Railway timetable dates from 1924. It is a reddish/rust and very dark green. The goat was the railroad company's symbol and was known as Rocky for the Rocky Mountains. Perhaps they were inferring that the Great Northern was as "sure of foot" as a mountain goat. The railroad ran through Glacier Park and actually painted the cab of some of its steam locomotives green and rust red to signify the route. (Courtesy of Bruce Eveland and the Fremont Dinner Train.)

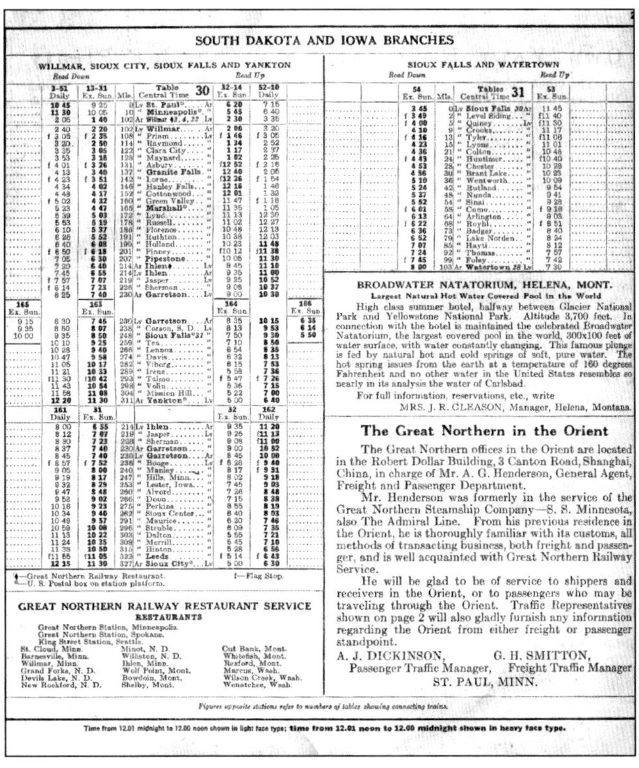

SOUTH DAKOTA AND IOWA BRANCHES

WILLMAR, SIOUX CITY, SIOUX FALLS AND YANKTON

Read Down — *Read Up*

	3-51 Daily	13-31 Ex. Sun.	Mls.	Table 30 Central Time	32-14 Ex. Sun.	52-10 Daily	
	10 45	9 25	0	Lv **St. Paul**⊙ ..... Ar	**6 20**	7 15	
	11 30	10 05	10	" **Minneapolis**⊙ . "	**5 45**	6 40	
	2 05	**1 40**	102	Ar Willmar ♦3, 4, 22 . Lv	**2 30**	3 35	
	2 40	**2 20**	102	Lv **Willmar** ...... Ar	**2 06**	3 20	
	f 3 05	f **2 35**	108	" Prism Lv	f **1 46**	f 3 05	
	3 20	**2 50**	114	" Raymond ..... "	**1 34**	2 52	
	3 35	**3 05**	122	" Clara City .... "	**1 17**	2 37	
	3 53	**3 18**	128	" Maynard ...... "	**1 02**	2 25	
	f 4 01	f **3 26**	131	" Asbury .... "	f**12 52**	f 2 18	
	4 13	**3 40**	137	" **Granite Falls** . "	**12 40**	2 05	
	f 4 23	f **3 51**	142	" Lorne .... "	f**12 26**	f 1 54	
	4 34	**4 02**	146	" Hanley Falls ... "	**12 16**	1 46	
	4 48	**4 17**	152	" Cottonwood ... "	**12 01**	1 32	
	f 5 02	**4 32**	160	" Green Valley .. "	11 47	f 1 18	
	5 23	**4 47**	165	" **Marshall**⊙ .... "	11 35	1 05	
	5 39	**5 03**	172	" Lynd .... "	11 13	12 39	
	5 53	**5 19**	178	" Russell .... "	11 02	12 27	
	6 10	**5 37**	186	" Florence ...... "	10 48	12 13	
	6 26	**5 52**	191	" Ruthton ...... "	10 38	12 03	
	6 40	**6 08**	199	" Holland ...... "	10 23	**11 48**	
	f 6 50	f **6 18**	201	" Pinney .... "	f10 12	f**11 38**	
	7 05	**6 30**	207	" **Pipestone** .... "	10 05	**11 30**	
	7 20	**6 40**	214	Ar **Ihlen**♦ Lv	9 45	**11 10**	
	7 45	**6 55**	214	Lv **Ihlen** ...... Ar	9 35	**11 00**	
	f 7 57	**7 07**	219	" Jasper Lv	9 25	**10 52**	
	f 8 14	**7 23**	226	" Sherman ...... "	9 08	**10 37**	
	8 25	**7 40**	230	Ar **Garretson** ... Lv	9 00	**10 30**	
165 Ex. Sun.		**163** Ex. Sun.			**164** Ex. Sun.		**166** Ex. Sun.
9 15	8 30	**7 45**	230	Lv **Garretson** ... Ar	8 35	**10 15**	**6 35**
9 35	8 50	**8 07**	238	" Corson, S. D. . Lv	8 13	**9 53**	**6 14**
10 00	9 35	**8 50**	248	" **Sioux Falls**⊙31 "	7 50	**9 30**	**5 50**
	10 10	**9 25**	259	" Tea .... "	7 10	**8 50**	
	10 28	**9 40**	266	" Lennox ...... "	6 54	**8 35**	
	10 47	**9 58**	274	" Davis .... "	6 32	**8 13**	
	11 05	**10 17**	282	" Viborg ...... "	6 15	**7 53**	
	11 21	**10 33**	289	" Irene .... "	5 58	**7 36**	
	f11 30	f**10 42**	293	" Talmo ...... "	f 5 47	f **7 26**	
	11 43	**10 54**	298	" Volin .... "	5 36	**7 15**	
	11 58	**11 08**	304	" Mission Hill ... "	5 22	**7 00**	
	12 20	**11 30**	311	Ar **Yankton**⊙ ... Lv	5 00	**6 40**	
	161 Daily	**31** Ex. Sun.			**32** Ex. Sun.	**162** Daily	
	8 00	**6 55**	214	Lv **Ihlen** .... Ar	9 35	**11 20**	
	8 12	**7 07**	219	" Jasper Lv	9 26	f**11 13**	
	8 30	**7 23**	228	" Sherman ..... "	9 08	f**11 00**	
	8 37	**7 40**	230	Ar **Garretson** .... "	9 00	**10 52**	
	8 45	**7 40**	230	Lv **Garretson** ... Ar	8 45	**10 00**	
	f 8 57	f **7 52**	236	" Booge Lv	f 8 26	f **9 40**	
	9 05	**8 00**	240	" Manley ...... "	8 17	f **9 31**	
	9 19	**8 17**	247	" Hills, Minn. ... "	8 02	**9 18**	
	9 32	**8 29**	253	" Lester, Iowa ... "	7 45	**9 03**	
	9 47	**8 48**	260	" Alvord ...... "	7 28	**8 48**	
	9 58	**9 02**	266	" Doon .... "	7 15	**8 38**	
	10 16	**9 23**	275	" Perkins ...... "	8 55	**8 19**	
	10 34	**9 40**	282	" Sioux Center ... "	6 40	**8 03**	
	10 49	**9 57**	291	" Maurice ...... "	6 20	**7 46**	
	10 59	**10 08**	296	" Struble ...... "	6 09	**7 35**	
	11 13	**10 22**	303	" Dalton ...... "	5 55	**7 21**	
	11 24	**10 35**	308	" Merrill ...... "	5 45	**7 10**	
	11 38	**10 50**	316	" Hinton ...... "	5 28	**6 56**	
	f11 55	f**11 05**	322	" **Leeds** ...... "	f 5 14	f **6 43**	
	12 15	**11 30**	327	Ar **Sioux City**⊙ ... Lv	5 00	**6 30**	

♦—Great Northern Railway Restaurant. f—Flag Stop.
⊙—U. S. Postal box on station platform.

SIOUX FALLS AND WATERTOWN

Read Down — *Read Up*

54 Ex. Sun.	Mls.	Tables 31 Central Time	53 Ex. Sun.
3 45	0	Lv **Sioux Falls** 30 Ar	11 45
f **3 49**	2	" Level Siding ... "	f11 40
f **4 00**	5	" Quincy Lv	f11 30
4 10	9	" Crooks ...... "	11 17
f **4 16**	13	" Tyler .... "	f11 08
4 23	15	" Lyons ...... "	11 01
4 36	21	" Colton ...... "	10 48
f **4 43**	24	" Huntimer ..... "	f10 40
4 53	28	" Chester ..... "	10 28
4 56	30	" Brant Lake .... "	10 23
5 10	36	" Wentworth .... "	10 09
5 24	42	" Rutland ..... "	9 54
5 37	48	" Nunda ...... "	9 41
5 52	54	" Sinai ...... "	9 28
f **6 01**	58	" Como ...... "	f 9 18
6 13	64	" Arlington .... "	9 03
f **6 22**	68	" Royhl ...... "	f 8 51
6 36	73	" Badger ..... "	8 40
6 52	79	" Lake Norden .. "	8 24
7 07	85	" Hayti ...... "	8 12
7 24	92	" Thomas ..... "	7 57
f **7 45**	99	" Foley ...... "	7 42
8 00	103	Ar **Watertown** 28 Lv	7 30

BROADWATER NATATORIUM, HELENA, MONT.

Largest Natural Hot Water Covered Pool in the World

High class summer hotel, halfway between Glacier National Park and Yellowstone National Park. Altitude 3,700 feet. In connection with the hotel is maintained the celebrated Broadwater Natatorium, the largest covered pool in the world, 300x100 feet of water surface, with water constantly changing. This famous plunge is fed by natural hot and cold springs of soft, pure water. The hot spring issues from the earth at a temperature of 160 degrees Fahrenheit and no other water in the United States resembles so nearly in its analysis the water of Carlsbad.

For full information, reservations, etc., write

MRS. J. R. CLEASON, Manager, Helena, Montana.

GREAT NORTHERN RAILWAY RESTAURANT SERVICE

RESTAURANTS

Great Northern Station, Minneapolis.
Great Northern Station, Spokane.
King Street Station, Seattle.

St. Cloud, Minn.	Minot, N. D.	Cut Bank, Mont.
Barnesville, Minn.	Williston, N. D.	Whitefish, Mont.
Willmar, Minn.	Ihlen, Minn.	Rexford, Mont.
Grand Forks, N. D.	Wolf Point, Mont.	Marcus, Wash.
Devils Lake, N. D.	Bowdoin, Mont.	Wilson Creek, Wash.
New Rockford, N. D.	Shelby, Mont.	Wenatchee, Wash.

The Great Northern in the Orient

The Great Northern offices in the Orient are located in the Robert Dollar Building, 3 Canton Road, Shanghai, China, in charge of Mr. A. G. Henderson, General Agent, Freight and Passenger Department.

Mr. Henderson was formerly in the service of the Great Northern Steamship Company—S. S. Minnesota, also The Admiral Line. From his previous residence in the Orient, he is thoroughly familiar with its customs, all methods of transacting business, both freight and passenger, and is well acquainted with Great Northern Railway Service.

He will be glad to be of service to shippers and receivers in the Orient, or to passengers who may be traveling through the Orient. Traffic Representatives shown on page 2 will also gladly furnish any information regarding the Orient from either freight or passenger standpoint.

A. J. DICKINSON, Passenger Traffic Manager, G. H. SMITTON, Freight Traffic Manager

ST. PAUL, MINN.

Figures opposite stations refer to numbers of tables showing connecting trains.

Time from 12.01 midnight to 12.00 noon shown in light face type; **time from 12.01 noon to 12.00 midnight shown in heavy face type.**

Table No. 30 from the 1924 timetable shows that there were four trains a day to and from Sioux City. The east–west connection with the main line was at Willmar, Minnesota. In northwest Iowa the tracks were through a portion where a large number of Dutch immigrants settled. It had a station stop in the Leeds area of Sioux City.

The Chicago, Burlington, and Quincy Railroad, although noted for its direct line from Chicago to Minneapolis, reached major markets in the Midwest and west. Its simple square and rectangles on its timetable cover were used and recognized for decades. This edition is from 1925. (Author's collection.)

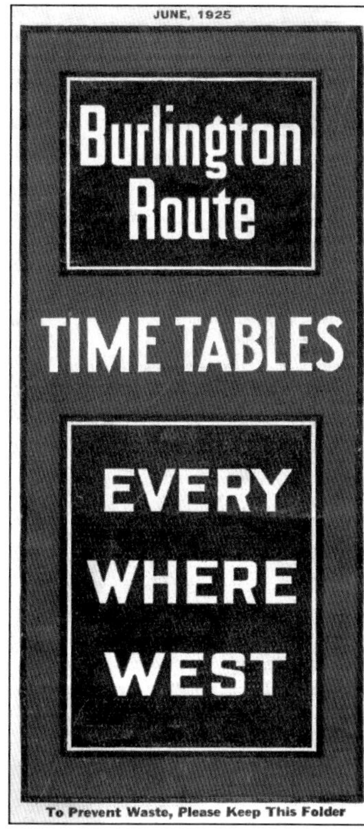

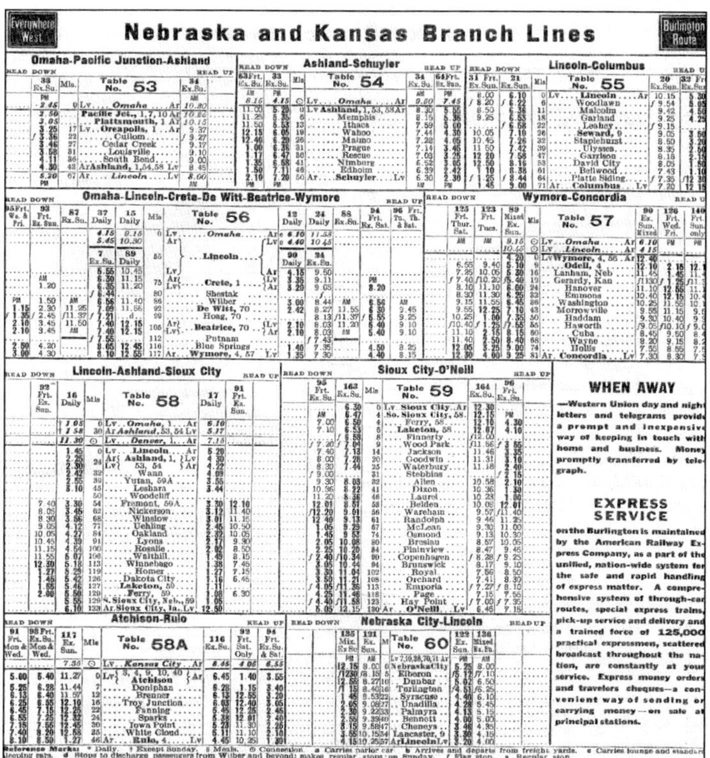

Two trains ran in each direction from O'Neill, Nebraska, to Sioux City. The line ran through prime farmland in eastern Nebraska. It is still used for freight today. There were connections at O'Neill with the Chicago and Northwestern until the 1960s. (Author's collection.)

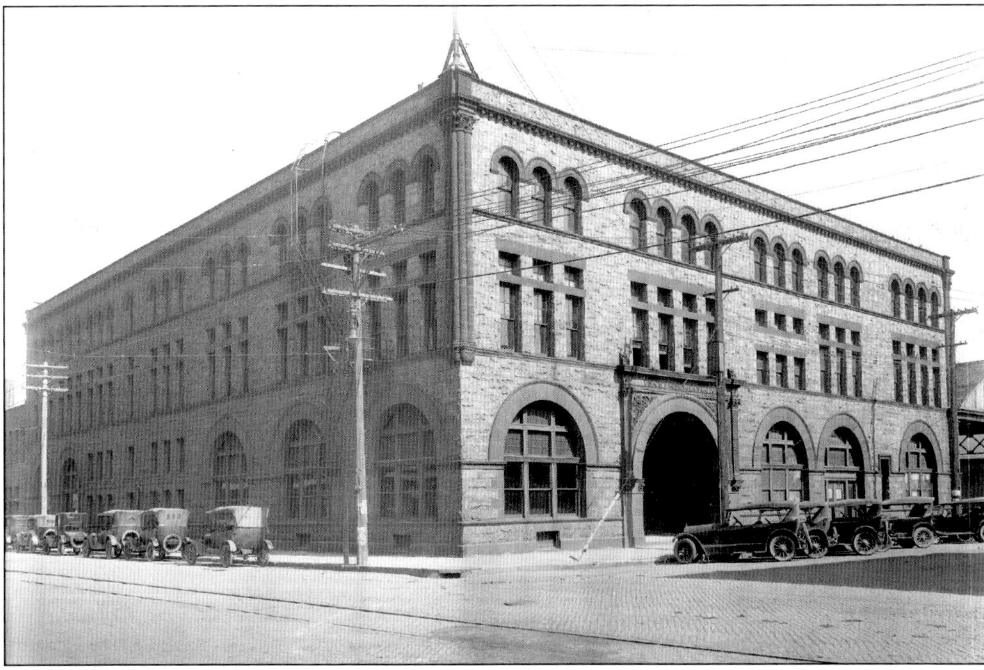

The Chicago, Burlington, and Quincy Railway and the Great Northern Railway used the same passenger station and depot. It was commonly known as the union station in Sioux City. The epithet was a misnomer. A *union station* is usually a term for a train station used by a number of railroads. (Courtesy of the Jack P. Fleckenstein Collection.)

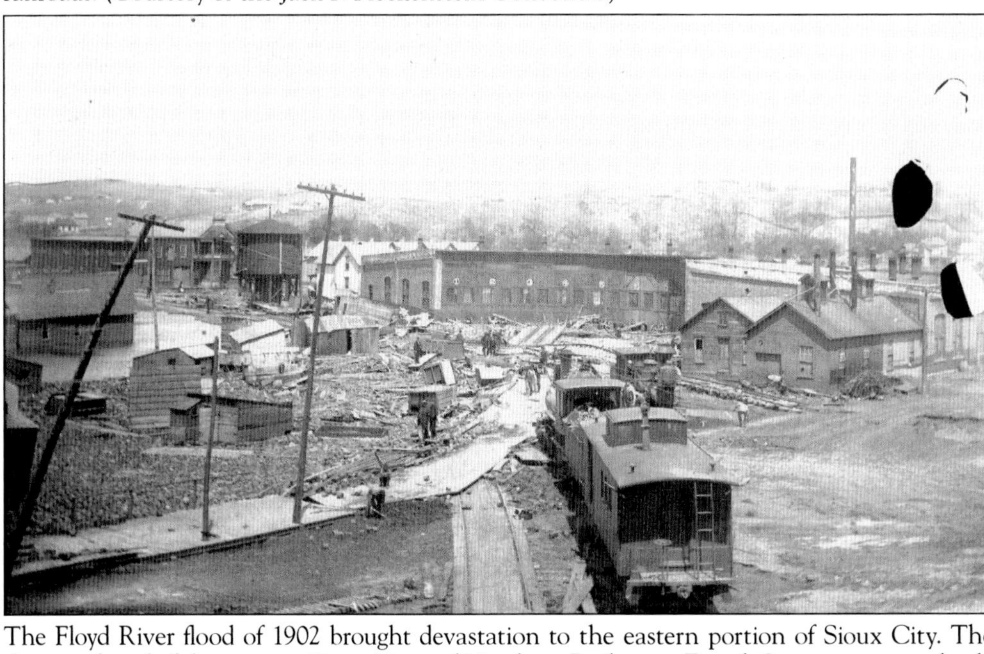

The Floyd River flood of 1902 brought devastation to the eastern portion of Sioux City. The shops and yard of the nascent Sioux City and Northern Railway at Fourth Street were completely destroyed. Only a caboose remains completely intact in this photograph. The flood contributed to the financial problems of the railroad and led to its takeover by the Great Northern. (Courtesy of the Sioux City Public Museum.)

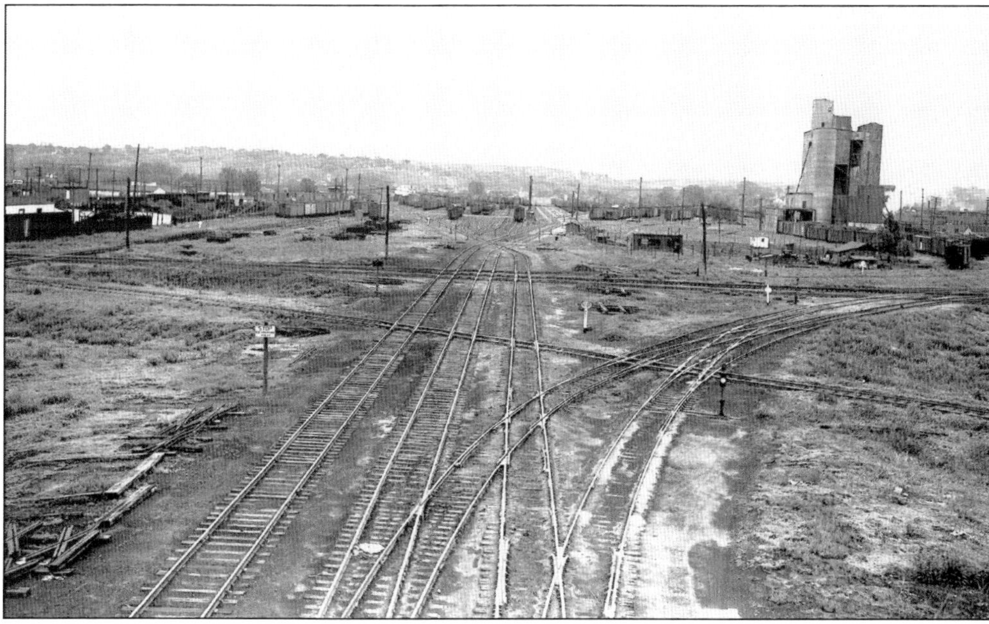

This view is looking to the east from the downtown area, or more specifically, from Wall Street. The stockyards are to the south, or right. (Courtesy of the Sioux City Public Museum, George Newman Collection.)

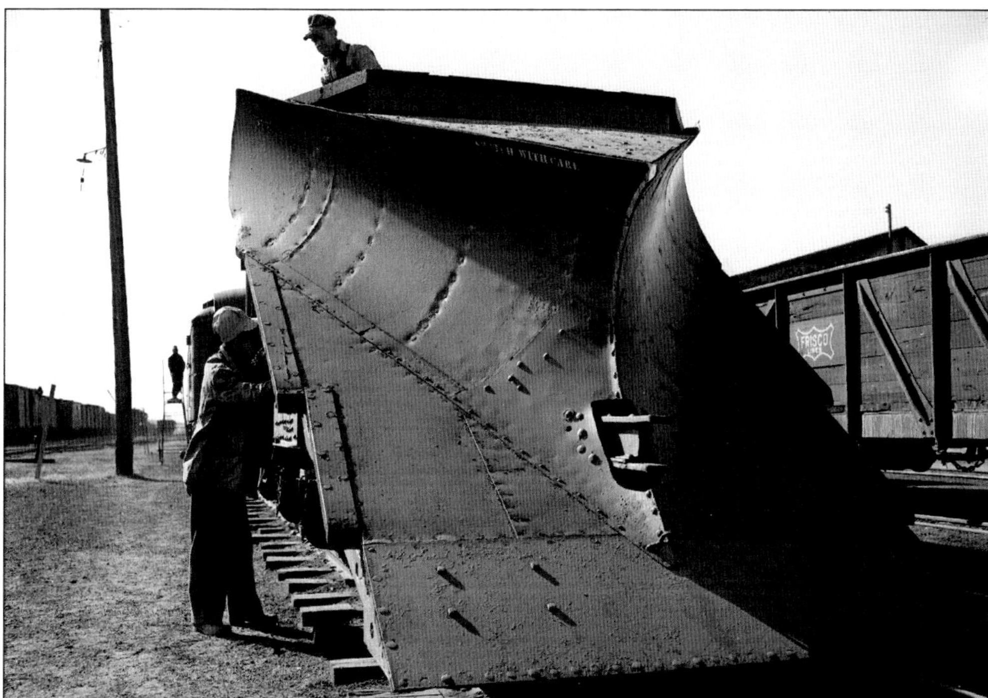

This large plow, though not labeled, is probably in the Great Northern Railway yard. Its successor BNSF still stations such a plow south of its yard in an area of some side tracks. In mountainous regions railroads used the famous rotary snow plows. Plows normally would be pushed by two steam locomotives. (Courtesy of the Sioux City Public Museum, George Newman Collection.)

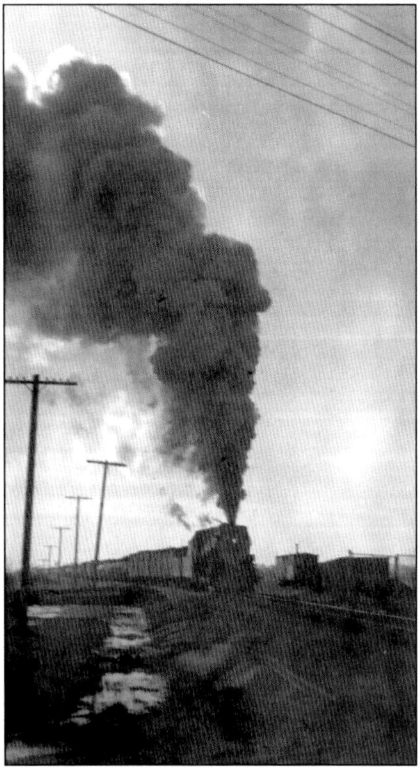

The black plume of smoke bears witness of this locomotive leaving the Sioux City yard. This Great Northern steamer demonstrates the efforts made to overcome inertia to move a heavy train. This scene took place several times a day in the 1930s and 1940s. (Courtesy of Paul H. Reistrup.)

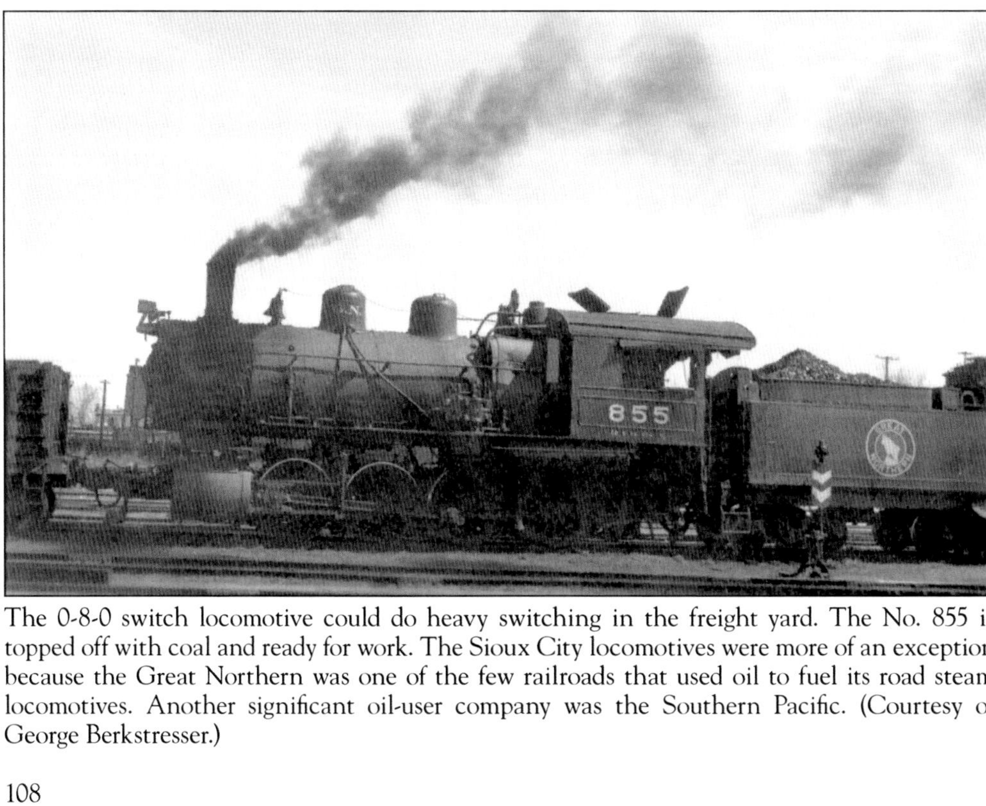

The 0-8-0 switch locomotive could do heavy switching in the freight yard. The No. 855 is topped off with coal and ready for work. The Sioux City locomotives were more of an exception because the Great Northern was one of the few railroads that used oil to fuel its road steam locomotives. Another significant oil-user company was the Southern Pacific. (Courtesy of George Berkstresser.)

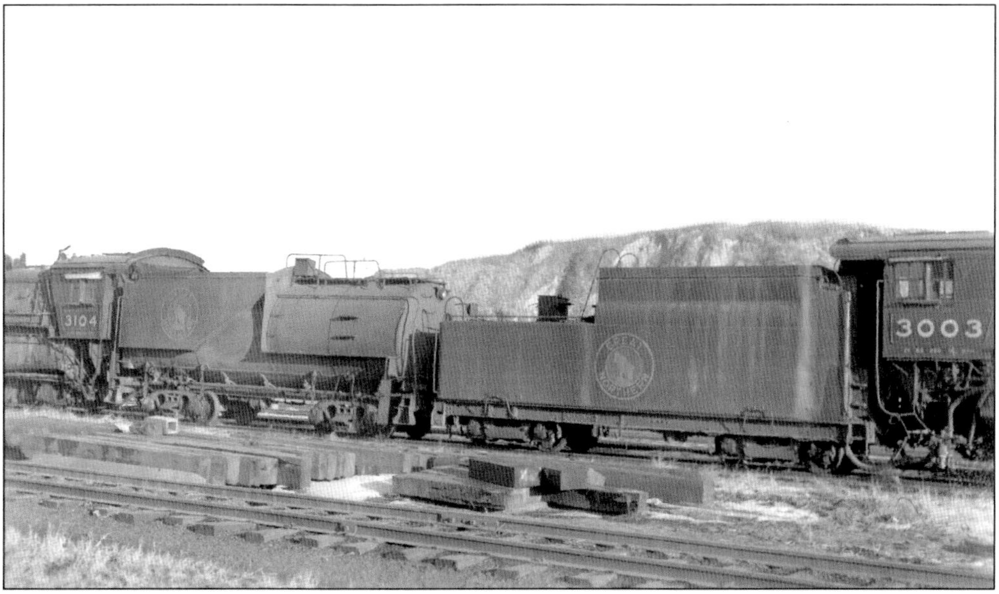

Two Great Northern steam locomotives sit tender to tender in the yard. The rounded portion of the left locomotive held the water used on the road. It is a clear view of a typical design. The liquid portion of tenders had baffles to keep the solution from swaying and push and pull on the locomotive. (Courtesy of George Berkstresser.)

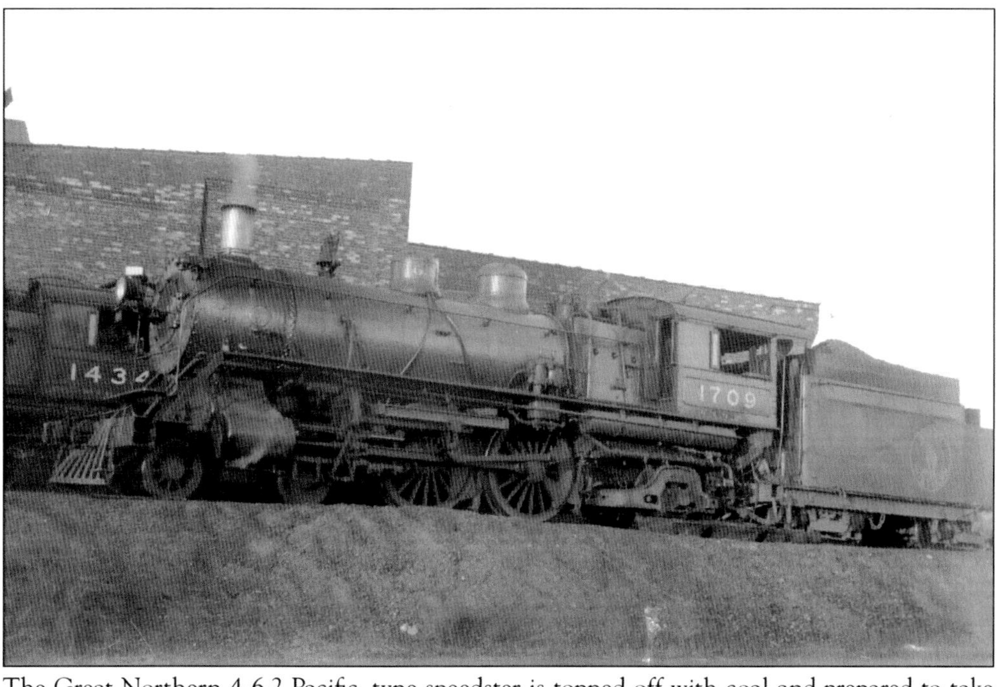

The Great Northern 4-6-2 Pacific–type speedster is topped off with coal and prepared to take a passenger consist to Willmar, Minnesota. It was photographed by Guy Thatcher in October 1940. The Thatcher collection is now property of the Siouxland Historical Railroad Association. (Courtesy of the Siouxland Historical Railroad Association.)

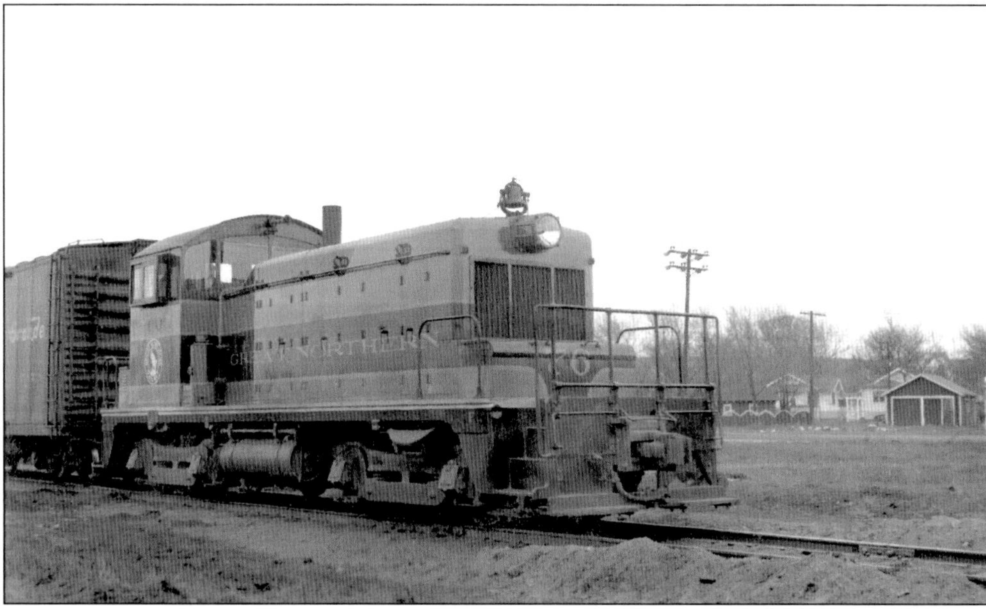

This classic Great Northern diesel-electric switch locomotive is pulling a boxcar. The Great Northern had a long freight yard in Sioux City. It also had to accommodate cars arriving from the Chicago, Burlington, and Quincy Railroad. (Courtesy of George Berkstresser.)

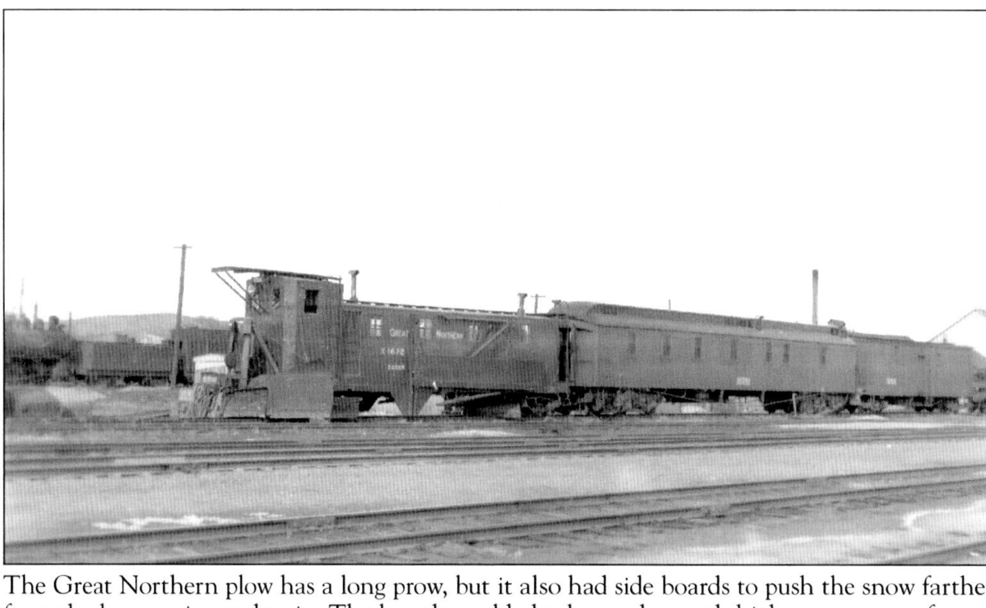

The Great Northern plow has a long prow, but it also had side boards to push the snow farther from the locomotive and train. The boards could also be used to push higher snow away from a parallel track. (Courtesy of George Berkstresser.)

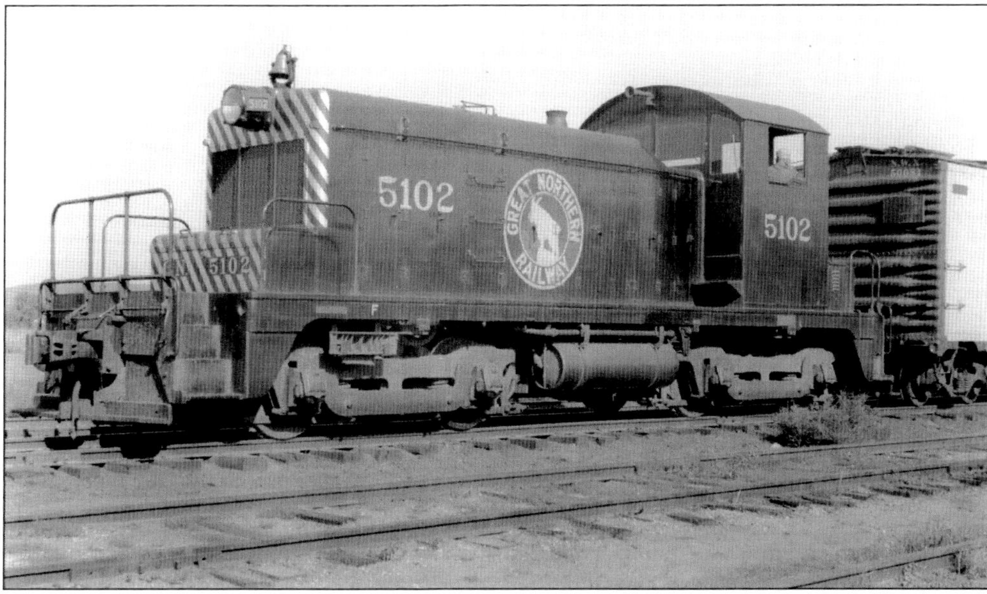

One of the smaller switch engines, the SW800, was used to move a shorter line of cars. These SW 1–type locomotives tended to remain in or near their own yard. (Courtesy of the Siouxland Historical Railroad Association.)

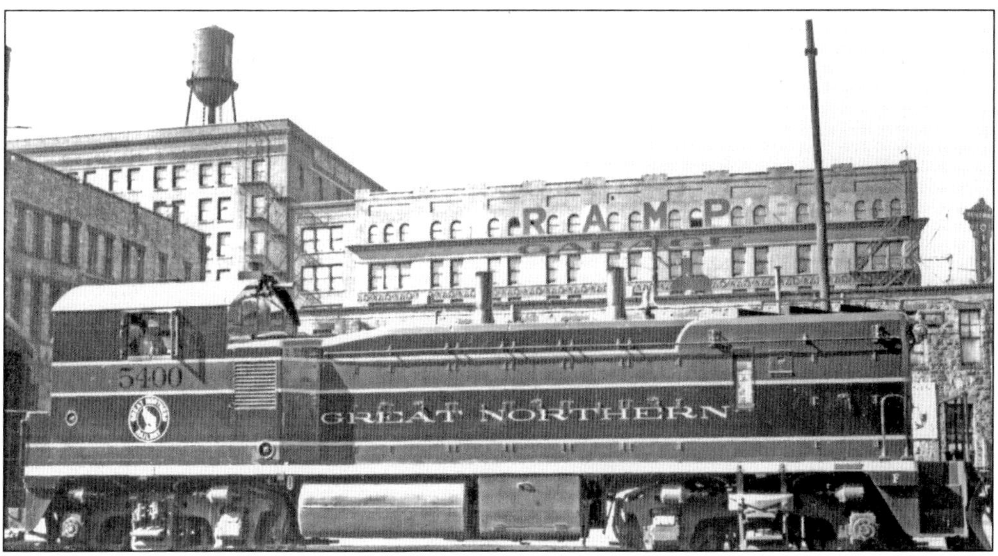

By the 1960s, the Great Northern changed from steam to diesel-electric switch locomotives in Sioux City. This Electro-Motive engine is located in downtown Sioux City. From the buildings in the background, it seems to be near the Milwaukee Road depot. It probably dropped some cars off to that railroad. (Courtesy of the Siouxland Historical Railroad Association.)

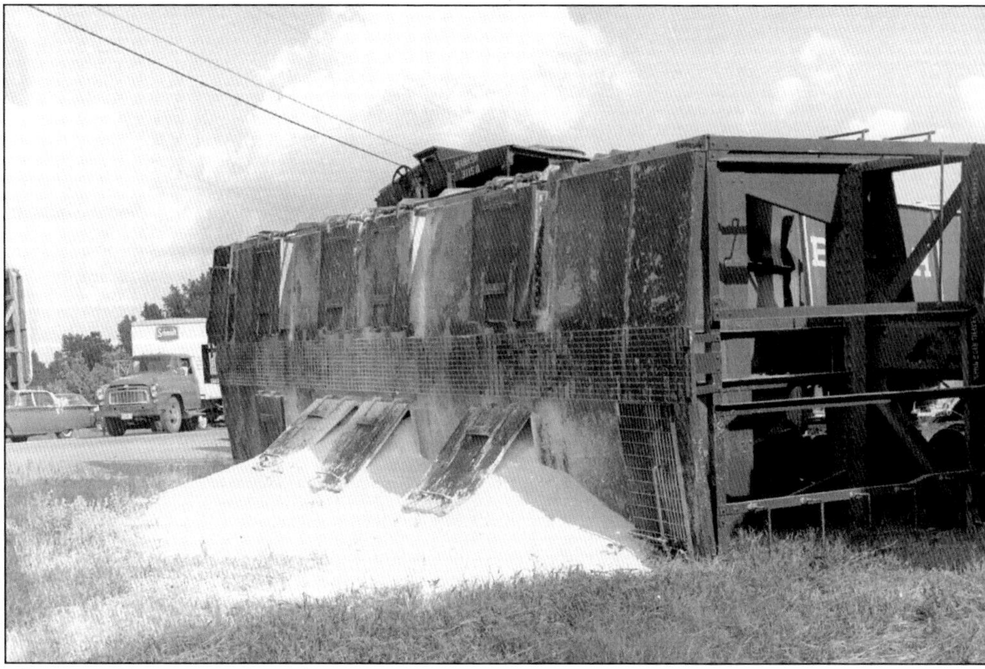

This closed-hopper car has fallen on its side and its cargo has been spilled along the track. It was hit by another hopper car that can be seen in the background. Switches in the wrong position in yards often resulted in this type of collision. (Courtesy of George R. Lindblade.)

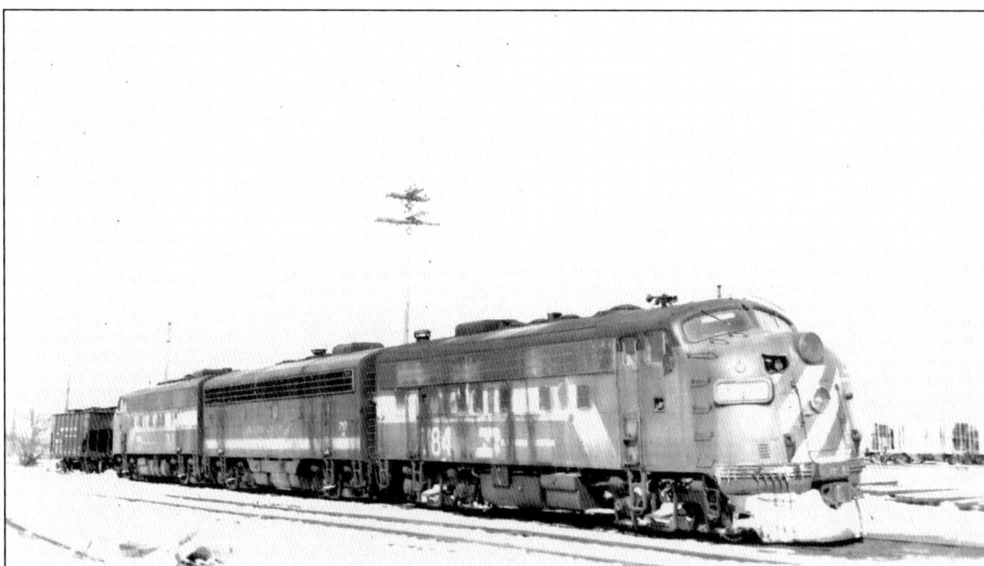

This three-unit FP7s or 9s covered wagons survived into the Burlington Northern merger of the early 1970s. The units could have originally belonged to any among the Great Northern; Northern Pacific; Spokane, Portland, and Seattle; or Chicago, Burlington, and Quincy. They have seen better days. (Courtesy of George Berkstresser.)

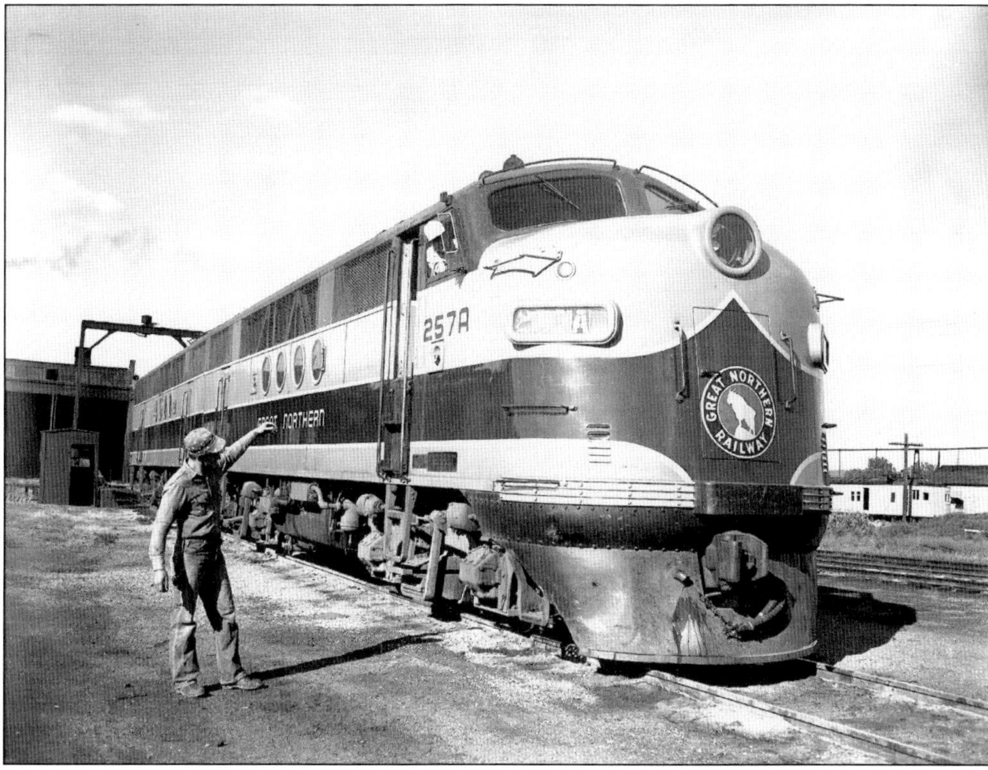

A Great Northern F 3 unit is leaving the turntable and roundhouse. It is being readied to return to Willmar, Minnesota, from Sioux City. The paint scheme was orange, very dark green, and yellow. (Courtesy of the Sioux City Public Museum, George Newman Collection.)

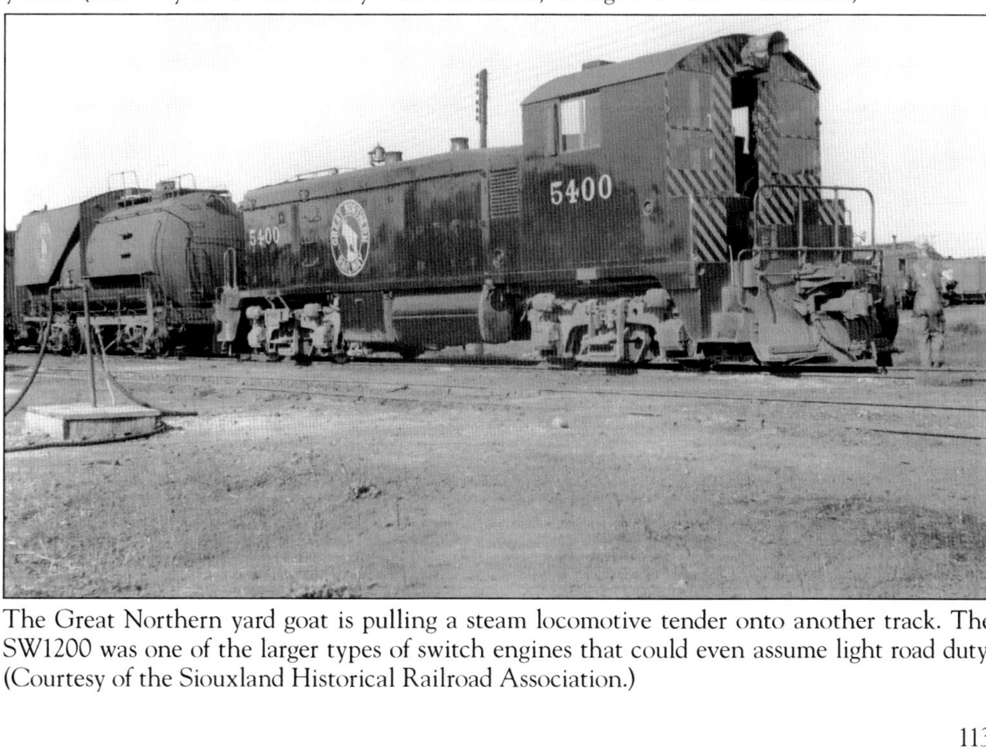

The Great Northern yard goat is pulling a steam locomotive tender onto another track. The SW1200 was one of the larger types of switch engines that could even assume light road duty. (Courtesy of the Siouxland Historical Railroad Association.)

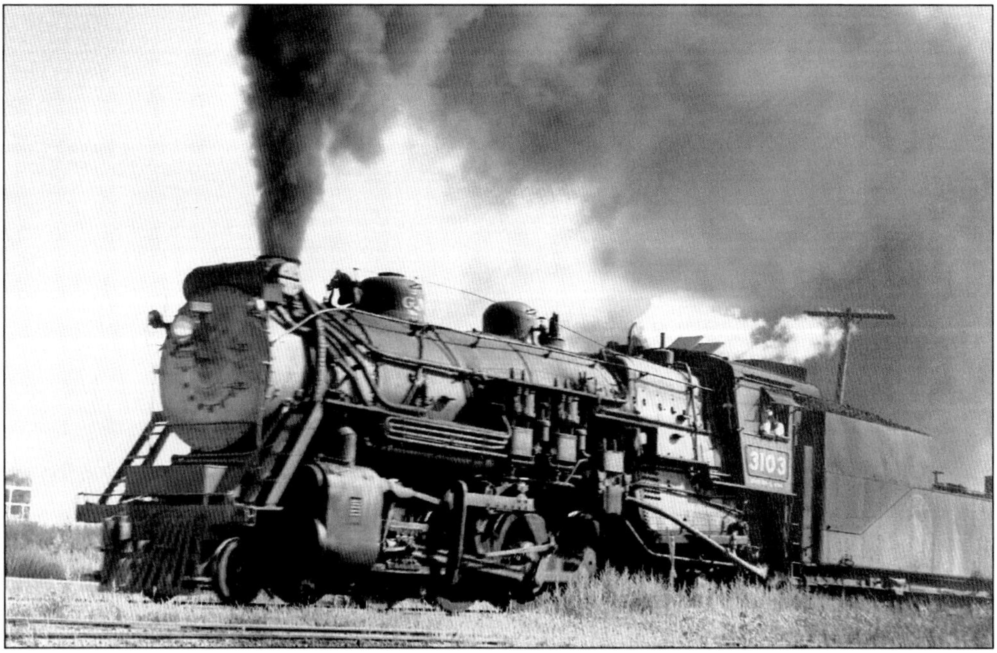

The Great Northern locomotive No. 3103 has claim to be the last regularly scheduled steam locomotive in Sioux City. Hearing of the occasion, a druggist in the Leeds part of Sioux City, near the yard, took the photograph in the early 1960s. Railfan steam excursions have come through Sioux City since then. (Courtesy of Leo Harris.)

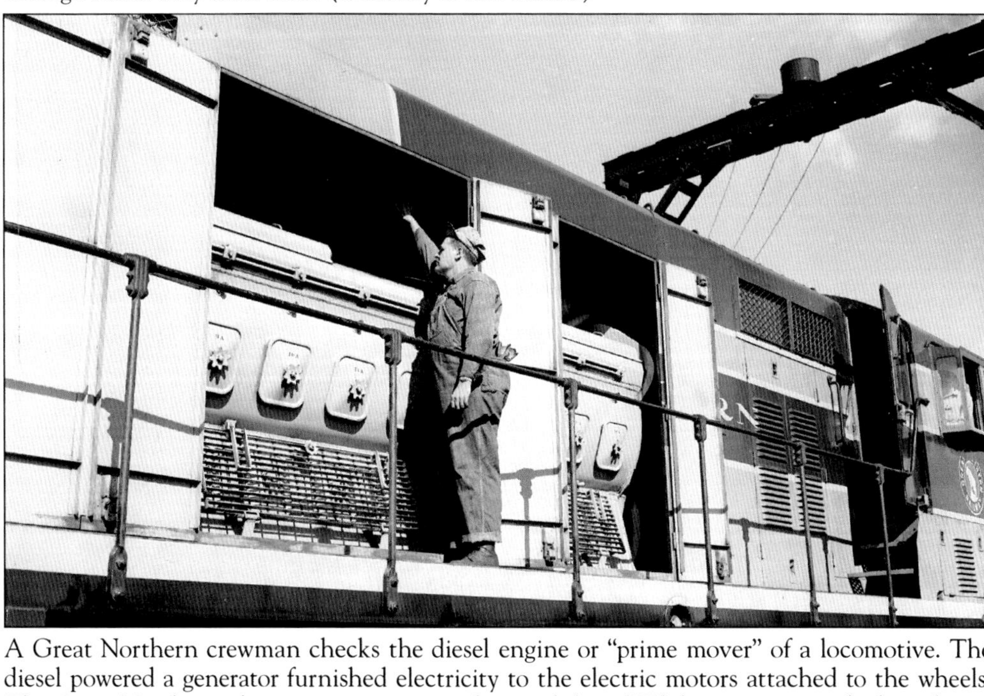

A Great Northern crewman checks the diesel engine or "prime mover" of a locomotive. The diesel powered a generator furnished electricity to the electric motors attached to the wheels. The Great Northern always ran its geeps and special duty (SD) locomotives with the cab end following. The locomotive, therefore, had to be turned on the turntable. (Courtesy of the Sioux City Public Museum, George Newman Collection.)

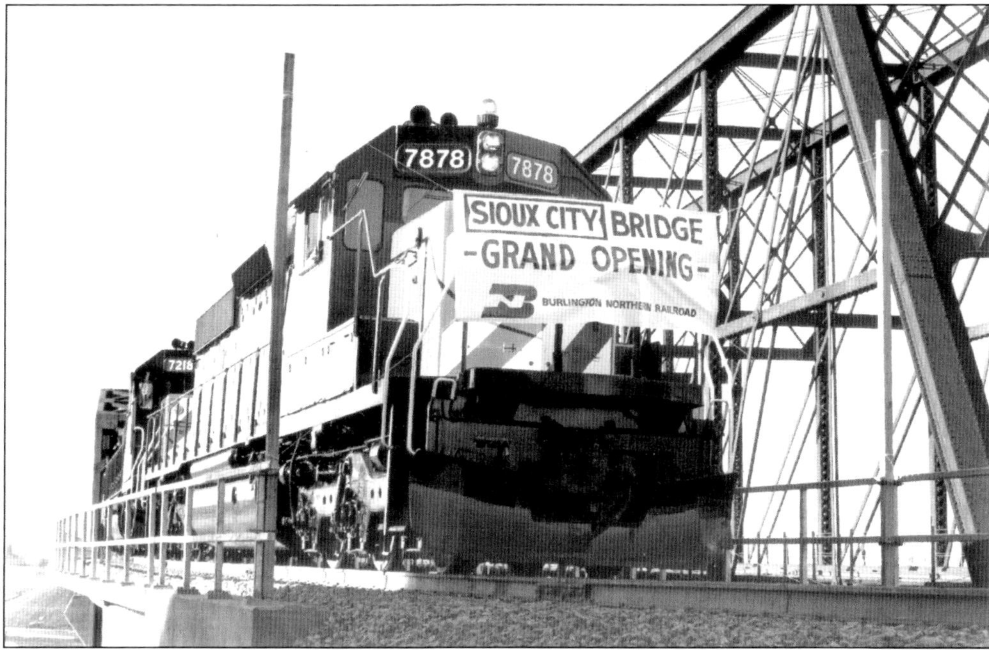

A modern bridge was completed for the Burlington Northern Railway in place of the almost-century-old structure built for the Chicago, St. Paul, Minneapolis and Omaha Railway. The first trains ran over the new bridge in December 1981. Now heavier locomotives and cars could make their way safely over the Missouri River. (Courtesy of the Sioux City Public Museum.)

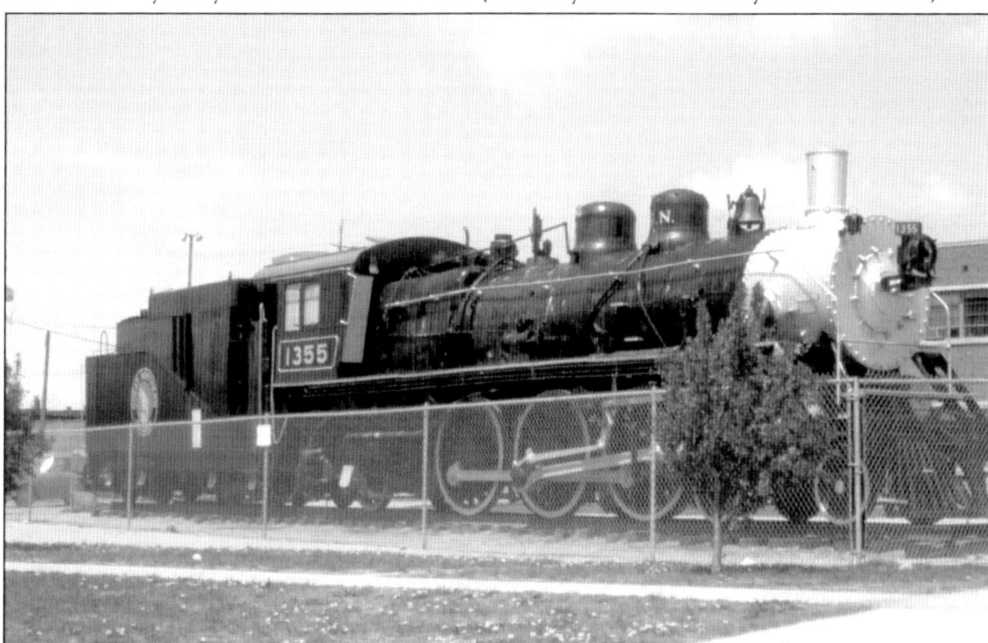

The Great Northern Railway donated *Chief Iron Horse* steam locomotive to Sioux City. It is seen here parked on the side of the Sioux City auditorium. It is now protected from the elements and housed in the roundhouse of the Siouxland Historical Railroad Association museum. (Courtesy of George R. Lindblade.)

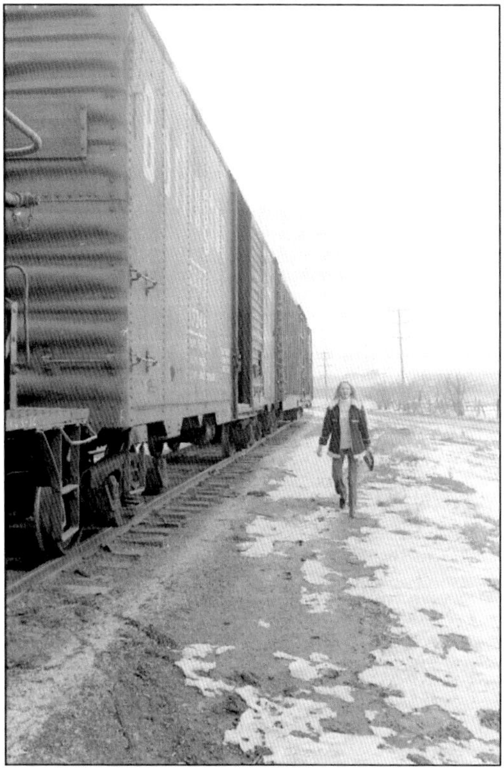

The first modern woman railroad employee in Sioux City walks along a freight train. Since freight trains could be a mile or so long, it could take a good amount of time to check all the cars. It was the type of work given a new employee. During the 19th century, daughters and wives of station agents often worked the telegraph. (Courtesy of George R. Lindblade.)

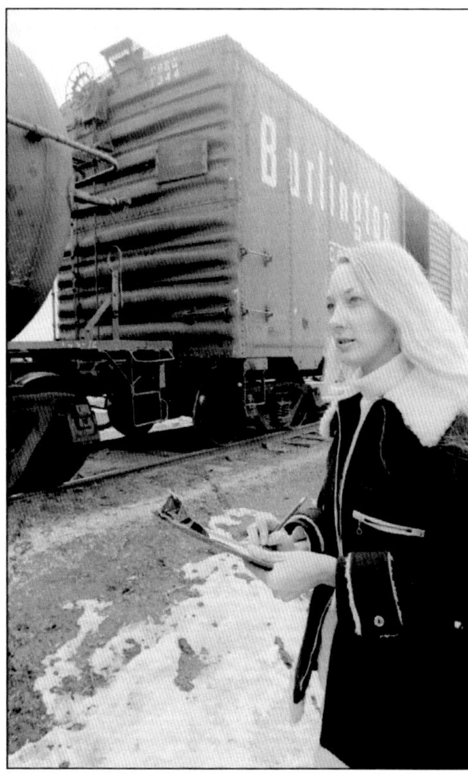

The first lady employee is checking the number and destination of freight cars in the Burlington Northern yard. Today the work is done automatically by computer and electronic car recognition. (Courtesy of George R. Lindblade.)

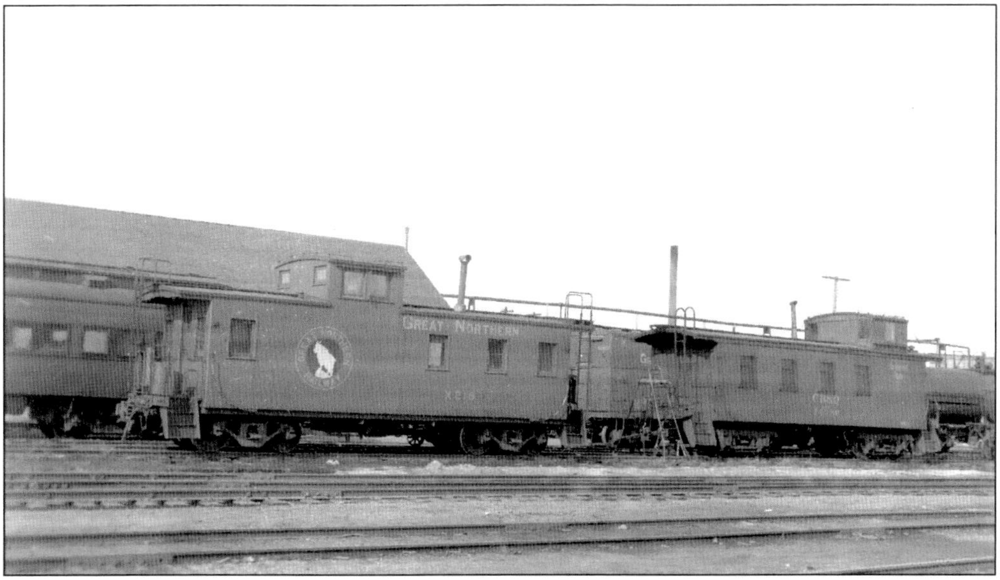

These two cabooses symbolize the joining together of the two Hill Railroads in Sioux City: the Great Northern Railway and the Chicago, Burlington, and Quincy Railway. The caboose on the left has Rocky, the mountain goat for the Great Northern. The one on the right has the Burlington Route rectangle herald. (Courtesy of George Berkstresser.)

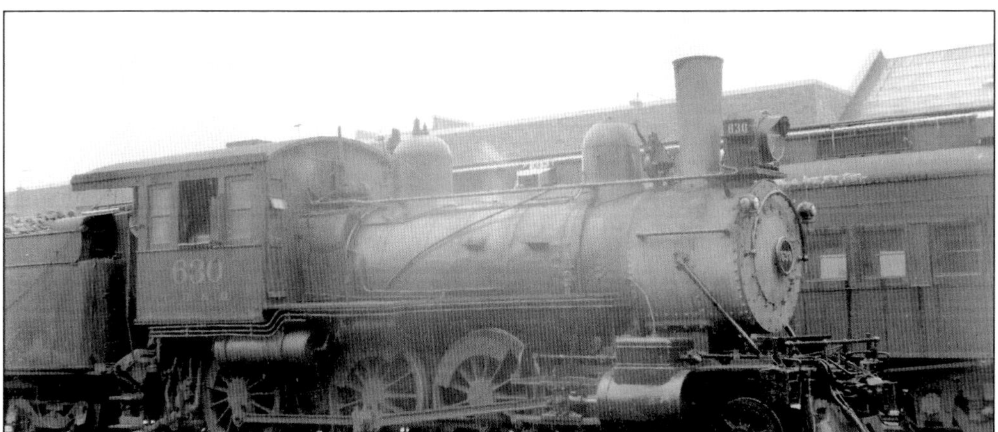

The 4-6-0 is left for light-duty passenger work as its time will end with the diesel-electric era. The No. 630 will run to the south after leaving passengers at the union station in downtown Sioux City. (Courtesy of the Siouxland Historical Railroad Association.)

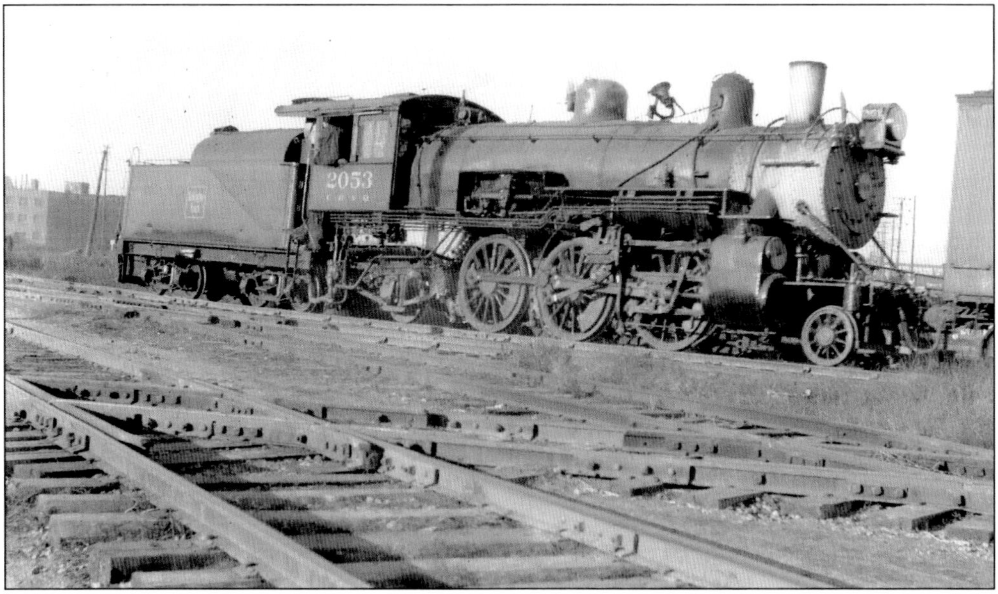

The Chicago, Burlington, and Quincy No. 2053 had relatively large drive wheels for a freight locomotive. The 2-6-2 wheel arrangement indicated a light-freight duty. There were relatively easy track grades on its usual route between Sioux City and Lincoln or O'Neill, Nebraska. (Courtesy of the Siouxland Historical Railroad Association.)

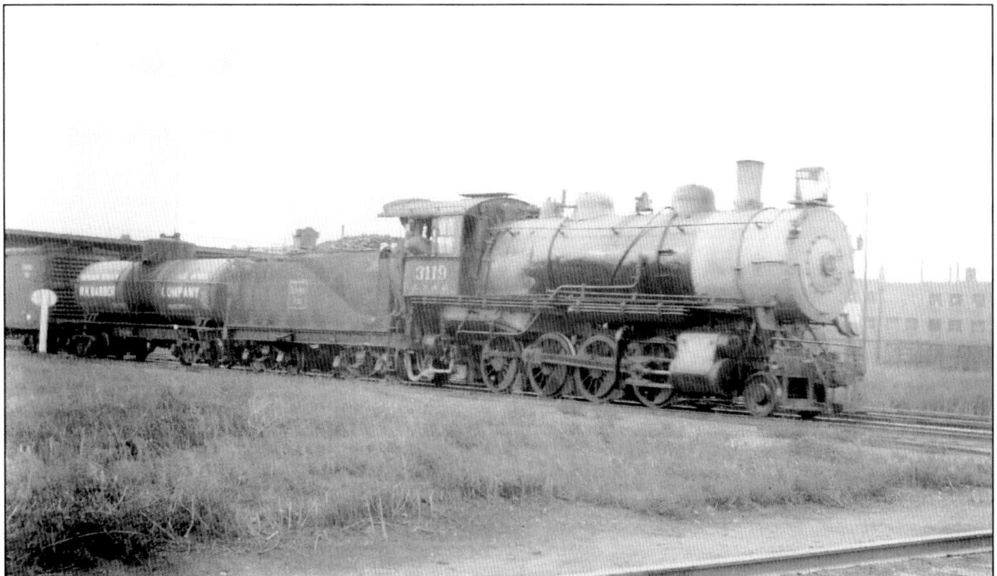

A Burlington Route 2-8-0 is pulling a freight train from the Missouri River bridge into the downtown area of Sioux City. It will turn around in the yard and make a return trip to Fremont or Lincoln, Nebraska. (Courtesy of the Siouxland Historical Railroad Association.)

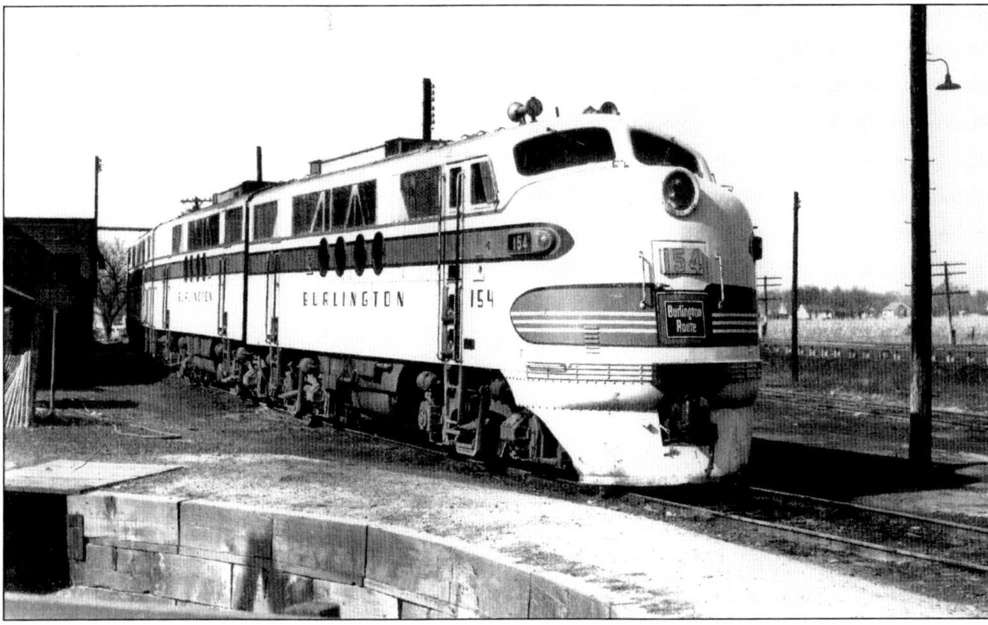

This group of three F units (most likely modified F-3s) are from the silver fleet of the Chicago, Burlington, and Quincy Railway. They appear to be in the Great Northern yard ready to pull a train southward. Sioux City was the midpoint northern terminus of the Burlington Route and the southern terminus of the Great Northern. (Courtesy of the Siouxland Historical Railroad Association.)

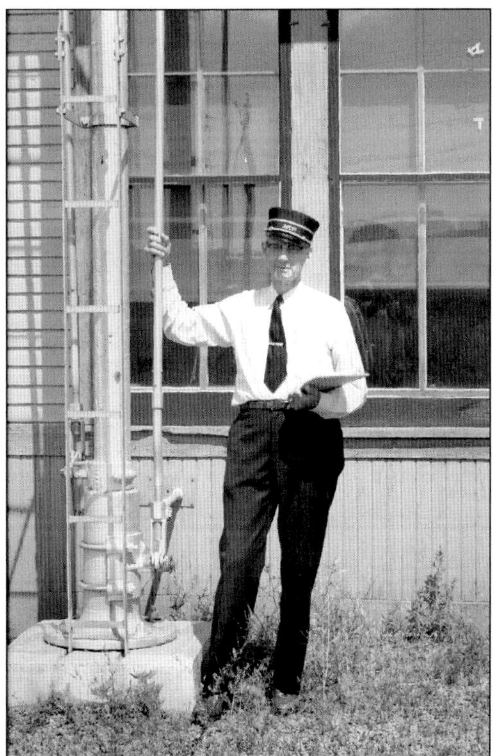

The Leeds portion of Sioux City had its own small railroad station and station agent. One could easily take a Great Northern train a few miles to downtown and return. The agent is standing outside holding onto the semaphore pole. (Courtesy of the Sioux City Public Museum.)

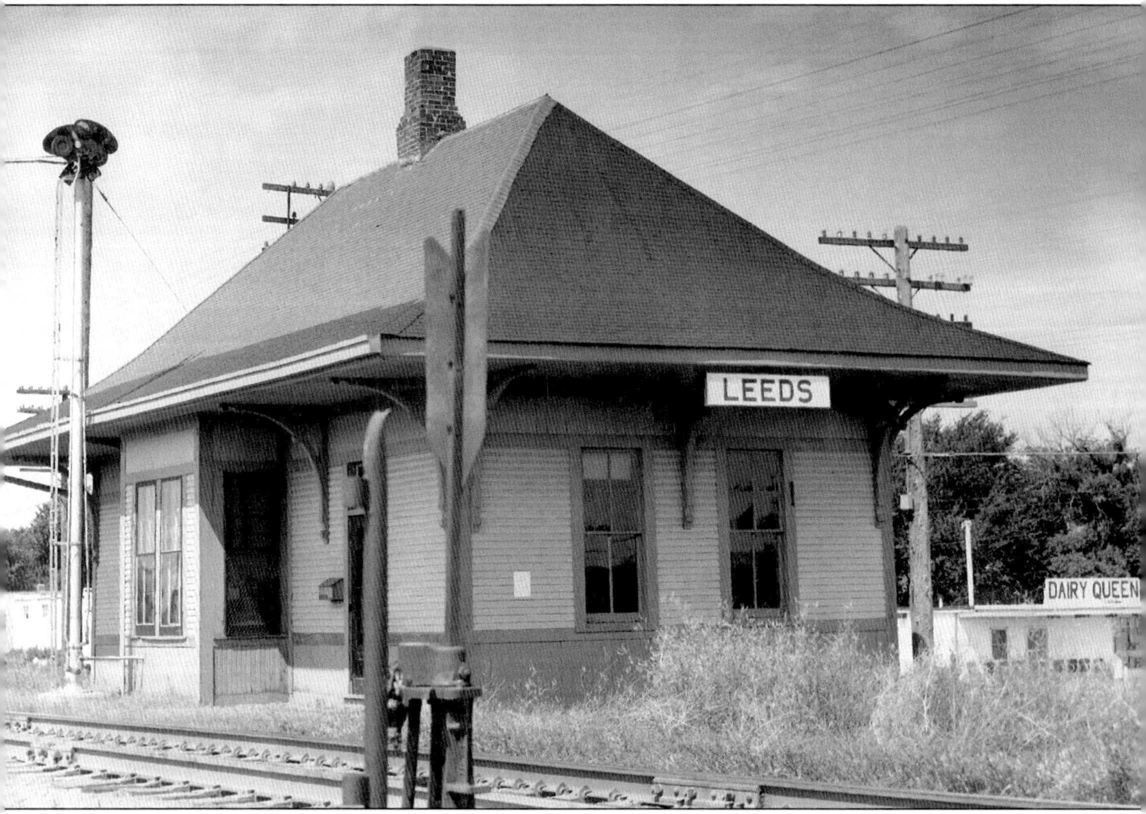

The small Leeds station has just about everything a larger one would have. The agent could observe an oncoming train from the bay window. He could also operate the semaphore with a lever inside the building. (Courtesy of the Sioux City Public Museum.)

Eight

Sioux City's Railroad Legacy

During the last two decades of the 19th century, Sioux City's economy grew with the possibilities made available by the advent of its railroads. In spite of the panic of 1893, the railroads accounted for its enormous prosperity. Even though the city had some of the nation's major carriers, the city fathers, aware of the railroad importance, wanted to create their own railroad companies.

Several Sioux City plans were considered. One called for the extension of the O'Neill line as far as Bismarck, North Dakota. Another plan, to be named the Sioux City, Pueblo, and Duluth Railroad, was to build tracks in a diagonal pattern from Sioux City through Nebraska, Kansas, and Colorado and northward through Minnesota to Duluth. With these railroads, Sioux City would create a larger hinterland to acquire agricultural products and an outlet for processed meat in particular. Sioux City intended to bypass and surpass Chicago as the Midwest's major city. It could then ship products to the Great Lakes and farther on to the East Coast and to Europe.

The Pacific Short Line Railroad was an attempt to build tracks to sell Sioux City meat products to the Pacific coast. Its tracks would go straight from Sioux City to Ogden, Utah. There connections would be made with the Southern Pacific to carry Sioux City products on to San Francisco—and possibly beyond. The Pacific Short Line went bankrupt during the construction of the Combination Bridge. The bridge, completed in 1896 by Sioux Citians paying an extra tax, remained a major crossing point of the Missouri River north of Omaha for over half a century.

During the 19th century, the railroads were the engine that made the United States an economic giant and world power. On a smaller scale, they did the same for individual communities across the land—especially Sioux City. The railroads made it possible for farmers to ship livestock over large distances to the Sioux City stockyards. At the same time, railroads made it possible for packing companies to send products without spoilage throughout the country—and even farther. The railroads and meatpacking industry, in turn, transformed Sioux City from a small supply and trading town on the difficult-to-navigate Missouri River into a rapidly growing, bustling, and modern municipality by the end of the 19th century. In short, the railroads built the foundation and brought about the legacy that Sioux City still stands upon today.

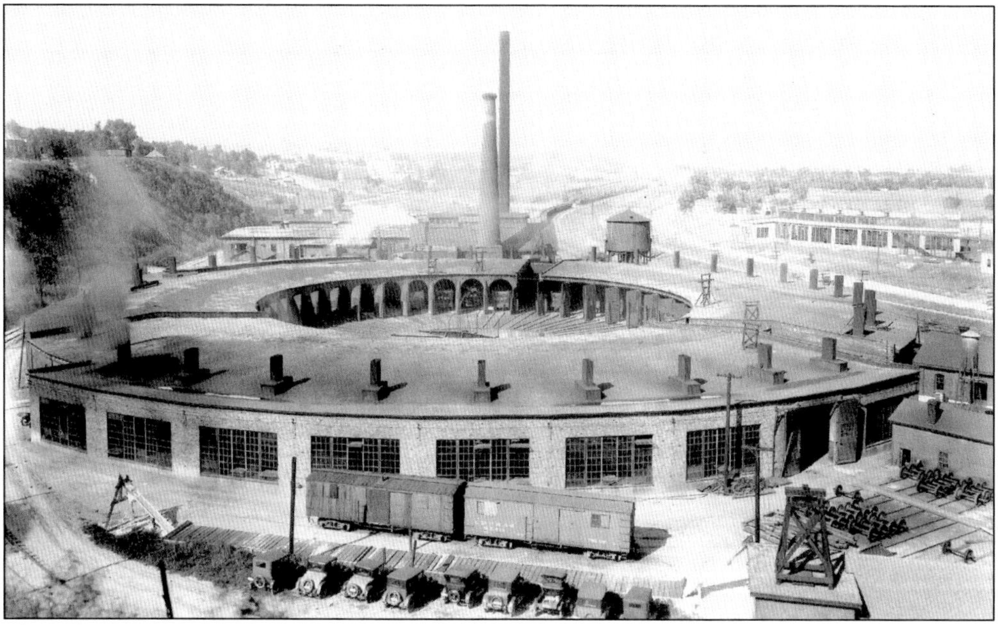

The Chicago and Northwestern roundhouse was located at Eighteenth and Howard Streets. It was a full-service roundhouse, and as an almost complete circle, it had 36 stalls. Both the Chicago and Northwestern Railway and the Chicago, St. Paul, Minneapolis, and Omaha used the facility. The small structure in the upper right was the Illinois Central roundhouse. Both were razed by 1950, with the advent of dieselization. (Courtesy of Jack P. Fleckenstein Collection.)

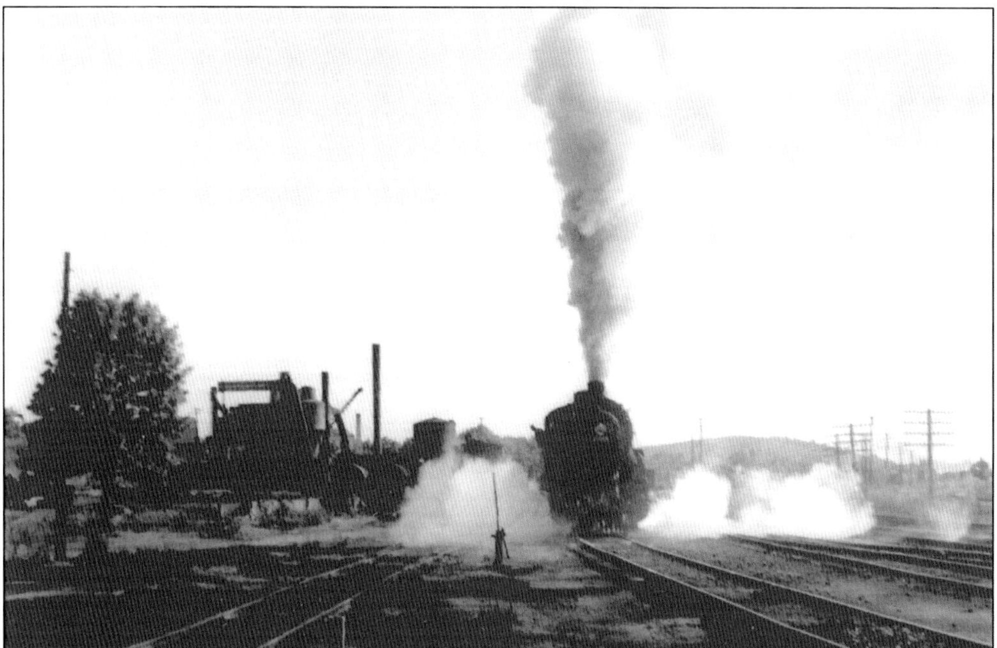

Chicago and Northwestern engine No. 1788 is on the outside track and is clearing its cylinders on its way out of town. It is a class Z, and its black smoke bears witness to its accelerating. A steam locomotive clearing its cylinders is always a magnificent sight. (Courtesy Paul H. Reistrup.)

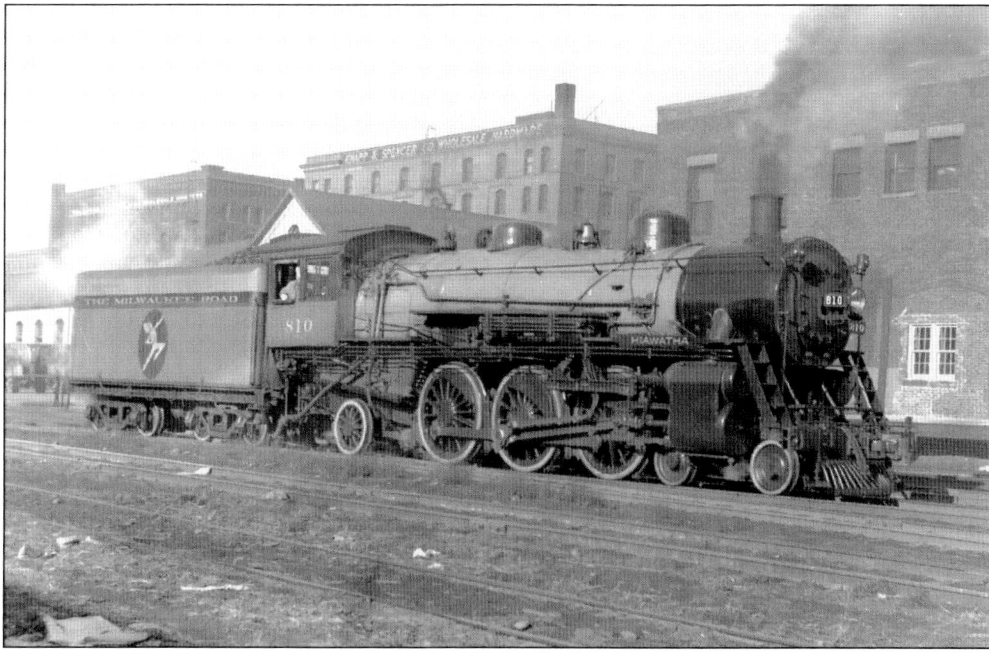

Milwaukee Road Pacific No. 810 is on a side track waiting to pick up its passenger consist. While it does not have a streamline shroud, it has the name Hiawatha on the side and pulls a streamlined tender. (Courtesy of the Siouxland Historical Railroad Association.)

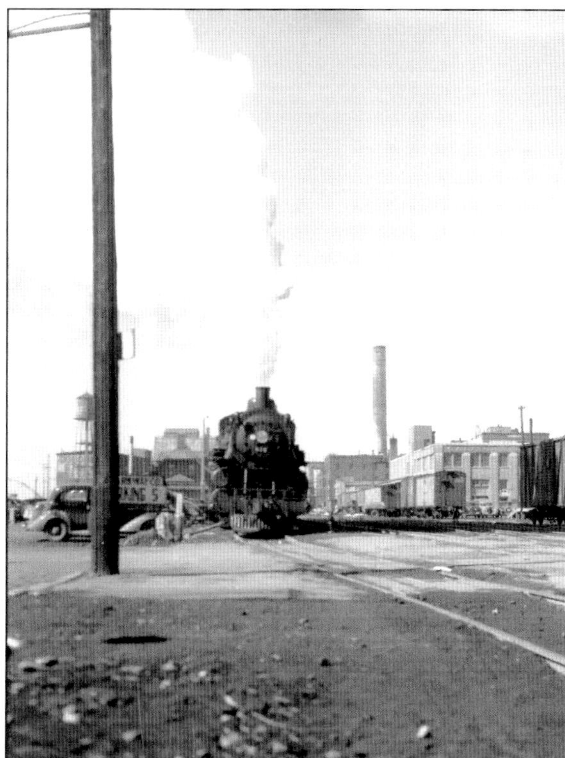

Milwaukee Road's No. 810 is underway out of downtown Sioux City with its Hiawatha passenger cars in tow. The Galinsky building is in the background. The photograph is probably from the late 1940s. In 1910, 88 passenger trains ran from Sioux City in every direction. In 1940, there were 44. (Courtesy of the Siouxland Historical Railroad Association.)

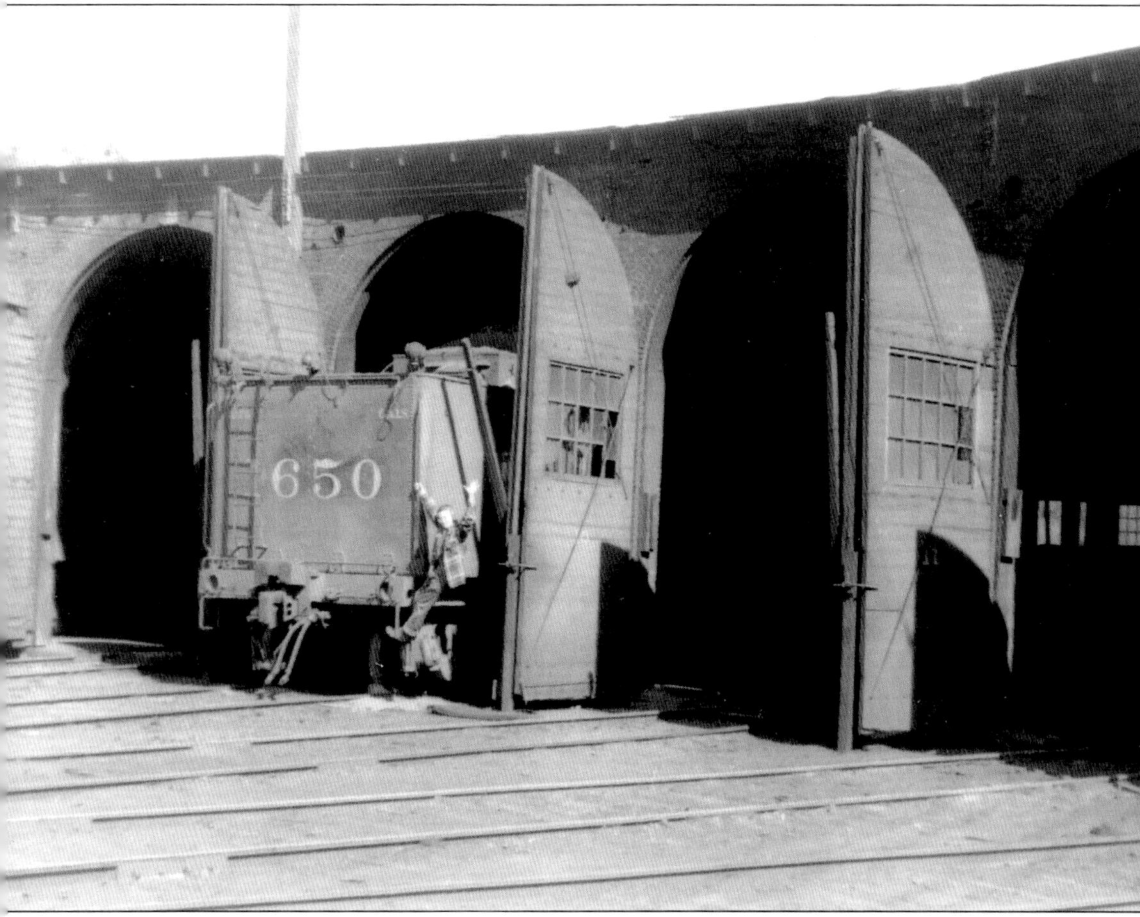

Chicago and Northwestern locomotive No. 650 is backing out of the roundhouse. The original number of this class E, 4-6-2 engine was 1650. The workers who drove locomotives out of the roundhouse were called hostlers. The turntable could guide a locomotive forward or backward into a stall. It is not usual for a locomotive to have a tender behind. In 1971 only one passenger train ran from Sioux City eastward on the Illinois Central. (Courtesy of Paul H. Reistrup.)

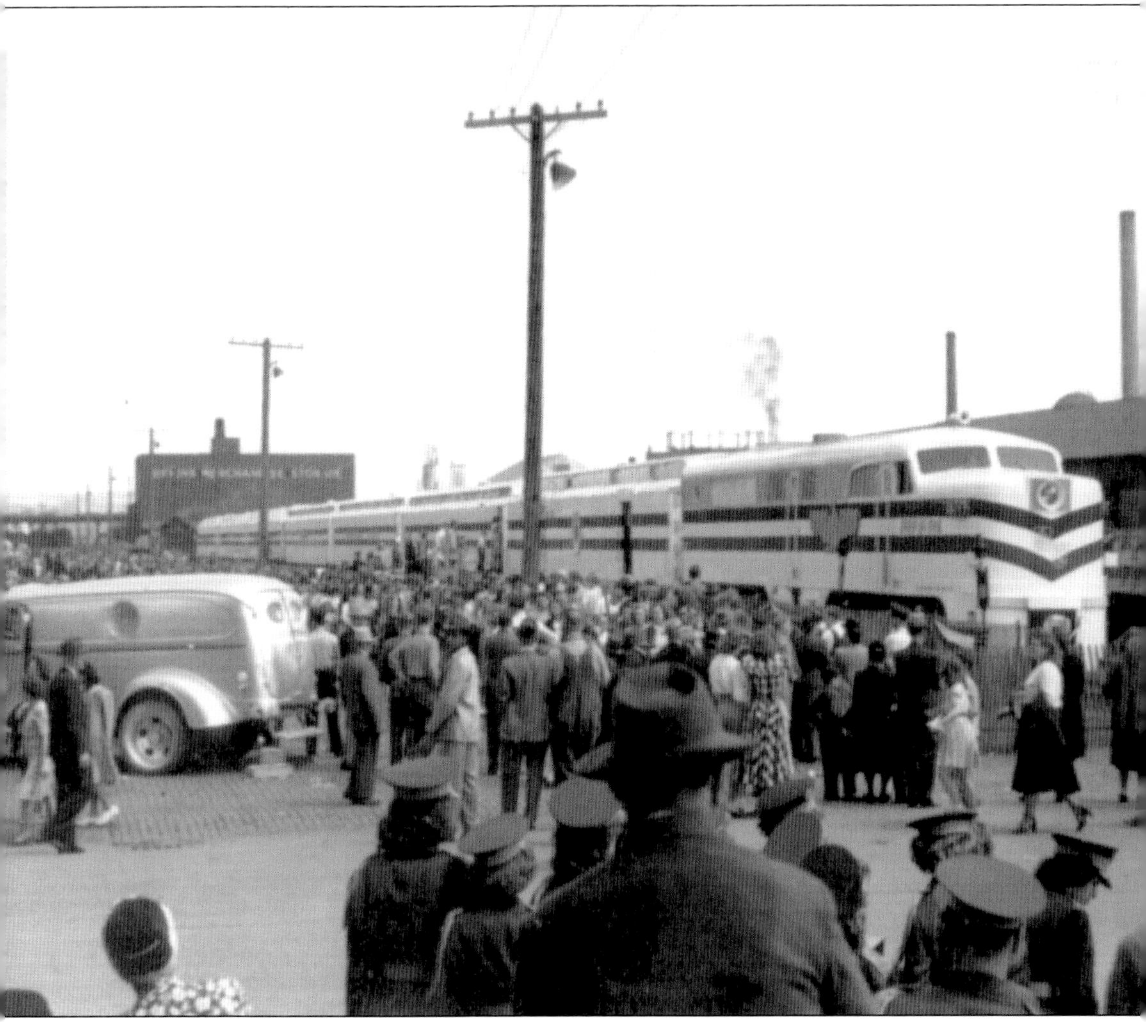

During 1952 the *Spirit of 1776* train toured around the country. The beautiful Alco model PA locomotive and the consist of seven cars attracted attention wherever it visited. Sioux Citians enjoyed seeing the train. It is quite fitting, because the freedom experienced by Americans permitted the great industrial growth spurred on by the railroads. And the railroads were the necessary condition for Sioux City to become the world's sixth largest meatpacking complex and western Iowa's largest city. (Courtesy of the Siouxland Historical Railroad Association.)

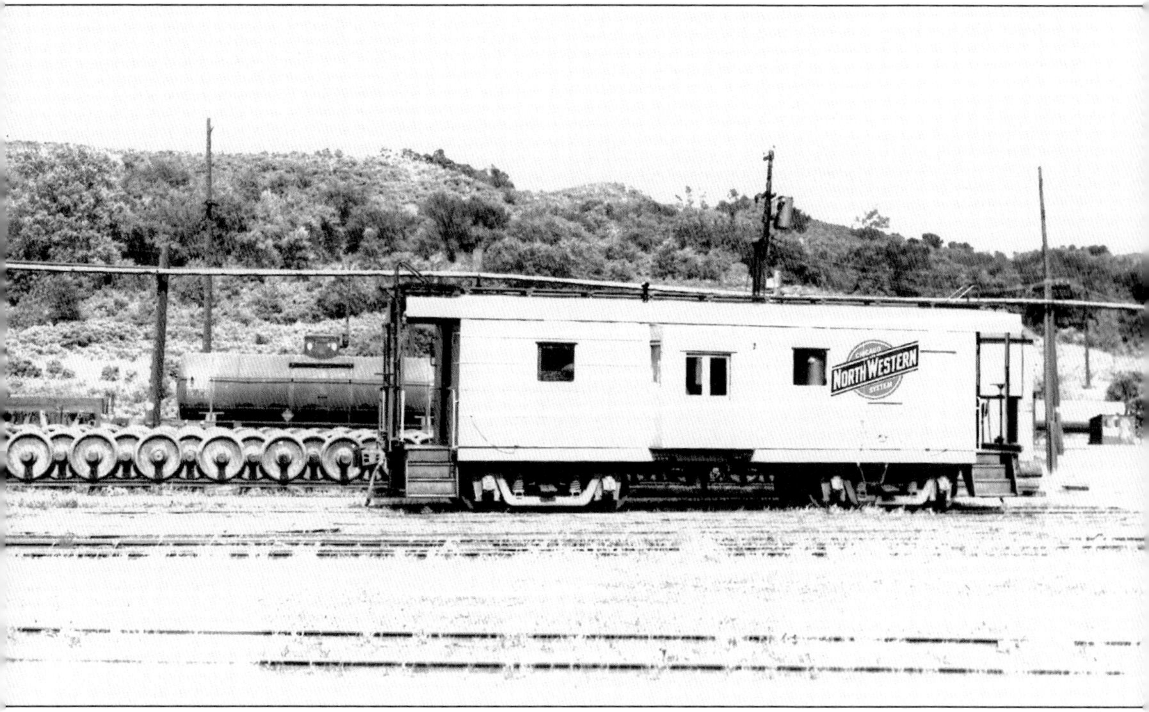

The caboose cupola originated in Iowa on the Chicago and Northwestern Railway. More modern cabooses on the Chicago and Northwestern had bay windows. The freight conductor lived in the caboose during a train run. He had to monitor an air pressure gauge and look out the bay windows for smoke emanating from wheels to avoid overheating and a derailment. The caboose, therefore, was always at the end of a freight train. (Courtesy of George Berkstresser.)

BIBLIOGRAPHY

Chicoine, Paul. "Rails Across the Sky." *Iowan*, 1980.

———. "The Sioux City Rapid Transit Co." *Model Railroader*. May 1986.

Daniels, Rudolph. *Trains Across the Continent: North American Railroad History*. Bloomington, IN: Indiana University Press, 2000.

Grant, Roger. *The Northwestern*. De Kalb, IL: North Illinois University Press, 1966.

Historical Guide to North American Railroads. Waukesha, WI: Kalmbach Books, 2000.

Poole, Marcia. *The Stockyards: A Way of Life*. Sioux City, IA: Lewis and Clark Interpretive Center, 2006.

Scribbins, Jim. *Milwaukee Road Remembered*. Waukesha, WI: Kalmbach Publishing Company, 1990.

Sorensen, Scott, and Paul Chicoine. *Sioux City: A Pictorial History*. Virginia Beach, VA: Donning Company, 1982.

State of Iowa. *Eleventh Annual Report of the Board of Railroad Commissioners for the Year Ending June 30, 1888*. Des Moines, IA: Geo E. Roberts, state printer, 1888.

Stevens, Jolene. *A Second Century Begins: A History of the Sioux City Stockyards*. Sioux City, IA: Record Printing Company, 1987.

Taylor, Orville Heber. "The Design of a Railway Terminal System for the Handling of Freight and Passenger Traffic in the City of Sioux City, Iowa." BA thesis, State University of Kentucky, 1914.